Māori

Māori, the indigenous language of New Zealand, has a number of interesting features in its structure. It is also an endangered, minority language, with an important role in the culture and identity of the Māori community. This comprehensive overview looks at all aspects of the Māori language: its history, its dialects, its sounds and grammar, its current status, and the efforts being made by the Māori community and the state to ensure its survival. Central chapters provide an overall sketch of the structure of Māori while highlighting those aspects which have been the subject of detailed linguistic analysis – particularly phonology (sound structure) and morphology (word structure), on which extensive linguistic work has been carried out. Though addressed primarily to those with some knowledge of linguistics, this book will interest anyone wishing to study the structure of a minority language, as well as those interested in endangered languages and their preservation.

RAY HARLOW is Professor of Linguistics at the University of Waikato, New Zealand. He has written and edited thirteen books, the most recent including *Māori* (1996) and *A Māori Reference Grammar* (2001).

Māori

A Linguistic Introduction

Ray Harlow

CAMBRIDGE
UNIVERSITY PRESS

CAMBRIDGE UNIVERSITY PRESS
Cambridge, New York, Melbourne, Madrid, Cape Town, Singapore, São Paulo

Cambridge University Press
The Edinburgh Building, Cambridge CB2 8RU, UK

Published in the United States of America by Cambridge University Press, New York

www.cambridge.org
Information on this title: www.cambridge.org/9780521808613

First published 2007

Printed in the United Kingdom at the University Press, Cambridge

A catalogue record for this publication is available from the British Library

ISBN 978-0-521-80861-3 hardback

Ki taku hoa,
ki a Terry

Contents

List of figures   *page* viii
List of maps   ix
List of tables   x
Acknowledgements   xii
List of abbreviations   xiii

Introduction   1

1   Māori literature and literature on Māori   5

2   A brief history of Māori   10

3   Regional variation in Māori   41

4   The phonology of Māori   62

5   The morphology of Māori   96

6   The syntax of Māori   135

7   The sociolinguistic situation of Māori   192

References   224
Index   239

Figures

2.1   Austronesian subgrouping (after Tryon 1994b:7).   *page* 13
2.2   The internal grouping of the Oceanic languages.   13
2.3   The subgrouping of the Polynesian languages.   14
2.4   The entry for *manufiri in POLLEX (Biggs 2000a).   34
4.1   De Lacy's (1997) feature tree.   65
4.2   Mean formant frequencies for the long and short vowels of a
      speaker born in the 1880s.   78
4.3   Formant frequencies of the long vowels of a speaker born in
      the 1880s.   78
4.4   Formant frequencies of the short vowels of a speaker born in
      the 1880s.   79
4.5   Mean formant frequencies for the long and short vowels of a
      second speaker born in the 1880s.   80
4.6   Mean formant frequencies for the long and short vowels of
      two speakers born in the 1970s.   81
7.1   Sign at the University of Waikato using different
      orthographic conventions.   209

Maps

2.1 The Austronesian family and major Austronesian language
groups, taken from Lynch *et al.* (2002:3) by permission. *page* 11

3.1 The North Island of New Zealand, showing (in italics) the
location of Maunsell's (1842) divisions and (in plain type)
other areas/tribes mentioned in this section. 42

Tables

2.1	POC to PPN consonant correspondences	*page* 16
2.2	The Māori reflexes of the PPN consonants	16
2.3	Some PAN items and their reflexes	19
2.4	Pronunciations of /f/ in the speech of a nineteenth-century informant (percentages rounded)	23
2.5	Aspirated articulations of /p, t, k/ from three informants (percentages rounded)	23
2.6	Case marking in intransitive and transitive clauses	25
2.7	Some examples of PPN lexical innovations inherited in Māori	33
2.8	Some sub-PPN innovations found in Māori	33
2.9	Some of the forms and words unique to Māori	33
3.1	Some examples of the lexical dialect differences reported in Rikihana (1976:8–10)	43
3.2	Examples of historical mergers in two Māori dialects	45
3.3	Biggs' examples of regional /ei/ $\sim$ /ai/ alternations	46
3.4	Biggs' examples of regional /ou/ $\sim$ /au/ alternations	47
3.5	Biggs' examples of regional /i/ $\sim$ /u/ alternations	47
3.6	Distribution of terms for 'woodpigeon' and 'stink-bug' in two regions of the North Island	50
3.7	Percentages of shared basic vocabulary between eight North Island dialects of Māori	51
4.1	The phonemes of Māori	63
4.2	Hohepa's (1967) assignment of feature specifications	64
4.3	De Lacy's (1997) feature specifications	66
4.4	Frequency of Māori phonemes	68
4.5	Frequency of short vowels	68
4.6	Merger of adjacent short vowels to form phonetically long vowels and diphthongs	75
4.7	Differing stress assignment according to Hohepa's and Biggs' rules	82
4.8	Some examples of items in Boultbee's word list	89

4.9   Examples of differences in editors' transcription of
       Boultbee's list   90
4.10 Examples of Kendall's (1815) orthography   90
4.11 Part of the Lord's Prayer in Kendall (1820)   91
5.1   Properties of verbal subcategories   108
5.2   Māori personal pronouns   112
5.3   Māori nouns with distinct plural forms   115
5.4   Examples of verbs with stem changes in passive   117
5.5   Tableau on derivation of *mahuetia* from de Lacy (2003a)   118
6.1   Marking of predicates in *ai*-strategy relative clauses   184
6.2   Distribution of relativisation strategies by target   187
7.1   Knowledge of Māori language among Māori schoolchildren   194

Acknowledgements

Sincere thanks are due to Terry Crowley, Julie Barbour, Margaret Maclagan, Jenny King, Peter Keegan, Jeanette King, Ann Harlow, who have read drafts of parts of this book and made very valuable comments.

My unending gratitude goes to my many Māori friends and colleagues, whose open-hearted hospitality and generosity throughout my years of study of Māori have made my involvement with their beautiful language an experience of great richness.

Kei aku rangatira, kei aku hoa, e kore rawa e mutu te mihi ki a koutou mō koutou i tautoko, i awhi i a au i roto i tēnei mahi āku. Tēnā koutou katoa.

Abbreviations

1Sg., 2Du., 3Pl., etc.	person and number (singular, dual, plural) in pronouns
Agt.	agentive
AN	Austronesian
Aph.	anaphoric particle
Caus.	causative prefix
CE	Central Eastern Polynesian
Comp.	complementiser
Det.	determiner
Dir.	directional particle
DP	determiner phrase
EP	Eastern Polynesian
Foc.	focus marker
Incl./Excl.	inclusive/exclusive in pronouns
Loc.	locative particle
MAONZE	Māori and New Zealand English research project
Neg.	negative
Nom.	nominalisation suffix
NP	Nuclear Polynesian, noun phrase
Nuc	nucleus
Obj.	object marker
OC	Oceanic
P	preposition
PAN	Proto-Austronesian
Pass.	passive suffix
PCE	Proto-Central Eastern Polynesian
PEP	Proto-Eastern Polynesian
Pers.	personal article
Pl.	plural
PMP	Proto-Malayo-Polynesian
PN	Polynesian
PNP	Proto-Nuclear Polynesian

POC	Proto-Oceanic
POP	postposed periphery
Poss.	possessive
PPN	Proto-Polynesian
Pred.	predicate marker
PrP.	preposed periphery
PTA	Proto-Tahitic
Sg.	singular
Subj.	subject
TA	tense/aspect marker
Top.	topic marker
TTW	Te Taura whiri i te Reo Māori 'The Māori Language Commission'
VP	verb phrase

Introduction

Māori is the indigenous language of New Zealand. Like all languages, it is in some respects unique, and in others quite typical. It is a member of one of the largest language families in the world, was brought to New Zealand by Polynesian voyagers, and so shares features with other members of its family. However, it has also its own history through its isolation in the most southerly regions of the South Pacific. Like many other minority languages, it has suffered through contact and competition with a major language, and its present situation and the issues involved in attempts to ensure its survival and revitalisation thus show similarities with those affecting many other languages around the world. At the same time, the circumstances surrounding all such disadvantaged languages are not identical, and there are unique aspects, and unique responses, to the place of Māori in New Zealand society.

In this book, aspects of Māori, its history, structure and present sociolinguistic situation, will be discussed in a way which is intended to provide the general reader with a good overview. In addition, however, the book aims to provide discussion of, and full bibliographical references for, the now considerable body of literature which exists on Māori. Some of this discussion will necessitate use of the technical apparatus of modern linguistics, which may make some sections rather less accessible to readers other than professional linguists and senior students of the subject. Overall, it is in the first instance this latter audience that the book is intended for, especially linguists interested in Oceanic languages and language maintenance issues. The primary, not to say unique, focus, will be the Māori language, but it is hoped that readers with interests in other languages will find much that is interesting, familiar even, and that resonates with those interests.

Māori belongs to the Polynesian subgroup of the huge Austronesian language family,[1] which consists of over 700 languages, and is spread geographically from Madagascar in the West to Rapanui (Easter Island) in the East, and from Hawai'i in the North to New Zealand in the South. Māori is thus the most southerly member of this family. Its closest relations are the languages of the Cook Islands, Tahitian and other languages of French Polynesia. Brought to New Zealand some 800–1,000 years ago by voyagers from Central

1

Polynesia, it is spoken now, at least to some level of fluency, by perhaps as many as 160,000 people, about 4 per cent of New Zealand's population of around 4 million. Spread as it has been over a country the size of New Zealand, it has developed some regional variation, though not to the point of mutual unintelligibility.

The figure of 160,000 is a respectable one. However, Māori must count as an endangered language, since in very large part natural intergenerational transmission has ceased. The majority of modern speakers of Māori are either of the generations born and brought up before or during the Second World War or younger people who have acquired Māori as a second language. Herein lies one of the aspects of Māori which is of relatively much greater interest to linguists than its 'size' might merit. For Māori, over the last thirty or so years, has been the subject of innovative language maintenance and revitalisation efforts, most of them the result of the initiative and drive of the Māori community itself.

Institutions such as *kōhanga reo*, 'language nests', the preschools which not only provide a Māori language environment, but also are administered and conducted entirely along Māori cultural lines, have served as models for similar enterprises in other minority language situations. The extension of this environment into primary, secondary, and even to some extent tertiary, education has excited interest among policy makers and researchers from around the world.[2]

Apart from its presence in education, Māori now enjoys a significant place in public policy and the media in New Zealand; however, the situation is still a long way from what would arguably be an appropriate status for New Zealand's only indigenous language.

At the same time, Māori, as well as being a relatively conservative language within its subgroup, and thus a good witness for many features of Eastern Polynesian, is of some interest also in linguistic typology and general descriptive linguistics. There can be few linguists who have not encountered some discussion of the morphology of the passive in Māori. Māori is a VSO language, exemplifying very well many of the relevant generalisations in the Greenbergian paradigm. On the other hand, its four relativisation strategies provide problems for proposed generalisations in that area of syntax.[3]

The chapters which follow aim at presenting to the reader an overview of the history, grammar and situation of Māori. Chapter 1 reviews the steady stream of writing on Māori which began nearly 200 years ago, making Māori one of the best recorded of the Polynesian languages, and presents a brief view of the language arts, both traditional and more modern, which find their expression through Māori. Such descriptive writings and the 'Classical Literature' of Māori provide a picture of its development over the last 150 to 200 years; chapter 2 sketches the history of Māori, drawing not only on what such sources reveal, but also on what sorts of developments, particularly in the sound system, can be traced from the ancestral language of the Austronesian family to modern Māori by means of the methods of reconstruction available in historical linguistics. Linguistic evidence contributes as well to the reconstruction of the movements which brought Austronesian speakers from the homeland of the family down into the South Pacific.

Since some of the regional diversity observable in Māori may be due to differences which existed in Eastern Polynesia before migrations to New Zealand, chapter 3 follows on from an account of the history of Māori with a survey of what can be said about its dialects. Chapters 4, 5 and 6 are those which present the structure of modern Māori, dealing with phonology, morphology and syntax respectively. It is in these chapters, more than anywhere else, that there will be some use of formulations and terminology which will be unfamiliar to general readers. This is necessitated by the fact that, as said, aspects of Māori have been the subject of research within theoretical linguistics, and these chapters will report on this work at the appropriate points. Nonetheless, these chapters endeavour to present a coherent and accessible picture of these aspects of Māori structure which can be read continuously by omitting more technical discussion where it occurs.

Finally, chapter 7 will concentrate on aspects of the sociolinguistic situation of Māori, partly historically, but primarily in the present, and the language maintenance measures being undertaken to try to ensure its survival and revitalisation. Contact with English over the last nearly-200 years has had a profound effect on Māori; the language itself has changed under this influence, but, most importantly, and particularly in the last 50 years, there has been vast language shift among the Māori population, to the point where, as mentioned above, the language is endangered, and very considerable efforts are being made to attempt to stem the tide of the shift and to preserve this unique yet typical expression of the human spirit.

NOTES

1. See Tryon (1994a) on the Austronesian language family, its composition, structure and vocabulary.
2. In November 2000, a conference, 'Bilingualism at the Ends of the Earth', held at the University of Waikato, Hamilton, New Zealand, as part of a collaboration between the University and the Xunta de Galicia, Santiago, Spain, attracted from all over the world participants with an interest in what is happening in New Zealand bilingual and immersion education. An international conference, 'Language, Education and Diversity', held in Hamilton in November 2003, at which a high proportion of papers addressed issues in Māori-medium education, similarly attracted very wide interest. Proceedings of these conferences are published as Barnard and Harlow (2001) and May et al. (2005) respectively.

People and organisations in New Zealand engaged in revitalisation efforts have very good connections with similar groups in other parts of the world, especially Hawai'i and native American communities, as well as parts of Europe, and reciprocal visits and exchanges of information and ideas, especially with respect to New Zealand's initiatives in Māori-medium education, are common.

3. See chapter 6 for discussion and references on these points.

1   Māori literature and literature on Māori

Māori is not the Polynesian language for which we have the oldest written records; that honour goes to Niuatoputapu and East Futunan.[1] However, it is the subject of substantial documentation over the last 200 and more years. Over the same period, Māori has become a written language, not only through such documentation, but also through the transcription of its rich oral tradition and its use in the nineteenth century, and again increasingly in the present, in domains which are typically literate.

Chapter 4 will sketch the development of the writing system now used for Māori. What this chapter will present is an account of the documentation of Māori since first contact with Europeans, and of the nature of Māori literature, traditionally oral, but in recent times forming an ever increasing, and ever diversifying, written corpus.

Literature on Māori

As noted, Māori is one of the best-documented of the Polynesian languages with written sources on the language dating from the earliest contact period.[2] Word lists compiled during James Cook's first voyage (1769–70) are simply the first of many such documents (see chapters 3 and 4). The first fuller documentation of the language was also the first publication in or on Māori (Kendall 1815). This was an attempt to provide a resource for Thomas Kendall's missionary colleagues and contains alphabets (rejoicing in the title *Na Letteree*), word lists and expressions. The second publication (Kendall 1820) benefited greatly from the input of Samuel Lee, a linguist at Cambridge, and contains rather more grammatical description.[3] These early 'textbooks' were followed by numerous others, of which the most important in the nineteenth century were Maunsell (1842), W. L. Williams (1862) and Aubert (1885). The twentieth century saw the production of considerable numbers of texbooks, the most important and influential being those by Biggs (1969), Waititi (1970, 1974) and Moorfield (1988, 1989, 1992, 1996). The Biggs work is still very much in the grammar-and-translation style of earlier works, but Waititi's and Moorfield's reflect much more modern methodologies.

All these works contain partial grammars, but it has not been until the 1990s that full reference grammars have appeared. Bauer (1993) is a grammar of Māori within the framework of the Routledge (originally Lingua) Descriptive Series. As such, it is a mine of information on every detail of Māori grammar, but often very hard to find one's way in because of the prescribed lay-out. Much more 'user-friendly' but similarly full of information is Bauer (1997). My own grammar (Harlow 2001) is not so exhaustive as either of Bauer's, but is aimed primarily at senior (BA and Honours-level) students of Māori, and intends to provide them with an account of all the construction types they will encounter in reading or speech.

Māori lexicography has progressed in parallel with the more descriptive works. The first major successor to the early word lists was the first edition of the Williams' Māori–English dictionaries (see W. L. Williams 1844). To this day, the most recent edition (H. W. Williams 1971) remains the major resource on Māori, though over the years it has been joined by a range of generally rather smaller dictionaries, including some English–Māori ones.[4] The most important addition to Māori lexicography in recent years has been H. M. Ngata's (1993) *English–Māori Dictionary*, the online version of which allows look-up in either direction (see chapter 7).

Despite this range of material, serious linguistic research on Māori really only began with Biggs' doctoral thesis (published as Biggs 1961), though Johansen (1948) had contained an insightful discussion of a number of points of grammar. Since then though there have been further doctoral[5] and Master's[6] theses, and a considerable body of published research on aspects of Māori grammar now exists in the linguistic literature, to which full reference is made at the relevant points in ensuing chapters.

Literature in Māori

Like all other Polynesian languages, except Easter Island,[7] Māori had no written form until the introduction of writing by missionaries, early in the nineteenth century. However, as in preliterate societies throughout history, there was, and to some extent still is, a rich orally transmitted and performed 'literature'. A wide range of poetic or chanted genres existed and continues to exist, and the range of prose genres includes tribal and local histories, genealogies (*whakapapa*), cosmogonies, 'folkstories',[8] and traditional knowledge.

Within modern Māori culture, a number of traditional oral genres have remained very much alive, and, in the case of poetic genres, new ones have been added. Apart from *karanga* 'call, especially a call of welcome' and *whaikōrero* 'oratory', composition these days is largely in writing, but performance is almost entirely oral.

The formal activities of the marae are the occasion of performance particularly of three genres, *karanga*, *whaikōrero* and *waiata* 'song', often of very traditional shape.[9] The marae is, strictly speaking, the open space on which a Māori community[10] carries out communal activities such as welcoming visitors, mourning the dead, meeting for discussion, celebrating birthdays, and so on. At one side of the marae is the meeting house,[11] in which guests are accommodated and in which further talk proceeds often deep into the night, and there is always a separate eating house close by.

Karanga is a women's genre and is the call of welcome to a group approaching the marae for whatever purpose. Once the visitors and hosts are seated across the marae from each other, *whaikōrero* follows, formal speeches of welcome, of remembrance, and of reference to the reason for the encounter. Often these speeches are highly formulaic, and exploit the whole range of traditional proverbs and sayings, as well as genealogical and historical links between the parties concerned.[12]

During the nineteenth century, large numbers of originally oral texts were committed to writing, very often by Māori themselves, and often at the request of missionaries or officials. The two best-known nineteenth-century collections are Grey ([1854] 1971), based largely on the work of Te Rangikāheke, a Te Arawa chief, and White (1887–91), drawn from a wide range of sources,[13] though these editors were less than entirely scrupulous in their use of sources.[14] A further important collection was the product of one of the last *whare wānanga* ('houses of learning') to survive (see chapter 7 for a brief note), a collection of manuscripts on which Smith (1913–15) is based, written at the instigation of the teachers themselves to ensure the survival of the traditional knowledge.

Numerous shorter stories were committed to writing in the nineteenth century, as were longer texts by other writers. Just two examples of the increasing amount of this material now readily available in published form are Ruatapu (1993) and Orbell (1992).

The most influential collection of poetry was assembled by Sir Apirana Ngata, and contains 400 commented song texts, most of them with a translation.[15] This collection contains examples of the very wide range of traditional chanted or sung genres. Many of these songs are no longer known or performed, but the performance of traditional styles, called generally *mōteatea*, still plays a significant role, particularly in support of *whaikōrero* in formal marae contexts. However, these styles have been supplemented in the twentieth century by the development of a songwriting tradition using modern tunes, many borrowed from English-language songs. Many of these songs, called *waiata-ā-ringa* 'action songs', are associated with body and hand actions. These are sometimes used in the formal marae setting, but play a much more important role at performance competitions, and as informal entertainment, as 'party songs'.

There can be few people interested in rugby football who have not seen the New Zealand team, the All Blacks, perform their famous *haka*. Often translated as 'war dance', the word refers to a genre of shouted text accompanied by vigorous body movement, and though expression of defiance is one of its functions, *haka* are also used to welcome guests, to make political points and to entertain (see Kāretu 1993).

In addition to these traditional genres, all of which are oral at least in performance, and many of which still flourish with new compositions, Māori is increasing being used in typically written genres. The main innovative genre in the nineteenth century was journalism, and numerous newspapers were founded (see chapter 7).[16] In more recent times, other, perhaps more literary, genres have emerged, especially children's literature, which is now being produced as support for *Kōhanga Reo* and *Kura Kaupapa Māori* (Māori immersion primary education) initiatives. Much of this is translated from well-known English sources, such as Dr Seuss or the 'Spot' series, but much is original and contains Māori themes in its narrative, including retellings of Māori mythology.

Some poetry is now being written with a view to its being read rather than performed orally, and most recently short stories[17] and a novel, *Makorea* by Katarina Mataira (2002), have appeared. This is a superb piece of writing in what is for Māori a new genre, covering the fictional, personal side of major political events in the South Island in the 1830s and 1840s. It is a remarkable feat and bold initiative on the part of Dr Mataira; while written poetry and short stories do have antecedents of sorts in the traditional oral genres, the only long prose genres recorded are tribal histories and mythologies. The composition of a long prose text which is deliberately fictional, and in which the characters and their concerns are so developed, is a major departure from traditional genres and has no inherited model.

All of these developments represent a radical extension of Māori in written domains, and are very much to be welcomed and encouraged. In parallel with the increasing use of Māori in domains such as law, medicine and education (see chapter 7), such work makes an invaluable contribution to the 'normalisation' of Māori. This is the process by which Māori becomes a 'normal' language, a language by means of which all aspects of life can be accessed in a normal manner.

However, while the volume of written Māori continues to diversify and increase, and while the academic study of the language and its use in some formal contexts will likewise continue, the future of Māori as a living means of ordinary communication is far from assured. We return to these issues in chapter 7, but for the moment it is ironic that, at a time of real flowering of written Māori, its fate as a spoken language is unsure.

1. Short word lists of these two languages were collected by Jacob Le Maire in 1616 in the course of the Schouten – Le Maire expedition to seek a new route to the East Indies (see Kern 1948). The Niuatoputapu language is now extinct and the *c.* 1,600 inhabitants of that island in northern Tonga speak Tongan. East Futuna, a French possession, has a population of nearly 16,000, who still speak the language recorded by Le Maire.

2. Similarly well documented from the time of early contact with Europeans is Hawaiian, see Schütz (1994). Other Polynesian languages in general do not have either such early attestations or such continuous writing on the language. See Krupa (1973).

3. On these early publications and the mss. which are associated with them, see Parkinson (2001a, 2001b, 2003, 2004).

4. E.g. P. M. Ryan (1974 and 1995 – this latter is hardly smaller, in that it boasts some 40,000 items; however, it is still a 'small' dictionary in approach, since it does not include examples of usage), Reed (1984), Biggs (1966, 1981, 1990a).

5. Hohepa (1967), Reedy (1979), Bauer (1981a).

6. E.g. Mutu (1982), Keegan (1996).

7. For an account of the Easter Island *rongorongo* writing system and an attempted decipherment, see Fischer (1997).

8. Particularly, *pakiwaitara* 'folkstories' show interesting structural features associated with orally transmitted and performed 'literatures'. For some discussion of this aspect of Māori literature, see Thornton (1985, 1989), Harlow (2000b), Mokena (2005). Dual-text editions of typical examples of such stories with commentary are found in Orbell (1968 and 1992).

9. The best account of marae protocol and custom, along with the language arts associated with these, is Salmond (1975).

10. Originally a kinship group, but now that very many Māori live in towns, often the group is defined by church, neighbourhood, educational institution, etc.; all universities and many schools, for instance, have marae.

11. There are several essentially equivalent terms in Māori for this house, e.g. *wharenui* 'big house', *whare tipuna* 'ancestor house' (so called because many houses are the embodiment of some ancestor whose name they bear), *whare whakairo* 'carved house'.

12. See especially Mahuta (1974), or, more accessibly, Salmond (1975).

13. The former has appeared in four editions, most recently in 1971. White's work has recently been made available in electronic form and published by the University of Waikato Library.

14. On Grey's collection, see Simmons (1966). For an example of White's cavalier approach to his material, see the introduction to Tiramōrehu (1987).

15. A. T. Ngata (1959, 1990), Ngata and Te Hurinui (1961, 1970). On Māori poetry see McLean and Orbell (1975) and McLean (1996). See further references to A. T. Ngata and his role in chapter 7.

16. Generally on publication in Māori during the nineteenth century, see H. W. Williams (1924), and Parkinson and Griffith (2004).

17. A number of short stories have appeared, for instance, through the encouragement of Huia Publishers (1995, 1997, 1999), who sponsored competitions for writers.

2   A brief history of Māori

The various types of records referred to in the previous chapter allow us to gain some picture of what has happened in Māori over the last two centuries. As will be seen later in this chapter, it is mostly in the area of vocabulary that developments have occurred over this period, though there is evidence of some change in details of phonology and grammar. In all three areas, contact with English has predictably been a major factor. At the same time, there have been extensive changes in the domains in which Māori is used. These will be discussed in chapter 7.

For an idea of the development of Māori before this period, we are reliant upon the reconstruction methods of historical linguistics.[1] As mentioned, Māori is the most southerly member of the Austronesian (AN) language family. There has been very considerable research carried out on the subgrouping relationships within this language family, as well as on the reconstruction of Proto-Austronesian (PAN) and of the proto-languages of lower-order groupings, especially, in our case, Proto-Oceanic (POC) and Proto-Polynesian (PPN). Such research, along with the investigation of the movements and cultures of the speakers of these languages, sheds a great deal of light on the history and origins of Māori.[2]

Space precludes a thorough account of all aspects of the remote history of the language family, for which there are in any case very good, accessible sources in the linguistic and anthropological literature.[3] This chapter will confine itself to an outline of this history, and will highlight the more significant aspects of the linguistic changes and developments which have led to modern Māori.

The Austronesian family and subgroups

The Austronesian language family is, in number of languages and geographic extent, the largest in the world. There are some 1,200 Austronesian languages,[4] which are spoken throughout an area stretching from Madagascar in the West to Rapanui (Easter Island) in the East. Map 2.1 shows the spread of the languages of the family, which include, as well as the dialects of Malagasy, many of the indigenous languages of Indonesia,[5] all the indigenous languages of the

10

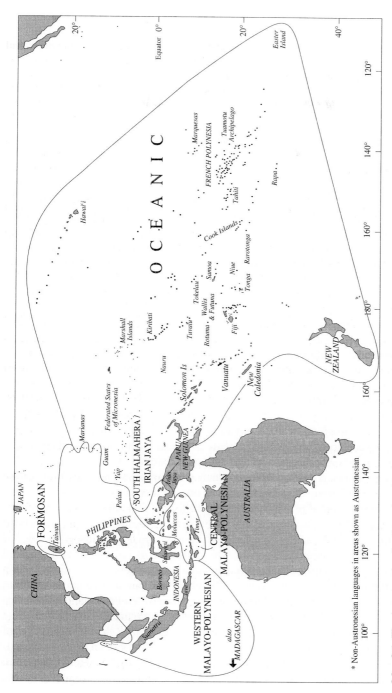

Map 2.1 The Austronesian family and major Austronesian language groups, taken from Lynch *et al.* (2002:3) by permission.

* Non-Austronesian languages in areas shown as Austronesian

Philippines and Taiwan, numerous languages on the South-east Asian mainland in Malaysia and Indo-China, many of the languages of Melanesia, and all of the languages of Micronesia and Polynesia.

Map 2.1 also shows the geographic distribution of the major subgroups. Although research continues, these subgroups are very widely recognised and are taken to be related as represented in Figure 2.1.[6]

In early writings, the term 'Malayo-Polynesian' was often used to refer to this family. However, it will be seen that the word has now a specialised meaning; it refers just to the subgroup containing all Austronesian languages outside Taiwan. As with all such subgroups, it is possible to identify innovations shared by the languages of the subgroup which point to a common history exclusive of other languages within the family. In many cases, this 'common history' is due to the languages concerned being descended from a single language, called the proto-language of the subgroup. In other cases, the subgroups are rather sets of languages arising perhaps as dialects of an earlier language, but reflecting an interlocking pattern of innovations, as in a dialect chain.

This distinction between 'innovation-defined' groups and 'innovation-linked' groups (linkages) is described in Lynch *et al.* (2002:92–3) in the introduction to their own treatment of the internal subgrouping of the Oceanic (OC) languages.

The Oceanic subgroup is well established; there are many shared innovations which serve to define it; there was a POC, spoken in the area of the north coast of New Guinea some 3,500 years ago (Lynch *et al.* 2002:97–8). However, the internal structure of the subgroup is not so clearly based on innovation-defined groupings, some of the groups showing distributions of features more in keeping with the model of 'innovation-linked' groups. Lynch *et al.* (2002:94–114) propose groupings of the Oceanic languages as presented in Figure 2.2. In this figure only the detailed subgrouping leading to the Polynesian (PN) language family is given. That is, Lynch *et al.* propose finer structure for the more westerly groups as well, but this is omitted here.

This patterning of relationships is generally felt to be the result of the fairly rapid spread through Melanesia of speakers of Oceanic who are associated with the so-called Lapita Culture.[7] As the figure shows, the closest relations of the Polynesian language family are the languages of Fiji and Rotuma. Indeed this group, the Central Pacific linkage, is thought to have been a dialect chain stretching over Fiji and into Western Polynesia (the region of Tonga and Samoa) out of whose eastern end Proto-Polynesian emerged. At the same time it seems clear that before PPN itself split up as shown in Figure 2.3, there was quite a long period of independent development during which the large number[8] of innovations which characterise the Polynesian languages as a group occurred.

The "classical" subgrouping of the Polynesian family, shown in Figure 2.3, was developed over some decades, culminating in the work of Pawley (1966,

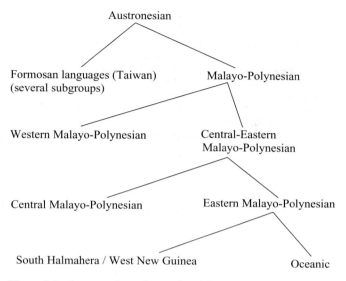

Figure 2.1 Austronesian subgrouping (after Tryon 1994b:7).

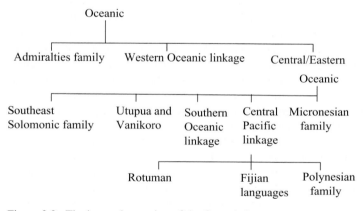

Figure 2.2 The internal grouping of the Oceanic languages.

1967) and Green (1966). Further work by, for instance, Howard (1981) and Marck (1996, 2000) has led to modifications in the area of the "Samoic" languages, but has served only to strengthen the earlier proposals with respect to the history and relationships of Māori.

To quite an extent, the historical relationships between these languages mirror the physical movements and settlement patterns of their speakers. The splitting

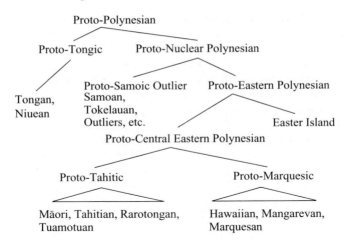

Figure 2.3   The subgrouping of the Polynesian languages.

up of the AN family and of the OC and PN subgroups, as summarised in the figures above, 'translates' into the spread and migrations beginning in Taiwan some 5,000 years ago, proceeding down into the Philippines and Indonesia, and eventually through Melanesia into Island Pacific (Tryon 1994b:29–31). Pawley and Green (1971) present the linguistic evidence for taking the Tonga–Samoa region to be the homeland of PPN. PPN developed there during a long period (perhaps as long as a millennium) of relative isolation from neighbours to the West before regional differences led to the split into Tongic and Nuclear (NP) varieties. Later still, perhaps around AD 300, migrations took a NP language into the central areas of Eastern Polynesia, from which an early further migration carried people and language to Easter Island, while those who stayed in the area of the Marquesas and Society Islands eventually spread out to occupy the other extremities of the Polynesian Triangle.

New Zealand is the last of the major island groups within Polynesia to have been settled, with the arrival of the ancestors of the modern Māori from the region of the southern Cook Islands and the Society Islands around 1,000 years ago.[9] The languages with which Māori is most closely related are those of the Cook Islands (except the island of Pukapuka, whose language is more closely related to Samoan) and the Society Islands, as seen in Figure 2.3, though it has not proved possible to determine finer subgrouping within the Tahitic family.[10] Also, whether the arrival of Polynesians in New Zealand was a single, perhaps chance, landfall by a single canoe, or whether there was not only multiple settlement but even prehistoric two-way voyaging between New Zealand and tropical Eastern Polynesia, is a subject of debate.[11]

Māori traditional history points in this latter direction. Virtually all Māori tribes identify with one or more canoes[12] which brought their ancestors from Hawaiki, the traditional homeland, and, in some views, the place to which the souls of the deceased return.[13] The name *Hawaiki* is a reflex of Proto-Nuclear Polynesian (PNP) **Savaiki*,[14] and is a concept in Māori traditional literature which serves mythical functions. However, reflexes of the name occur at least four times in the Pacific applied to actual locations. Best-known, of course, is its application to the so-called 'Big Island', and by extension to the whole state of Hawai'i.[15] Similarly well-known is the name Savai'i for one of the main islands of Samoa. Less well-known are the region of Avaiki in Niue, and the existence of Havai'i as an older name for the island Ra'iātea in French Polynesia. Clearly, the 'canoe traditions' and the remembered and mythologised name of the homeland reflect historical migration(s) to New Zealand from tropical Central Polynesia. Individual canoe traditions point to specific locations, such as Rarotonga in the southern Cook Islands, as the starting point of migrations.

The linguistic developments

Not only do the methods of historical linguistics allow the establishment of such relationships between languages and in some part the reconstruction of prehistoric movements, but also the Comparative Method provides partial pictures of the phonology, grammar and lexicon of the proto-languages of the succession of families and subgroups.

Sound changes

As with the structure and history of the language family, this section will not deal in any detail with developments from PAN down to PPN. The reader is referred to published sources on these, especially Lynch *et al.* (2002), and Tryon (1994a).[16] What will be described in more detail is the phonological history from PPN to modern Māori, though there are some general features of the earlier developments that deserve comment here.

The overall trend from PAN to PPN is one of simplification of both phoneme inventory and phonotactics, in particular, mergers and losses characterise every stage from PAN to Proto-Malayo-Polynesian (PMP) to POC to PPN, a development which culminated in Māori, along with many other PN languages, having phoneme inventories among the smallest in the world. Table 2.1 shows the reflexes in PPN of the POC consonant system.[17] The reductions observable here are typical of the whole history from PAN onwards.

The twenty-three consonants reconstructed for POC reduce to thirteen for PPN through loss of the voice distinction in stops, merger of five nasals to three, direct loss of two consonants, *inter alia*. A result of the losses of *y and *R

Table 2.1. *POC to PPN consonant correspondences*

POC	p	b[18]	t	d	k	g	pʷ	bʷ	q	m	n	ñ
PPN	f	p		t		k	f/p[19]	p	?	m	n	

POC	ŋ	mʷ	c	s	j	l	dr	r	w	y	R
PPN	ŋ		h	s	t	l	r/l	r	w		Ø

Table 2.2. *The Māori reflexes of the PPN consonants*

PPN	p	t	k	m	n	ŋ	w	f	l	r	s	?	h
Māori	p	t	k	m	n	ŋ	w	f/h/w		r	h	Ø	

was that PPN developed phonemically long vowels. For instance, POC *apaRat 'wet season when northwesterlies blow and sea is rough' became PPN *afaa 'storm'.[20]

Phonotactically, too, the development from POC to PPN represented a simplification; POC was already simpler than PAN in this respect. PAN admitted a restricted range of two-phoneme medial consonant clusters, as well as single final consonants. The latter were preserved in POC, but medial consonant clusters were simplified by the loss of the first member. Thus PMP *gapgap 'stammer' had become POC *kaka(p)[21] (> Māori *kaka*),[22] and PMP *beRŋi 'night' became POC *boŋi.[23] PPN however, along with many other OC languages, allows no final consonants. This is in fact the reason for the bracketed letter in the reconstruction, POC *kaka(p). Though it is known that PMP had a final /p/ in this word, and thus POC should also, since final consonants were normally retained, no reflex with final /p/ has been found in an OC language.

While no PPN or Māori word (for Māori is like PPN in this respect) ends in a consonant, many stems which originally had such final segments, and which lost them in absolute final position, in fact retain them in suffixed forms. We return to this below *à propos* of the allomorphy of the Māori passive inflection (see chapter 5). For the moment, here are two examples: Māori *tangi* 'to mourn' has passive *tangihia* from POC *tangis (+-ia); Māori *inu* 'drink', passive *inumia*, from POC *inum (+-ia).

The development from PPN to Māori is again characterised by mergers and losses.[24] Table 2.2 shows the regular reflexes in Māori of the PPN consonants.[25] The five vowels of POC, *a, *e, *i, *o, *u, are regularly retained right through to modern Māori.

The PPN consonant inventory of thirteen is reduced to ten in Māori. The glottals of PPN are lost, though at different stages of the history, and PPN *l and *r merge as /r/. This merger is one of the defining innovations of the Nuclear Polynesian subgroup, these sounds appearing nearly always as either /l/ or /r/ in the languages of this group. The loss of *h is likewise shared by all languages of the Nuclear Polynesian subgroup, thus quite early. The loss of *ʔ is, however, later, being a feature of Proto-Central Eastern Polynesian (PCE) and its descendants. In fact, PPN *ʔ was lost at least three times independently within the PN family.[26]

The continual reduction in consonant inventory which can be observed throughout the development from PAN to Māori is striking.[27] It raises questions as to how it came about and what effect the reduction of phonological resources has on the efficiency of these languages. These reductions have had two principal effects. Firstly, homophony has increased; for instance, the Māori form *tau* continues both PPN *tau 'suitable' and other meanings and *taʔu 'season, year'; *ara* 'way, awaken' reflects *ʔara 'awaken' and *hala 'way'. The second consequence is the increased incidence of phonemically long vowels.[28] Since PPN syllable structure was (C)V(V), which is retained in Māori,[29] the loss of *h and *ʔ medially brought two vowels together. If these were like vowels, they were thereafter always realised as a single long vowel. Thus, PPN *faʔaki 'tell' becomes Māori *whāki*, phonetically [fɐːki], PPN *kehe 'different' becomes *kē*.

Trudgill (2004) explores the questions mentioned above. In particular, he asks whether 'there [is] any connection between [the] geographical penetration deeper and deeper into the formerly uninhabited Pacific and the loss of consonants'. The contributing factors he explores are the smallness and isolation of particularly the Polynesian communities, which at least allow, if they do not necessarily cause, such reductions. Small communities have a great deal of shared knowledge, so that decreasing redundancy does not impair communication, and isolated communities do not have the opportunity to borrow sounds.[30]

Table 2.2 shows the reflexes in Māori of the PPN consonants. These correspondences are highly regular, with the exception of the case of PPN *f. In contrast to the other consonants, PPN *f shows three reflexes in Māori, /f/, /h/ and /w/.[31] The instances of PPN *f > Māori /w/ are very few, but show some regularity. In common with the other Central Eastern Polynesian languages, Māori shows the results of a dissimilatory change: PPN *faf- > /wah/. Thus, PPN *fafine > Māori *wahine* 'woman'. A total of five lexical items are affected, the others being Māori *waho* 'outside', *waha* 'mouth', *waha* 'carry', *wahie* 'firewood', all from PPN *faf-.[32] Grace (1985:60–1) connects this change with another similar one which is both less regular and more wide-spread in the PN family. In East Futunan, some Northern Outlier languages and Central Eastern Polynesian languages, some instances of PPN *f become *v/w* in the

environment before vowel + *s. Thus PPN *fesi 'hate' becomes East Futunan
vesi, and Māori *wehi* 'fear, awe'. Given their distribution, however, the two
changes cannot be related despite their superficial similarity.

The distribution of /h/ and /f/ reflexes of PPN *f in Māori is much more
involved. Biggs (1978:707) provides the summary: '[For PPN *f] Māori has
wh [hw] or [f] or [ø] initially before unrounded vowels and **h** medially and initially before round vowels.' To quite an extent, this characterises the situation,
though some commentary is necessary. In common with other Central Eastern
Polynesian languages, Māori underwent a change: *f > h before rounded vowels. Thus, PPN *nofo 'sit, dwell' becomes Māori *noho*, and *futi 'draw up' >
huti.[33] Beyond that, though, Biggs' statements identify only tendencies, not
regular reflexes. Thus, while very many instances of medial *f do merge with
*s as /h/ in Māori, as in, for example, PPN *afi 'fire' > *ahi*, there are cases, even
in very similarly shaped words, where *f remains distinct as /f/: *afe 'stir, as a
light body in the wind' > *awhe* 'stir, disturb (as by wind)', *ʔafi 'embrace' >
awhi. A further group of words shows regional variation, having /f/ in some
dialects and /h/ in others: *koofatu 'stone' > *kōhatu* ~ *kōwhatu*, *tufa 'spit' >
tuha ~ *tuwha*.[34]

Conversely, while initial *f before unrounded vowels is generally preserved
in Māori as /f/, e.g. *fale 'house' > *whare*, there are words where initial *f
is reflected as /h/, e.g. *hao* 'enclose in net' from *faʔo, and yet others where
both forms are attested: *faapuku 'fish sp.' > *hāpuku* ~ *whāpuku* 'groper', *fea
'where' > *hea* ~ *whea*.

The situation is not unique to Māori. In those closely related languages in
which *f and *s have not merged completely,[35] similar disarray can be seen.
Harlow (1998) proposes that the synchronic situation is the result of a slow
change in progress, i.e. the merger of *f and *s, which has been following
similar paths in the Eastern Polynesian languages, but has reached different
stages of lexical diffusion in the individual languages.

Intertwined with the development of *f is that of PPN *s. With one exception,
all Eastern Polynesian languages show a shift of *s to /h/, with which *f merged
either entirely or partially.[36] The exception is the language of Tongareva, Penrhyn Island, in the northern Cook Islands, where all *f and a few *s merge to /h/,
but most *s retain a sibilant pronunciation (in the area [ç] ~ [ʃ]).[37] Further, a
number of items, preserved in early publications and manuscripts which reflect
the language spoken in the Far North of New Zealand before the spelling system
settled into the modern conventions,[38] suggest that at least some Māori /h/ had
a sibilant pronunciation. Thus spellings occur such as *shoroe* (= modern *horoi*)
'wash', *shoopa* (= modern *hupe*) 'mucus',[39] both reflecting *s. Given that similar sources also contain spellings such as *hoyea* (= modern *hoea*) 'paddle',
which reflects *f, it is tempting to see the continuation into the early nineteenth
century in northern New Zealand of a sibilant pronunciation of *s, distinct from
both retained /f/ and *f shifted to /h/. Unfortunately, it cannot be this neat, as

Table 2.3. *Some PAN items and their reflexes*[40]

PAN	POC	PPN	Māori	Meaning in Māori
daqey	*raqe*	*laʔe*	*rae*	'forehead'
kasaw	*gaso*	*kaso*	*kaho*	'rafter'
ikan	*ikan*	*ika*	*ika*	'fish'
h₂aŋin	*aŋin*	*aŋi*	*āngi*	'light air'
baqeRu	*paqoRu*	*foʔou*	*hāu*	'new'

occasional early spellings of, for instance, the place name *Hokianga* (from *foki 'return') beginning with *Sh-*, also occur.

Table 2.3 shows a handful of examples of lexical items inherited in Māori from PAN, tracing their shape through intermediate stages, and illustrating some of the regular developments. However, notwithstanding these generally very regular reflexes of PPN phonemes in Māori, there are incidences of sporadic change, partly shared with the languages most closely related to Māori. Indeed, sporadic changes have been identified which have occurred at a range of points in the descent of Māori from PPN, and are thus shared variously by larger and smaller subgroups. There are in addition some types of sporadic change peculiar to Māori which are thus late. The most thorough account of such sporadic changes for the whole family is Marck (2000), in which exhaustive examination of the 1996 version of Biggs (2000a) has allowed the identification of a variety of types of sporadic change and their assignment to the particular proto-languages in which they must have occurred. For instance, in the case of PPN *tafulaʔa 'whale', which became *tohorā*, Māori shares with other NP languages the change of *u to /o/ in the second syllable, but the change of the first vowel *a > /o/ only with Tahitic languages. The history of this word thus seems to have been: PPN *tafulaʔa > PNP *tafolaʔa > PCE *tafolaa > Proto-Tahitic (PTA) *toh(f)oraa > Māori *tohorā*. Similarly, PPN *tufuŋa 'expert, priest' became PTA *tahuŋa and finally Māori *tohunga*, by a shared Tahitic change *u > *a in just this word, and a sporadic assimilation *a > /o/ in Māori only. Such assimilations, especially of *a to a mid vowel in the environment of a high vowel are not uncommon in Polynesian languages – though, with the exception of Tongan, where this assimilation was highly regular, they are always sporadic. Other examples in Māori include *whenua* 'land' from PPN *fanua, involving an assimilation which seems to have led to the existence of a doublet in PNP *fanua ~ fenua.

Among the sporadic changes peculiar to Māori are idiosyncratic shifts like PPN *lima 'hand' > Māori *ringa*, though the homophonous (and clearly related) form PPN *lima 'five' retains its *m in Māori *rima* 'five'. Proto-Eastern Polynesian (PEP) *aanuanua 'rainbow', reflected regularly in Rarotongan, Tahitian and Marquesan as *ānuanua*, irregularly became *āniwaniwa* in Māori. Strikingly, this latter innovation is shared by the closely related Mōriori (*aniniwa*), but not the former (*ririma* 'hand').[41]

In addition to the instances of sporadic change, such as those cited above, which can be traced through reconstructions and comparisons, there is evidence of considerable sporadic change in the existence of doublets recorded in Māori sources. Even a casual glance at Williams (1971) will reveal many examples of items which are attested in two or even more slightly varying shapes. Instances such as *matihao* = *maihao* 'finger, toe', *paremo* = *parengo* 'slip', abound. The variation in shape in such doublets/triplets may be of any type: omission of a consonant, change of consonant, change of vowel. Some of the cases recorded in Williams (1971) may be due to nonce errors on the part of some scribe. However, the authenticity of most cases cannot be doubted, and, in virtually all such cases, one at least of the forms represents a sporadic change. In some instances, it is possible to determine which of a set of forms is inherited, thus *rango* ~ *ngaro* 'fly (n.)', is descended from PPN *laŋo with cognates reflecting this form in many sister languages.

In a number of cases, the variation of form is regionally determined, being an aspect of an eastern vs western distinction in Māori dialects.[42] This is very much the case with respect to an alternation /f/ ~ /h/, which is seen in a range of words. For instance, *whea* 'where' is characteristic of dialects in the west of the North Island, vs *hea* in the east, both from PPN *fea 'where'. Similarly, *pōwhiri* ~ *pōhiri* 'welcome, invite'.[43] Other variations by region, however, also occur, e.g. the *rango* ~ *ngaro* pair mentioned above follows again the east–west division, as do pairs such as *pōhatu* ~ *kōhatu* 'stone',[44] and *kari* ~ *keri* 'dig'.

A similar variation distinguishes South Island and North Island dialects in a few words: for North Island *pouaru* 'widow' and *pounamu* 'greenstone, jade', South Island sources record *poueru* and *pounemu*,[45] probably an assimilation to the neighbouring high vowels.

The language shows a great range of variation in the types of alternation of form which individual words exhibit. Further research may lead to a useful classification. For the moment, however, two such alternation types deserve comment.

Metatheses

It is striking how many instances of doublets in Māori involve metathesis. Certainly, other languages exhibit this phenomenon, especially as a type of sound change,[46] and in, for instance, English, doublets such as *relevant* ~ '*revelant*', *enmity* ~ '*emnity*' occur between idiolects, or as sporadic spoonerisms within idiolects. However, in general, whether as change or as synchronic alternation, metathesis is rare. In Māori on the other hand, as recorded in Williams (1971), examples abound, though the reasons for this phenomenon remain unknown. In at least one case, that of *ngaro ~ rango* 'fly (n.)', it is a matter of dialect difference, and further research may reveal that other cases are similar. However, some are not so clearly regional; in the superficially similar pair *engari ~ erangi* 'but', both forms occur in the Bible translation, which is based primarily on Northland Māori, and in the writings of Te Rangikāheke, from the central North Island.[47]

What is striking, as well as the level of incidence of metathesis, is the range of phonological units which can undergo metathesis.

(1) Vowels in adjacent syllables: *ikeike = ekieki* 'high, lofty', *mahine = maheni* 'smooth' show alternation of the two non-low front vowels; *pape ~ pepa* 'make a slip in reciting a *karakia* (a charm/prayer/spell)', *hangehange ~ hengahenga* 'a shrub' show alternation of the two non-high unrounded vowels; *hukinga ~ hikunga* 'head of a valley'.

(2) Consonants in adjacent syllables:[48] *honuhonu ~ nohunohu* 'nauseous', *kāheru ~ kārehu* 'spade', *paewhenua ~ paenehua* 'dock (the weed)',[49] *ngaro ~ rango* 'fly (n.)', roller for canoe', *erangi ~ engari* 'but', *pūrokuroku ~ pūkorukoru* 'gather up, of garments'.

(3) Adjacent whole syllables: *rewha ~ whare* 'eyelid',[50] *ngahere ~ ngarehe* 'forest', *pūtangitangi ~ pūngitangita* 'prickle', *kōmuramura ~ kōramuramu* 'eat at odd times'.

(4) Of particular interest perhaps are three examples which look like metathesis of features, not segments or syllables: the pair *tenga ~ kenakena* 'Adam's apple' shows metathesis of place of articulation in the consonants, while leaving nasality in place. A further pair showing the same consonants is: *ngatu* (the original form, having cognates in Rapanui and Hawaiian) *~ nakunaku* 'crushed'. Similarly, the pair *inohi ~ unahi* 'scale of fish' seems to show metathesis of rounding, but not of height, which remains (more or less) constant in the alternate forms.

Consonant deletion

The other sporadic process which has produced lexical alternations, but has done so in a semi-systematic fashion, has the appearance of a very circumscribed conditioned consonant deletion.[51] Many tribal names in Māori begin with a prefix meaning roughly 'the descendants of'. This prefix appears in two forms: *Ngāti ~ Ngāi*, of which the second appears only before names in /t/. Thus, *Ngāti Porou, Ngāti Ruanui*, etc., but *Ngāi Tahu, Ngāi Tūhoe*, etc. A few tribal names whose eponymous ancestor's name began with /t/, also use *Ngāti*, such as *Ngāti Tūwharetoa*, but no instance of *Ngāi* occurs before a consonant other than /t/. Similarly, the morpheme *motu* 'island' has a second form *mou* which seems to occur only in compounds where the second element begins in /t/: *moutere* 'island' (beside *motutere*), *Moutohorā* 'Whale Island'.

Other examples of alternations resembling these are *whaka-* ~ *whā-* (the causative prefix), the passive of some reduplicated verbs – on both of which see chapter 5 – and some further individual lexical items, such as *matatau* ~ *mātau* 'know', *pararaki* ~ *pāraki* 'land wind'.

Recent phonological and phonetic change

We have at our disposal written records of Māori covering the past two centuries.[52] These of course allow us to gain a picture of the development of the language in lexicon and to a lesser extent grammar over that period, but provide little information on recent sound change. New Zealand is, however, fortunate in possessing a unique resource for tracking the development of both its languages in these respects over the last *c.* 140 years. In the 1940s, the Mobile Disc Recording Unit of the New Zealand Broadcasting Service recorded a series of interviews around the country. The population sampled in this way was extremely varied, including both Māori and Pākehā (New Zealander of European extraction), and people of all ages, some born as early as the 1860s. The exploitation of this resource both with regard to the development of New Zealand English and for the picture it can give of Māori over this period is centred on the University of Canterbury, Christchurch.[53] The research on Māori using these recordings is in its infancy, but preliminary investigation of some features reveals change in Māori phonetics, arguably as a result of contact with English.[54]

Two such features are the pronunciation of /f/, spelt <wh>, and the aspiration of /p, t, k/.[55] Both studies involved the detailed analysis of the speech of a native speaker born in 1885 and recorded in 1947. The second study then compared the earlier speaker's pronunciations with those of two informants recorded in 2001, one born in 1934, and the other in 1972.

In the case of /f/, four differing pronunciations are found in the speech of the older informant: [h], [ø], [ʍ] and [f], with [ø] being by far the most common. Table 2.4 shows the incidence of the four pronunciations as reported in Maclagan and King (2002).

All the instances of [h] as a realisation of /f/ occur before /a/, very frequently in the prefix /faka-/, which is always unstressed. About four out of five times, the /a/ is rounded in this context.

Granting that this is an observation of a single speaker's practice, and that further research is necessary, this pattern contrasts strikingly with modern Māori pronunciation, in which [f] as a realisation of /f/ is very common and the other pronunciations, though they occur, are far less frequent.

A similar shift is observable with respect to the aspiration of the three voiceless stops of Māori. The earliest recordings show little or no aspiration of these

Table 2.4. *Pronunciations of /f/
in the speech of an informant
born in the nineteenth century
(percentages rounded)*

[ø]	50%
[ʍ]	18%
[f]	13%
[h]	20%

Table 2.5. *Aspirated articulations of /p, t, k/ from three
informants (percentage rounded)*

	Informants		
	born 1885, recorded 1947	born 1934, recorded 2001	born 1972, recorded 2001
aspirated stops	6%	49%	88%
unaspirated stops	92%	49%	12%

sounds while the more recent recordings show progressive increase in this feature. Table 2.5 reports Maclagan and King's (2001) observations.

Both developments are very pausibly laid at the door of contact with English,
in which of course [f] is the only allophone of Māori <wh> which occurs at all
frequently, [ʍ] as a pronunciation of 'wh-' words being marginal at best, and
voiceless stops are regularly aspirated except after /s/. Equally plausibly due to
contact with English is the merger of original /au/ and /ou/ ([əʊ] and [oʊ]), so
that for instance *pau* 'exhausted, used up' and *pou* 'post' are now homophones
for many speakers. Both sounds occur in New Zealand English but only as
allophones, the second occurring before /l/.

Grammatical developments

As with the changes and developments in the sound system of Māori, so comparison with related languages is able to reveal something of the history of
aspects of its grammar. Reconstruction of (parts of) the grammar of PAN and
of POC are summarised in Lynch *et al.* (2002:57–63, 67–89, see also references there), and will not be recounted here. Further, those features of Māori
which are shared widely by PN languages and which are reconstructible to
PPN, such as reduplication, the double possessive system (*a* vs *o* marking),
the structure of noun phrases, etc., are discussed in other chapters. Rather, this
section will take PPN as a starting point and draw attention to two types of

phenomena: those features of Māori grammar which are relevant to the issue of case marking and grammatical relations in PPN transitive clauses; and grammatical features found in Māori (and, in most instances, in other languages of the family) but not reconstructible to PPN, i.e. innovations in the history of Māori.

As will be seen in chapters 5 and 6, Māori grammatical structure, like that of PN languages generally, relies heavily on particles, small words, usually preposed to the phrase they mark, which indicate the grammatical role of the phrase and meanings such as tense. It is these particles more than the category of the lexical head of a phrase which determines the phrase's category. One consequence of this property is that words and phrases of categories other than verbal, with appropriate marking, may be encountered as predicates. Furthermore, as will be observed, basic phrase order in Māori, as in most of the PN languages within the Polynesian Triangle, places the predicate phrase first in a clause as its unmarked position, followed by its arguments and other phrases. Examples illustrating these brief general points will be seen in the next sections.

Māori and PPN ergativity/accusativity

Given the extent to which we understand PPN phonology and lexicon,[56] and to a lesser extent other aspects of PPN syntax and morphology, it is striking that the reconstruction of the structure of simple transitive clauses remains controversial. In particular, cases have been made both for PPN having *ergative* marking in its simple clauses and for *accusative* marking being the norm. This distinction is of central interest in the area of linguistic typology and has generated considerable literature (see, for instance, Song 2001:138–210 and references there). Accusative constructions mark the subject of transitive clauses in the same way as those of intransitive clauses. Ergative marking, however, treats the object of transitive clauses in the same way as the subject of intransitive clauses, and provides a distinct marker, be it a case form, a particle, or agreement pattern, for the subject of transitive clauses. In discussion of this aspect of PN languages, the major works are Clark (1976) and Chung (1978) but these represent contrary points of view on this matter.

Many Polynesian languages of all subgroups exhibit (at least)[57] two patterns of case-marking with transitive verbs, to the extent that there is no difficulty in reconstructing both to PPN. Using the now conventional symbols for the arguments of intransitive and transitive predicates, Table 2.6 displays the two patterns along with the intransitive pattern.[58]

That is, in the pattern transitive 1, the A (agent, experiencer, 'logical subject') is unmarked, as is the single argument of intransitive predicates, while the O ('object', patient, source of experience) is marked with particles which also have a range of oblique functions. In transitive 2, it is the O which is unmarked,

Table 2.6. *Case-marking in*
intransitive and transitive clauses

intransitive	V	S	
transitive 1	V	A	ʔi/ki + O
transitive 2	V(-Cia)	ʔe + A	O

while the A is marked by means of a particle which has only this function. In transitive pattern 2, the verb can be, but need not be, marked with an allomorph of the suffix labelled '-Cia'[59] in Polynesian linguistics. This suffix is reflected in the Māori passive, on which see chapter 5.

Tongic languages and many of the non-Eastern languages of the Nuclear Polynesian subgroup have pattern 2 as the canonical transitive pattern, and restrict pattern 1 to so-called 'middle' verbs, i.e. verbs of mental attitude, like perception, liking, wanting, and others where the object is not directly affected, such as 'follow', 'help'.[60] In most two-argument clauses, however, the noun phrase marked with reflexes of *ʔe is the 'subject', and the unmarked noun phrase (the O) is the object. In Eastern Polynesian languages on the other hand, pattern 1 is available for all transitive verbs, and pattern 2 is clearly a passive; the noun phrase marked with reflexes of *ʔe is oblique and denotes the passive agent, while the unmarked noun phrase (the O) is the subject.[61]

Languages like Tongan, Samoan and similar languages in which the object of a transitive clause is marked in the same way as the subject of an intransitive clause thus show ergative marking.[62] Māori, Tahitian, Hawaiian, etc., on the other hand, are accusative languages. 'What was PPN like?' is the question.

As mentioned, Clark (1976) and Chung (1978) offer conflicting answers. Clark argues that PPN was ergative, that is, like Tongan in this respect, and that languages like Māori have innovated by extending pattern 1 to all two-argument verbs, and reanalysing pattern 2 as passive. Chung, on the other hand, following earlier work by Hohepa (1969a) and Hale (1970), argues that PPN was more like Māori, that is, essentially accusative in its case marking, and that the modern ergative languages innovated by reanalysing the passive as the canonical transitive construction. More recently, Clark (1995) has suggested a compromise position, according to which PPN was ergative, but those features of PPN which Chung identifies as pointing to accusative patterns are relics of an earlier stage of the language. This brief characterisation here does scant justice to the question and the arguments. For these, the reader is referred to Clark's and Chung's original works.

Māori plays a central role in this discussion, largely because it is not immediately clear that it is in fact an accusative language. Two papers argue that Māori is actually an ergative language. Sinclair (1976) and Gibson and Starosta (1990), working respectively in Relational Grammar and Lexicase frameworks, arrive at the conclusion that what is usually regarded as passive in Māori is actually the basic transitive construction, and that the 'active' is an anti-passive construction. Chung (1977) argues successfully against Sinclair's conclusion, and there is a broad consensus now that Māori does indeed have accusative case marking. However, there are a number of features of Māori grammar which exhibit ergative-like patterning. The more important of these are presented more fully in chapter 6, but are mentioned briefly here because of this historical context. Further research may reveal whether these are relics of an earlier stage in which ergative patterns were more widespread in the language, or are pointers to a drift towards ergativity of the sort suggested by Hohepa (1969a).

The active–passive voice distinction found in Māori is exemplified in these two versions of the same sentence[63] – the same in that the assignment of roles, tense and verb remain constant:

> *Ka hoko te matua i ngā tīkiti.*
> aor buy the parent Acc the+pl ticket
> 'The parent buys the tickets.'

> *Ka hoko-na ngā tīkiti e te matua.*
> aor buy-Pass the+pl ticket Agt the parent
> 'The tickets are bought by the parent.'

The second sentence, the passive, shows three differences from the active: the presence of a suffix on the verb; Nominative marking for the O (the tickets); and the marker *e* for the A (the parent). This is the Māori reflex of the PPN transitive pattern 2 of Table 2.6, while the active reflects pattern 1.

Bauer (1997:536–8), in a section entitled 'Ergative Traces in Māori', mentions four constructions in which a verb not marked for passive is nonetheless accompanied by an O (or at least a patient) case-marked Nominative. The four constructions are:

(1) 'Weak imperatives with *me*'. After the tense/aspect marker *me* 'should', a verb normally does not take passive morphology, even though other aspects of the clause are clearly passive. Using the same example as just above:

> *Me hoko ngā tīkiti e te matua.*
> TA buy the+Pl. ticket Agt. the parent
> 'The tickets should be bought by the parent.'

(2) 'Clefting with *he mea*'. This refers to a construction, often called 'pseudo-passive', which has the shape illustrated in the following version of our sentence:

> *He mea hoko ngā tīkiti e te matua.*
> a thing buy the+Pl. ticket Agt. the parent
> 'The tickets were bought by the parent.'

The Nominative-marked NP (the tickets) is O, the A is marked with *e*, yet the verb (buy) does not show passive morphology.

(3) 'Actor Emphatic'. This important construction, to which I return below and in chapter 6, appears to be an innovation of the Eastern Polynesian languages. It is characterised by having the A in initial position marked as a possessor, the O is case-marked Nominative, and the verb occurs, yet again, without passive morphology:

> *Nā*   *te*   *matua*   *ngā*   *tīkiti*   *i*   *hoko*.
> 'belongs.to' the   parent   the+Pl.   ticket   TA   buy
> 'It was the parent who bought the tickets.'

As can be seen from the gloss, this construction (which is available also for the future) serves to focus the A.

(4) 'Neuter verbs'. This term refers to a class of verbs in Māori and other PN languages, often also called 'statives'. Verbs of this subcategory can be accompanied by a patient which is case-marked Nominative and, optionally, an agent marked oblique by the particle *i*:

> *I*   *pakaru*   *te*   *wini*   *i*   *a*   *Hēmi*.
> TA   be.broken   the   window   Agt.   Pers.   H
> 'The window was broken by Hēmi.'/'Hēmi broke the window.'

In all four of these cases, it is true that a patient occurs case-marked Nominative, that if there is an agent it is marked by a particle of some kind, and that the verb is not explicitly marked passive. However, in all four cases, it is the Nominative-marked noun phrase which exhibits subject-like properties,[64] and the agent is oblique. Also, all four constructions are marked in some way and cannot really be taken to represent the canonical transitive marking for Māori. The first is restricted to just one tense/aspect marker; the second is restricted in tense to past; the third is a focussing construction, thus pragmatically marked; and the fourth is lexically restricted to a small group of verbs.

In addition to these four which Bauer mentions, there are a few other features of Māori which suggest an ergative orientation rather than accusative:

(5) Marking of the subject of nominalisations: Māori preserves the PN dual possessive system (*a* vs *o* marking, on which see chapter 6), and has two processes for the nominalisation of verbs and adjectives, zero-derivation and derivation by a suffix '-*Canga*'.[65] The subject of the nominalised predicate is marked as a possessor. What is of interest is the fact that in general the A of a canonical transitive predicate is marked as a so-called '*a*-category' possessor, and all others, including the single argument of intransitive predicates[66] and the O of transitive verbs,[67] are marked with *o*. That is, selection of the marker (*a* or *o*) groups the intransitive subject with the transitive object against the transitive subject, an ergative feature. Consequently, the ambiguity of English

expressions such as 'the shooting of the hunters', which can be read as meaning either that the hunters do the shooting or that they get shot, is not found in Māori:

> te   pupuhi-tanga   *a*   ngā   kaiwhakangau
> Det. shoot-Nom.   of   Det.Pl. hunter
> 'the shooting of the hunters' (A)

> te   pupuhi-tanga   *o*   ngā   kaiwhakangau
> Det. shoot-Nom.   of   Det.Pl. hunter
> 'the shooting of the hunters' (O)

> te   mate-nga   *o*   ngā   kaiwhakangau
> Det. die-Nom.   of   Det.Pl. hunter
> 'the dying/death of the hunters' (S)

(6) '*Ko wai e . . . ?*' This question form consists of a fronted noun phrase whose head is the interrogative *wai* 'who' and a verb phrase marked with the particle *e*. The role of the noun phrase depends on the transitivity of the verb: if the verb is transitive, the 'who' is O, but if intransitive, the 'who' is S. That is, this construction pairs S and O, not S and A.

> Ko   wai   e   haere?
> Focus who   TA   go
> 'Who is to go?'

> Ko   wai   e   karanga?
> Focus who   TA   call/invite
> 'Who is to **be invited**?'

(7) The frequency of the passive in text, a point to which we return in chapter 6. It has long been recognised and remarked on that the passive is used much more frequently in Māori than in, for instance, English, and even, in certain types of text, more frequently than the corresponding active.[68] This is among the features which Sinclair (1976) and Gibson and Starosta (1990) use as arguments for their position that Māori is an ergative language. It is argued, on the basis of the frequency of the passive *inter alia*, that it is the 'passive' which is the basic construction for transitive clauses, and thus that the 'active' is derived, a sort of anti-passive.

Typological categorisations such as ergative/accusative are frequently far from cut and dried in many languages, and Māori is a good example of this. The consensus is now that the basic case-marking of Māori is accusative, but as seen above there are numerous case where departures from this pattern are found.

Grammatical innovations in Māori

Māori shares, of course, all the innovations of its subgroups, Nuclear Polynesian, Eastern and Central Eastern Polynesian, but is in fact rather conservative
vis-à-vis its closest relatives. Pawley's (1966) lists of those grammatical features which constitute arguments for the existence of the Nuclear Polynesian
and Eastern Polynesian subgroups as in Figure 2.3, are still the best summaries
of these innovations. Many of these are irregular developments in the shape of
some grammatical morphemes, such as PNP *nei 'here' from PPN *ni. Others
are new grammatical morphemes, such as the PEP negative verb *kore, or the
innovative PEP progressive tense/aspect marker *e . . . ana. All of these still
occur in Māori and will be referred to again in chapter 6.

This section will restrict itself to pointing to some of the more important ways
in which Eastern Polynesian languages, and Māori in particular, differ from PPN
in syntax, especially at sentence level, apart from the issue of case marking in
transitive clauses, and to grammatical changes which can be identified in Māori
in more recent times.

In general, the picture Māori presents us of the structure of phrases and the use
and marking of oblique phrases preserves what must be reconstructed for PPN.
However, in two aspects of the phrase which heads the predicate, Māori shows
two important innovations, both shared by other members of its subgroups.

PPN, like many other Oceanic languages, had clitic subject pronouns which
formed part of the verb phrase. Tongan, for instance, retains this feature, having
clauses like:[69]

> *Naʻá ku   lea.*
> TA   1Sg. speak
> 'I spoke.'
>   (Churchward 1953:68)

Eastern Polynesian languages lack these entirely. Compare Māori

> *I   kōrero au.*
> TA speak 1Sg.
> 'I spoke.'

Indeed, the EP pronominal system represents a considerable reduction vis-
à-vis PPN. W. H. Wilson (1985) presents the details of the relevant reconstructions and innovations, connecting these latter to developments in some of the
Polynesian Outlier languages. With the exception of the singular pronouns,
which have a special suffixal form when governed by possessive prepositions,
all pronouns in Māori have only one shape.[70] This is in all cases the reflex of the
PPN free form, which existed alongside clitic subject pronouns, as mentioned,
and other reduced forms which occurred in possessive constructions.

The treatment of predicative prepositional phrases is a further area of innovation in EP languages. In PPN, possessive and locative prepositional phrases could occur as the head of a predicate phrase introduced by a tense/aspect marker (and clitic subject pronoun, where appropriate). Taking again the Tongan constructions to exemplify this feature:

> *'Oku 'o e 'eikí.*
> TA   P   the   chief
> 'It is the chief's.'
> (Churchward 1953:112)

> *'Oku mau   'i heni.*
> TA   1Pl.Excl.   P here
> 'We are here.'
> (Churchward 1953:102)

In EP languages on the other hand – with the exception of a construction, now rarely used in Māori, in which a prepositional phrase naming the route or means of transport can be used with tense/aspect markers to mean 'to go by that means or route' – a system of tensed predicative prepositions has replaced the constructions exemplified above for Tongan.

Thus, while

> *Me mā runga tereina rātou.*
> TA P   on   train   3Pl.
> 'They should go by train.'

has the prepositional phrase *mā runga tereina* 'by train' made 'verbal' by marking with the tense/aspect marker *me* 'should', possessive and locational predicates have the form of a prepositional phrase:

> *Nā te   rangatira.*
> P   the   chief
> 'It is the chief's.'

> *Kei konei mātou.*
> P   here   1Pl.Excl.
> 'We are here.'

These prepositions are tensed in so far as there are paradigms in Māori and closely related languages contrasting *i* 'at past', *kei* 'at non-past' and *hei* 'at future'[71] for the locative expressions, and, at least in Māori, *nā/nō* vs *mā/mō* for what W. H. Wilson (1985) calls 'realis vs. irrealis' possession.[72]

Particularly the predicative possessive prepositions *nā/nō* and *mā/mō* have developed further non-possessive functions in the EP languages, which will be exemplified in Māori in chapter 6. However, it is worth mentioning here the construction available in all EP languages, including Rapanui, for focussing the A of a transitive clause. This is the Actor Emphatic, referred to briefly above as one of the features of Māori showing ergative-like case marking.

> Nā Mere tēnā pukapuka i   tuhi.
> P Mere Det. book   TA write
> 'It was Mere who wrote that book.'

This construction seems to have undergone reanalysis or at least extension in all languages in which it now occurs. I have argued (Harlow 1986) that the original form of the innovation was

> Past: $N\bar{a}$ + NP$_1$ i + V NP$_2$, and

> Future: $M\bar{a}$ + NP$_1$ e + V NP$_2$,

where NP$_1$ is a human Agent and NP$_2$ is a definite Patient. Māori has extended this pattern, so that non-human Agents are possible, as are indefinite Patients. Also, since NP$_2$, though a Patient, is grammatically subject, it can, like subjects generally, also occur immediately after the initial phrase. Other languages, while doing the same, have also extended the construction to the present, and show a reanalysis of the Patient NP as an object, marking it with i.[73]

Since its migration to New Zealand, the Māori language has undergone grammatical innovations independently of its closest relatives. In very recent times, the influence of English has made itself increasingly felt, owing in large part to the high proportion of L2 speakers of Māori. The types of change to which the present situation of Māori and the demography of its speakers have led will be alluded to in chapter 7.

Finally in this section, two spontaneous grammatical developments in Māori deserve mention. The second of these has occurred during the period of contact with English, but cannot be attributed to influence from that language.

From PCE, Māori inherited a number of tense/aspect markers (on which see chapter 6), particles which mostly precede the head of a verbal phrase and thus form the predicate of clauses. In addition, Māori makes use of the tensed locative prepositions referred to above (kei 'at, present', i 'at, past') plus the zero-nominalisation of a verb to form a verbal phrase with progressive aspect.

Thus beside

> e   haere ana . . .
> TA go   TA . . .
> 'is/are/was/were going'

there are equivalent phrases:

> *kei te   haere ... i   te   haere*
> P   the   go   P   the   go
> 'is/are going'   'was/were going'

While these constructions are available in all varieties of Māori, there is an eastern preference for *kei te / i te* while western and northern dialects prefer *e ... ana* (see chapter 3). Further, although there is very considerable overlap in the ways in which these alternatives are used, there are constructions in which there is a clear preference for *e ... ana* (see Harlow 2001:59).

As will also be seen in chapter 6, relative clause formation in Māori involves a variety of strategies including the occurrence of a resumptive pronoun within the clause, which is coindexed with the antecedent. One of the types of clause in which this occurs is that where the position relativised on is that of the fronted agent in the so-called Actor Emphatic, mentioned above. Thus:

> *te   tangata$_i$ nā-na$_i$ i   tito   te   waiata*
> Det. person   P-3Sg. TA compose Det. song
> 'the person who composed the song'

In texts of all ages, one finds examples in which the third person resumptive pronoun is singular, irrespective of the number of the antecedent. Thus:

> *ngā   tāngata$_i$ nā-na$_i$ i   tito   te   waiata*
> Det.Pl. person.Pl. P-3Sg. TA compose Det. song
> 'the people who composed the song'

In older (e.g. nineteenth-century) texts, this is in fact the only possibility. However, in more modern Māori, and increasingly at the present, number agreement not only is an option, but is becoming the preferred form:

> *ngā   tāngata$_i$ nā   rātou$_i$/rāua$_i$ i   tito   te   waiata*
> Det.Pl. person.Pl. P   3Pl./3Du.   TA compose Det. song
> 'the (several/two) people who composed the song'

The Māori vocabulary

Like most languages, Māori shows a number of historical layers in its vocabulary. Leaving aside for the moment developments in the Māori vocabulary due to recent history and concentrating on 'indigenous' words, it is easy to identify words inherited from PAN, those which stem from some lower-level proto-language, such as PPN, and those which are unique to Māori. Table 2.3 above provides a very few examples of words of the first type, and Tables 2.7–2.9 contain some instances of the others.

Table 2.7. *Some examples of PPN lexical innovations inherited in Māori*

Māori	English	PPN
moa	'Dinornis sp.'	*moa 'fowl'
moana	'sea'	*moana
maunga	'mountain'	*maʔuŋa
riri	'angry'	*lili
rākau	'tree'	*raʔakau

Table 2.8. *Some sub-PPN innovations found in Māori*

Māori	English	proto-language	words in languages from other subgroups
kore	'not'	*kole PEP	*'ikai* Tongan, *lē* Samoan
kōtare	'kingfisher'	*kōtare PTA	*sikotā* Tongan, *ti'otala* Samoan
pāpaku	'shallow'	*pāpaku PNP	*mamaha* Tongan, *lakelake* Niuean
tini	'many'	*tini PCE	*lahi* Tongan, *tele* Samoan

Table 2.9. *Some of the forms and words unique to Māori*

Māori	English	corresponding words in closely related languages
mōhio	'know'	*kite* Rarotongan, *'ite* Tahitian, *'ike* Hawaiian 'see, know' In Māori, *kite* means 'see, find'
ringa	'hand'	*rima* Rarotongan and Tahitian, *lima* Hawaiian 'hand, five' In Māori, *rima* means only 'five'
āniwaniwa	'rainbow'	*ānuanua* Rarotongan, *ānuenue* Tahitian and Hawaiian
kekeno	'seal (animal)'	*'ūrī'aiava* Tahitian, *'īlio-holo-i-kauaua* Hawaiian
mātao	'cold'	*makariri* Rarotongan, *ma'ariri* Tahitian, *ma'alili* Hawaiian (*makariri* is also a Māori word, for 'cold', of weather and water)

An invaluable tool in the study of this aspect of the history of Māori is the Polynesian Lexicon Project (POLLEX, Biggs 2000a), which consists of a constantly revised and updated file of some 4,400 lexical items reconstructed to various proto-languages plus the Polynesian data supporting the reconstruction.[74] Nearly a third of the items are PPN reconstructions, while the rest are assigned to a variety of both higher (e.g. PAN) and lower (e.g. PNP) levels. In some 600 cases, no assignment is essayed. Figure 2.4 shows a typical entry, that for the etymology of the Māori word *manuhiri/manuwhiri* 'guest, visitor'.

```
.CE     MANU-FIRI
TICK    0----+-+000+-0--0-+-+----+0--000-----
0000000000000000000.
*0      25/10/95.
*CE*    :Visitor, guest, stranger.
FIJ-    <Manu ciri. :Wandering bird (Mythological)>.
HAW     Malihini. :Stranger, newcomer, guest.
MAO     Manuwhiri. :Visitor, guest.
MQA     Manihi`i. :Hote, étranger; convives.
RAR     Manu`iri. :Stranger, visitor, guest from distant
                   parts.
TAH     Manuhiri. :Guest, visitor.
TAH1    Manihini. :Guest, visitor.
TIK-    <Manu. :Wanderer, traveller>.
TUA     Marihini. :Guest, visitor.
TUA1    Manihini. :Guest, visitor.
```

Figure 2.4   The entry for *manufiri in POLLEX (Biggs 2000a).

The first line shows the proto-language to which the form is reconstructed, in this case PCE, and the reconstructed form itself. For reconstructions to PPN or higher-level proto-languages, like PAN, the given form is the reconstructed PPN form. For lower levels, as in this case, the form is that reconstructed to the lower level. The next line ('TICK') is a code for which languages have been checked for the occurrence of a cognate. Next follow the date of entry and the meaning reconstructed for this form. The remaining lines record the data from PN languages on which the reconstruction is based, using the now effectively standard three-letter abbreviations for language names. Since this file was begun at a time when coding was restricted to ASCII characters, there are one or two conventions of note. <9> is used for <ŋ> in those languages, like Tuamotuan, which use this symbol as a letter, and <Q> is used for the glottal stop in reconstructed forms, though <`> is used in the data.

Marck's (especially 2000) work represents really the only large-scale research exploiting this resource, and concentrates on the collection of sporadic sound changes attested in the data, and on the evidence which the list provides for subgrouping. There has as yet been nothing done to determine whether, for instance, there are any generalisations which suggest themselves as to the domains of vocabulary that were acquired at different stages of Māori's history.

Apart from the lexical innovations reflected in those 'indigenous' Māori words which seem to have no cognates outside New Zealand (e.g. those in Table 2.9), important changes occurred in the vocabulary as a result of the migrations from tropical Island Polynesia to temperate New Zealand. Confronted with an environment containing features, flora and fauna not previously known, Māori vocabulary adapted by a combination of neologism and semantic shift.[75]

A well-known case of the latter type is change of meaning of inherited *moa 'fowl, chicken' – creatures which the migrants seem not to have brought with them – to designate the now extinct large flightless birds (*Dinornis*) which were encountered on arrival, and which were widely hunted for food. Some of these reached heights of three metres, quite unlike the *moa* of the homeland. A further example was the extension of the meaning of *huka* (from PNP *fuka) 'foam' to encompass also 'frost, snow'. Similarly, *roto* (from PPN *loto 'lagoon, pool') became the usual word to designate a lake such as was scarcely encountered on the tropical islands, but which was a very important body of water in New Zealand.

Neologism as a device for adaptation of the inherited vocabulary to the new environment consisted in the application of the derivational processes available to Māori – affixation, compounding and reduplication – to words already in the vocabulary.[76]

Kawakawa '*Macropiper excelsum*' is a reduplication of *kawa '*piper methysticum*, the drink derived from this shrub'. New Zealand *kawakawa* is in many respects physically like the plant designated *kawa* (or cognates of *kawa*) in related languages, but lacks the narcotic properties enjoyed in the tropical climes. *Kōwharawhara* and *pūwharawhara* '*Astelia banskii*' are words formed by both affixation (*kō-* and *pū-*) and the reduplication of *fara 'pandanus', a plant similarly not found in New Zealand. *Kahikatea*, a compound of inherited *kafika 'Malay apple' and *tea* 'clear, white (adj.)', designates the white pine.

Other areas of vocabulary which underwent development involved canoe terminology and vocabulary to name the various types of greenstone, jade, which were extracted, traded and exploited for tools and ornaments.

The next major event to have an influence on the vocabulary of Māori was contact with European languages. The first reliably recorded arrival of Europeans in New Zealand was the visit of the Dutchman Abel Tasman in 1642. However, it was not until after the visit of James Cook in 1769 that effective contact occurred through successions of whalers, sealers, missionaries, traders, settlers, and eventually government officials.[77] These contacts of course brought Māori and their language face to face with a huge range of goods, and cultural and religious ideas and practices which had been completely unknown previously.

The language adapted in predictable ways to the new circumstances. Of course, borrowing from English (and, to a very small extent, other languages, e.g. *miere* 'honey' from French *miel*) played a major role.[78] As will be seen, the phonology of Māori is very different from that of English, so that the incorporation of words of English origin entailed considerable modification. In particular, since Māori has no voice contrast in its stops, voiced stops collapse with voiceless ones (though English /d/ often surfaces as Māori /r/): *pēke* 'bank, bag', *kuihi* 'goose', *tīhema* 'December', but also *kāri* 'card'. Māori has no sibilants, so English sibilants are primarily represented by /h/, with the affricates sometimes adapted as /ti/,[79] occasionally /ri/ (for English /dʒ/): *hāhi* 'church', *hōiho* 'horse', *penihana* 'pension', *tiamana* 'German, chairman', *hori* 'George'. Māori /r/ serves for English /r, l/, as well as for some /d/ and /dʒ/: *reta* 'letter', *miraka* 'milk'. The phonotactics of Māori admit no consonant clusters or word-final consonants, so English consonant clusters are either split up by means of epenthetic vowels or simplified by the loss of all but one of the consonants: *aihi kirīmi* 'ice cream', *miraka* 'milk', *perehipitīriana* 'Presbyterian' exemplify the use of epenthetic vowels; *kōtimana* 'thistle (< Scotsman)', *poutāpeta* 'post office', *pēke* 'bank' show simplification of clusters. English final consonants are accommodated by having a supporting vowel added: *raiti* 'light', *pāmu* 'farm', *pere* 'bell'.

There is some difficulty in determining what words were borrowed in the earliest period of contact. Our sources for that period are essentially of two types: word lists compiled by missionaries and other Europeans; and ecclesiastical materials, such as biblical translations and prayer books, and, by the middle of the nineteenth century, political and administrative documents. It is likely that word lists under-report borrowing, since their compilers would have been more interested in recording indigenous Māori words than reporting actual usage, while the other types of document perforce contain numerous nonce 'borrowings', as their authors struggled to express new ideas and concepts. The first reliable source is an extended narrative by Renata Kawepō Tama Ki Hikurangi of a journey undertaken with Bishop Selwyn in 1842–3.[80]

This text contains twenty-nine borrowed items, which not only are typical of the semantic fields of items borrowed into Māori throughout its contact with English, but also illustrate other aspects of this process. Many of the items are ecclesiastical terminology, such as *pīhopa* 'bishop', *hapa* 'communion, i.e. Eucharist' (from English 'supper'); articles of clothing, e.g. *hāte* 'shirt', *hū* 'shoe'; terms relating to trade, goods and containers, e.g. *moni* 'money', *kāho* 'cask', *karaihe* 'looking glass', *kēna* 'can', *paraikete* 'blanket', *tupeka* 'tobacco'. In some of these fields, new vocabulary was also generated by the extension of the meaning of existing Māori words, occasionally leading to doublets. Renata uses both *pēti* and *moenga*[81] for 'bed', and *parāoa* 'flour, bread' beside *taro* 'bread'. Modern Māori religious terminology contains, as well as borrowed items such as those already appearing in Renata's text, *tapu* for 'holy', *karakia* for 'church service' by extension of the original meanings 'ritual restriction' and 'incantation', respectively.

When words are borrowed into a language, they take on a life of their own, which may involve the acquisition of meanings not expressed by the word in the source language. Two examples from Renata are *hereni*, *herengi* (which also illustrates the variability of form shown by many borrowed items) 'shilling', thence 'money generally', and *wiki* 'week', which became a verb meaning 'to pass Sunday'.

Similar borrowings and adaptations continued to be made throughout the period of contact with English, until quite recently, when Māori encountered the third major event to influence the language. As a result of the efforts made over the last twenty years or so to maintain and revitalise the language (on which see chapter 7), Māori is now being used in a wide range of domains which used to be virtually the exclusive preserve of English. This has led to the need for deliberate vocabulary development and terminological work to equip it for its new uses. The language remains, of course, in contact with English, but now the work of extending the Māori lexicon is governed by an ideology of purism which prohibits borrowing. The devices used are thus varieties of adaptation of existing lexical resources, providing the language with its most recent layer of vocabulary in a history which has left traces all the way from PPN through the language's travels and challenges to the present day.

NOTES

1. Good introductions to historical linguistics and its methods can be found, for instance, in Campbell (1999), Crowley (1997) and Fox (1995).
2. See also Benton (1991).
3. See particularly Ross (1994) and Tryon (1994b) – both of which are chapters in Tryon (1994a) – Lynch *et al.* (2002), Kirch and Green (2001). These works also contain information and further references on the corroborative evidence from archaeology.
4. Tryon (1994b:6).
5. The Indonesian province of Papua, along with Papua New Guinea and Solomon Islands, is home also to numbers of non-Austronesian languages, often referred to as Papuan languages.
6. This analysis is due primarily to the work of Robert Blust, see for instance Blust 1977, 1978, 1984, 1987, 1993.
7. Lapita Culture is the term in archæology for a range of sites associated with a particular type of pottery found from New Britain in the West to Tonga in the East. See, for instance, Lynch *et al.* (2002:98–9), Pawley (1996).
8. See Pawley (1996).
9. See papers in Sutton (1994), and especially Sutton's preface, pp. 1–18.
10. See Biggs (1994a).
11. Again, see papers in Sutton (1994), also chapter 3 below for an account of the linguistic evidence relevant to this question.
12. Tribal traditions pointing to several founder canoes would of course be incompatible with a single prehistoric arrival. However, there is the possibility that what is remembered in the canoe traditions may be movements within New Zealand after initial settlement. See Simmons (1976) for a full discussion of these traditions.
13. See Orbell (1985).
14. See Taumoefolau (1996) for an interesting proposal as to the etymology of this name.

15. In Hawaiian spelling, the symbol ' is used for the glottal stop, the reflex of Eastern Polynesian *k, preserved as /k/ in Māori. Similarly, the glottal stop in both Samoan and Tahitian corresponds to Māori /k/.
16. See also Blust (1990), which summarises the reconstructed PAN phonology and refers to a number of the broader developments sketched here.
17. Based on Pawley (1972, 1996) and Lynch *et al.* (2002).
18. POC *b, d, g, bʷ, j, dr are taken to have been prenasalised voiced stops. *c, s, j are palatals, and *pʷ, bʷ, mʷ labiovelars.
19. The status of POC *pʷ and its reflexes is by no means so clear as that of the other labiovelars. See Lynch (2002).
20. This example is from Biggs (2000a).
21. Unless otherwise stated, the meaning of reflexes is the same as that of the equivalent word/s in the proto-language.
22. In a number of cases, such reduplicated monosyllables are simplified in POC and acquire a following vowel, e.g. PAN *butbut > POC *(pu)puti > Māori (*hu*)*huti*, all meaning 'pluck'.
23. These examples from Lynch *et al.* (2002:66).
24. Still the best account of Polynesian historical phonology is Biggs (1978).
25. Some regional variants of Māori show different reflexes of some PPN sounds or have undergone mergers beyond those shown in Table 2.2. On this, see chapter 3.
26. In Niuean, in Proto-Central Eastern Polynesian and at least once among the languages of the Samoic-Outlier group of Figure 2.3.
27. Some PN languages go even further. Hawaiian has, for instance, only eight consonant phonemes, having further merged PPN *f and *s to /h/, and *n and *ŋ to /n/.
28. On the synchronic analysis of this feature of Māori phonology, see chapter 4.
29. Māori also has long diphthongs, so there are also some syllables of the form (C)VVV, see chapter 4.
30. As Trudgill himself points out, many of those Polynesian languages, called Outliers, which are spoken in Melanesia in close contact with non-Polynesian languages, have increased their phoneme inventories in this way, some radically.
31. Māori /f/ is spelt <wh>, and is of all the consonants the one showing the greatest variation in pronunciation. See chapter 4. Biggs (1978:707) speculates that PPN *f was an unvoiced fricative, possibly with both labio-dental and bilabial allophones.
32. Māori does have words with the phoneme sequence /faf/. However, with the exception of the item *whawhe* 'encircle, interfere with', which cannot be traced to PPN *faf- (see Biggs 2000a: under FAFE), the other instances are reduplicated forms, e.g. *whawhai* 'fight' from *whai* 'pursue'.
33. On the synchronic phonotactic rule */fo,u/, and for that matter */wo,u/, see chapter 4.
34. See chapter 3.
35. In Rarotongan, for instance, *f and *s have merged completely to /ʔ/, and in Hawaiian, to /h/.
36. In some languages, e.g. those of the southern Cook Islands, this /h/ shifted to /ʔ/.
37. Described as a voiceless alveopalatal fricative in Yasuda (1968:21).
38. By about 1840; see chapter 4.
39. These examples are from Kendall (1815).

40. The reconstructions in this table are from Biggs (2000a).
41. Mōriori is the indigenous language of the Chatham Islands, a group belonging to New Zealand but situated some 650 kilometres to the east of the South Island. On this language and its relationship to New Zealand Māori, see chapter 3.
42. For more detail, see chapter 3.
43. There are, however, very many words where all dialects retain /f/ from *f, e.g. *whare* 'house', and yet others where all dialects agree on /h/ from *f, e.g. *ahi* 'fire'.
44. At least historically. However, the form in /k/ has been literally gaining ground in recent time at the expense of the /p/ form, though this latter is attested in older eastern and southern sources, as well as place names in the east. Strikingly in this case, both forms have cognates outside New Zealand, see Harlow (1994a:114). Note also that this is a word which shows the regionally determined alternation: /f/∼/h/, so that *kōwhatu* also occurs.
45. Harlow (1987: under *poenemu* and *poueru*).
46. E.g. Spanish *peligroso* 'dangerous' from Latin *periculosus*, English *wasp* from earlier *wæps*.
47. Biggs (2000a) connects this word with PPN *ŋali 'better, preferred'. In modern Māori *engari* is now used virtually exclusively. On Te Rangikāheke, see chapter 1.
48. If the vowels of the adjacent syllables concerned are identical, this case cannot be distinguished from metathesis of whole syllables. This section illustrates only cases where clearly only consonants have undergone metathesis.
49. The /h/ in the second form, for /f/, is due to the phonotactic constraint on /f,wo,u/, on which see chapter 4.
50. *Whare* in this sense only in the South Island, where *rewha* also occurs, see Harlow (1987: under *refa* and *whare*).
51. See Harlow (1991b) for further examples and more detail.
52. See chapter 1.
53. The MAONZE (Māori and New Zealand English) project is funded by the Marsden Research Fund, administered by the Royal Society of New Zealand on behalf of the government. The ongoing project on New Zealand English is called ONZE (Origins of New Zealand English): see Gordon *et al.* (2004).
54. See chapter 4 for further references to the MAONZE project.
55. For more detail on both studies, see Maclagan and King (2002 and 2001, respectively).
56. See below, and especially Biggs (2000a).
57. Eastern Polynesian languages have a third pattern called Actor Emphatic, on which see below in this chapter and chapter 6.
58. Both the verb-initial order and the marker of A in pattern 2 are PN innovations, see Pawley (1996).
59. C = a variable over several consonant phonemes which occur in allomorphs of this suffix.
60. On this class of verbs in Māori, also called 'experience' verbs, see below, chapter 5.
61. See especially Chung (1978) for the evidence for these analyses.
62. In Samoan, etc., these NPs are marked by zero. In Tongan there is an 'absolutive' particle, *'a*, which can mark intransitive subjects and transitive objects.

63. These two examples are from Biggs (1969:31 and 33), also cited in Chung (1977:355). The glosses here are as in Chung: aor(ist), Pass(ive suffix), Acc(usative).
64. Interestingly though, the fronted agent of the Actor Emphatic construction can control a reflexive.
65. As with the passive suffix ('-*Cia*') mentioned above, '-*Canga*' conventionally stands for the set of allomorphs of this suffix. See chapter 5.
66. Most intransitive predicates. The *a* marking is available if the predicate, even though intransitive, is highly agentive.
67. If not marked as an object by means of *i/ki*.
68. See, for instance, Clark (1973:576–80) and Chung (1978:66–71) and references therein. See also chapter 6.
69. The 'subject' treated in this way is the A of transitive clauses and the S of intransitive ones, not the absolutive marked noun phrase.
70. See chapter 5. Some other EP languages have taken this reduction of allomorphy even further. While Māori preserves the pair *koe* ~ -*u* '2Sg.' (*nōu* 'belonging to you'), Tahitian, for instance, has eliminated the alternation: '*oe* occurs both as the free form and with possessive prepositions – *nō* '*oe*.
71. In fact, those other languages which show this phenomenon reflect a *tei rather than a cognate of Māori *kei*.
72. The existence of *a* and *o* forms here is due to the double possessive system referred to briefly above and dealt with in detail in chapter 6. The forms in *n*- seem to be an EP innovation based on an earlier **ni* + possessive pronoun found in some non-Eastern NP languages, e.g. Pileni (Næss 2000:60). The forms in *m*- are inherited from PPN. Most EP languages – e.g. Tahitian, Hawaiian, Cook Islands Māori – have merged the *n*- and *m*- forms to *n*-.
73. Thus, Rarotongan *Nā*+NP$_1$ *e*+V+*ana i*+ NP$_2$ is possible and focusses the subject of a present-tense, accusative-marked transitive clause.
74. Similarly useful, but now very outdated, is Tregear's (1891) comparative dictionary.
75. See especially Biggs (1991 and 1994b). See also Harlow 2004), which covers not only this period of vocabulary change but also the effects of contact with European languages and of modern developments in the status and use of Māori.
76. On these processes, see chapter 5.
77. See Salmond (1991, and particularly 1997).
78. See, particularly, Duval (1992 and 1995), Moorfield and Paterson (2002) and J. S. Ryan (1972).
79. As will be seen in chapter 4, Māori /t/ has a palatalised allophone before /i/, which in turn is often shortened to [j] before stressed vowels. Thus a string like /tiaki/ is phonetically rather like the 'cheque' of which it is the 'nativised' form.
80. Hogan (1994) provides an accessible edition of the text along with translation and commentary.
81. Derived from *moe* 'sleep' and the suffix -*nga*, here 'place where', see chapter 5.

3   Regional variation in Māori

The Eastern Polynesian speech form which was to become the Māori language was brought to New Zealand as long as 800–1,000 years ago, and so far as we can tell spread rapidly over the whole of both major islands. Even assuming for the moment that this arrival was originally of a single group of people bringing a completely homogeneous speech form with them, it is not surprising that over time differences began to appear in this language in different areas. That is, Māori is not a single speech form, but has dialects. As will be seen, the differences lie predominantly in the lexicon and in some aspects of phonology, and are never such that mutual intelligibility is impaired.

That the language showed such variation has been noticed and commented on ever since there have been written records. Joseph Banks, for instance, included in his journal of the first voyage of the *Endeavour* (1769–70) lists of words labelled 'northern' (forty-two items) and 'southern' (twenty-six items) along with Tahitian equivalents.[1] In fact, most of the items in the two Māori lists are clearly the same, but it is significant that even after such short contact with the language Banks was aware that there were regional differences he felt needed recognising.

Since that time, missionaries and writers of grammars and dictionaries, among other commentators, have all referred to the existence of regional variation, and in many cases given some few examples.[2] For instance, James Watkin, the first missionary in the Otago region (southern third of the South Island approximately), wrote, on his arrival there in 1840, that 'I soon found that the dialect spoken here differs materially from that of your Island [i.e. the North Island]',[3] and set about preparing his own materials for liturgical and teaching uses, since the books he had with him from the North Island he found unusable.

Maunsell (1842:viii) distinguishes seven 'leading dialects' in the North Island, those indicated in italics on Map 3.1, adding that Rotorua forms part of his East Cape variety. The long tradition of lexicography by the Williams family, of which H. W. Williams (1971) is the fullest and most recent product, began shortly after with W. L. Williams (1844). The first four editions, all under the name of William Williams, mark a large number of items as coming from one or the other of six dialects, covering much the same areas as Maunsell's

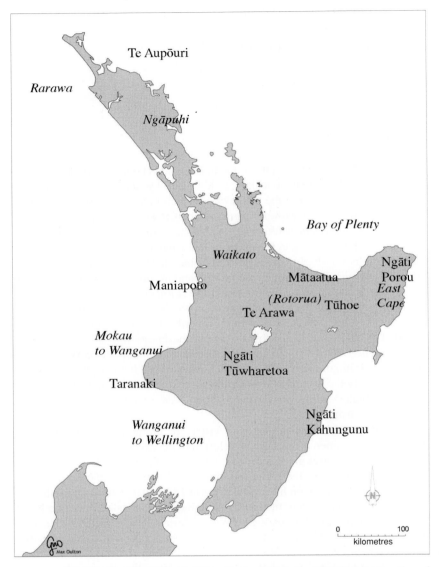

Te Aupōuri

Rarawa

Ngāpuhi

Bay of Plenty

Waikato

Ngāti
Porou
East
Cape

Maniapoto

Mātaatua

(Rotorua) Tūhoe
Te Arawa

Mokau
to Wanganui

Ngāti
Tūwharetoa

Taranaki

Ngāti
Kahungunu

Wanganui
to Wellington

N

0   100
kilometres

Max Oulton

Map 3.1 The North Island of New Zealand, showing (in italics) the location of
Maunsell's (1842) divisions and (in plain type) other areas/tribes mentioned
in this section.

Table 3.1. *Some examples of the lexical dialect differences reported in Rikihana (1976:8–10)*

English	Te Arawa	Waikato-Maniapoto	Ngāpuhi	Mātaatua	Ngāti Porou
head	ūpoko māhunga	māhunga pane	mātenga pane	māhuna	māhunga
cat	pūihi	ngeru	tori	poti ngeru	poti

classification, with the added proviso (in the 1852 edition:v) that words unmarked in this way are either from Ngāpuhi or 'common to most tribes'.

More recent editions of the dictionary have to a very large extent discontinued this practice, on the grounds that 'intercommunication between the different tribes, by obliterating niceties of dialect, has made the investigation of such niceties a matter of extreme difficulty' (H. W. Williams 1971:xxix, in the preface to the fifth edition 1917). Nonetheless, these more recent editions do in fact mark a few items as peculiar to specific areas.

Many more recent materials than Maunsell's book give some space to the regional diversity of Māori. For instance, Rikihana (1976:8–10) mentions the few phonological differences (to which we return below), and gives a table of ten English words, contrasting their translation equivalents in five Māori dialects (see Table 3.1).

As a final example of this type of data on dialects, Benton (1982), a teaching resource containing structured lists of almost 800 of the most frequently occurring words in a corpus of children's literature in Māori, also includes an indication of the dialect origin of a number of forms. For example, the entry for *makariri* 'cold, esp. weather' goes on to give the following equivalents: '[*Au = kōpeke, *W = māeke, *E = mātao]'.[4] Given this constant reference in publications of these kinds, and given further not only all native speakers' awareness of the existence of such regional variation, but also the importance attached to these differences as markers of tribal identity, it is striking, not to say an indictment, that there are only two short publications devoted primarily to the study of the dialects of Māori. Harlow (1979) and Biggs (1989), on which much of the following sketch of Māori variation depends, both provide some data, while lamenting that the dialects have not yet been the object of much more exhaustive study.

Biggs' (1989) article makes a very valid point in answer to the view expressed in the Williams dictionary and cited above that increasing intercommunication has lessened the variation to be observed. Biggs points out that the regional variations in Māori are associated not only with place, but at least as significantly with tribes. Thus, wherever they might live, people tend to preserve at least those features of their dialect which serve to mark their tribal connections. In the case of people who have moved from their own tribal area, this is of course simply a matter of retention of their own dialect. However, there is a marked tendency for learners to take up and deliberately use features of their own tribal dialect even when this is not the form of Māori they would mostly hear around them in the places where they live. Dialect loyalty and tribal identification are important in their implications for the efforts made to revitalise and 'modernise' Māori which will be discussed in chapter 7.

Harlow (1979), as well as summarising earlier reports, presented the results of a simple survey of eight North Island dialects using a modified Swadesh 200-word list,[5] and eliciting responses to the list from native speakers. As well, lists for South Island Māori and Mōriori were constructed from documentary sources.

There are similarly few works which have as their purpose the documentation of a particular variety of Māori. Harlow (1987) is an edition with commentary of a word list of some 1,400 items compiled in the early 1840s by the missionary Watkin referred to above. As such it is an important source of information on the variety of Māori which he encountered. This edition also brings together other sources (many of them only in manuscript) which bear on the same dialect and attempts a brief characterisation of the southern dialect on the basis of these materials.[6]

D. Wilson (1991) is primarily a sociolinguistic study of a small community in Northland, and includes data on, for instance, language choice. However, Wilson also elicited data from her informants on aspects of the Māori spoken in the community which are known from other sources to vary across the country.

A much broader project which attempts to provide a description of the lexicon of Māori as spoken in Northland generally is the Taitokerau Dictionary[7] project being conducted at the James Hēnare Māori Research Centre at the University of Auckland.

The nature of regional variation in Māori

Though in no respect very great, variation is found in all aspects of the language, phonology, grammar, lexicon and idiom. The divergent pronunciations and usages never impede mutual intelligibility, but are to quite an extent exploited as shibboleths, identifying speakers' regional and tribal origins. The following account is intended to give an impression of the nature and extent of the regional variation in Māori; a full picture of Māori dialectology is not only beyond the scope of this section, but also impossible in the absence of good research.

Phonological differences

Most varieties of Māori have the same segmental phonology with five vowels and ten consonants, as presented below in chapter 4: /a, e, i, o, u, p, t, k,

Table 3.2. *Examples of historical mergers in two Māori dialects*

Most dialects	Bay of Plenty	South Island	
/ana/	/ana/	/ana/	'cave'
/aŋa/	/ana/	/aka/	'shell'
/aka/	/aka/	/aka/	'root'
/puka/	/puka/	/puka/	'form (for filling in)'
/puŋa/	/puna/	/puka/	'anchor'
/puna/	/puna/	/puna/	'spring'

m, n, ŋ, r, f, w, h/. There are, however, two varieties in which mergers have occurred. In parts of the Bay of Plenty (Mātaatua, Tūhoe, see Map 3.1), *n and *ŋ merged to /n/, while in the dialect of most of the South Island,[8] *k and *ŋ merged to /k/. Both these varieties thus had similar inventories, the standard one minus /ŋ/, though the distribution of /k/ and /n/ is of course different. Thus correspondences such as those in Table 3.2 are found.

Both mergers occurred before the existence of any records, the Bay of Plenty merger being referred to by Maunsell (1842), and the South Island one already evident in the very earliest sources, e.g. George Forster's list of bird names compiled during the visit of Cook's ship *Resolution* to the far south in 1773 (Begg and Begg 1966:122).

Other phonological differences between regional variants of Māori are either a matter of the pronunciation of particular phonemes, or cases of differing distribution of phonemes in specific lexical items.

In the region of Taranaki and Wanganui (see Map 3.1 above), /h/ is realised as a glottal stop [ʔ], and /f/ as a glottalised [ʔw]. In fact, in general, the phoneme /f/ shows perhaps the greatest variation among the sounds of Māori. Reference has been made in chapter 2 to the history of this sound. In modern Māori, the majority of speakers use [f]; however, besides the very deviant pronunciation just mentioned, there is a strong tendency for speakers in Northland to avoid [f], using bilabial articulations, and, in the prefix *whaka-*, [h]. Sporadic pronunciations of /r/ as [l] (usually [ɾ]) occur in speakers from a variety of regions, but seem to have been particularly a feature of South Island speech,[9] and possibly of some Northland speech; D. Wilson (1991:72–3) draws particular attention to this feature of the speech of her Northland community.

Otherwise, it is in the form of obviously related words that dialects can vary. In particular, there are four pairs of phonemes which in certain environments show a western vs eastern distribution. A broad division of Māori dialects into western and eastern was proposed by Biggs (1961:2–3), and is supported not only by the phonological features to be described, but also by a few preferences

Table 3.3. *Biggs' examples of regional /ei/ ~ /ai/ alternations*

Waikato (i.e. western)	Ngāti Porou (i.e. eastern)	
teina	*taina*	'younger sibling same sex' < **tahina*
kei	*kai*	'at (present)'? < **ka *i*
hei	*hai*	'at (future)' **sei*
wheeiro	*whaairo*	'be seen, understood' (? < **fai-iro*)

in grammar, and some lexical variation. Nonetheless, within each division, more local variation remains marked. Biggs' western dialects are those of Northland (Rarawa, Ngāpuhi, Te Aupōuri of Map 3.1), Waikato, Maniapoto, Taranaki, Whanganui, while the eastern division includes those of Tūhoe, the whole of the East Coast of the North Island from Ngāti Porou southwards, and the speech forms of the South Island. The varieties spoken in Te Arawa and Ngāti Tūwharetoa show features of both divisions.

The alternations are:

(1) Western /ei/ ~ eastern /ai/:[10] in the words in which this alternation occurs, it is sometimes the eastern form which is conservative, and sometimes the western. Biggs (1989:67) gives the examples in Table 3.3.

The etymologies given by Biggs are plausible, though in the case of *teina* ~ *taina* it is more likely that the immediate ancestor of Māori had already made the assimilation from PPN *tahina to *teina, since the more closely related languages such as Rarotongan and Tahitian all show *teina*. In any event, it is clear from these examples that in some words eastern dialects have innovated with a shift /ei/ > /ai/, while in others the opposite innovation occurred in western dialects.

(2) A parallel development is evident in a very few words illustrating an alternation /ou/ ~ /au/, as shown by Biggs (1989:67) in Table 3.4.

(3) Western dialects preserve *u; eastern show a shift to /i/. Biggs (1989:67) describes this as an irregular eastern preference for /i/ 'following a front consonant'. However, a glance at the list of his examples (Table 3.5) suggests that it is perhaps rather the presence of other labial/rounded sounds in the word which has conditioned a dissimilation.

(4) /f/ ~ /h/: the developments affecting PPN *f in Māori have been discussed in chapter 2. For the present issue, it is important to recall that there are three types of word in Māori reflecting PPN *f: those where all dialects have /f/, e.g. *whare* 'house' < *fale; those where all dialects have /h/, e.g. *ahi* 'fire' < *afi; and those which show an alternation /f/ ~ /h/. Apart from examples such as *kōhuhu* ~ *kōwhiwhi* in Table 3.5, in which the /f/ ~ /h/

Table 3.4. *Biggs' examples of regional*
/ou/ ~ /au/ alternations

Western	Eastern	
-tou	-tau	'pronoun plural marker' < *-tou
māpou	māpau	'tree sp.'
tūmou	tūmau	'permanent' < *tūmau

Table 3.5. *Biggs' examples of regional /i/ ~ /u/*
alternations

Western	Eastern	
tupu	tipu	< *tupu 'grow'
kōhuhu	kōwhiwhi	< *kōfufu 'tree sp.'[11]
pupuru	pupuri	< *pulu 'grasp'
tuturu	tuturi	< *tulu 'drip'
tupa	tipa	< *tupa 'scallop' ('landcrab' in PPN)

alternation is due to the difference in the vowels, the distribution of /f/
and /h/ forms corresponds to the western/eastern division: *manuwhiri* ~
manuhiri 'guest', *whea* ~ *hea* 'where'.

Beyond these semi-regular alternations, there are numerous examples of
idiosyncratic regional alternations in the form of lexical items, some of which
have already been mentioned in chapter 2, as they can represent innovations vs
retentions of inherited forms. For instance, the distribution of the pair *ngaro* ~
rango 'blowfly' (< *laŋo) is regionally based, my own data recording *ngaro*
in Waikato and Northland and extending as far east as Tūhoe, with inherited
rango preserved on the East Coast and in the South Island. Similarly, *toke* ~
noke 'worm' shows a distribution following Biggs' western/eastern division.
The modern and historical distribution of *pōhatu* ~ *kōhatu* ~ *kōwhatu* has
already been referred to in chapter 2; however, a similar alternation *rūkahu* ~
rūpahu 'lie' has kept to what must have also been the earlier western/eastern
division for both sets of words. Other examples, to which we will have to
return along with others mentioned here, are the words for 'right (not left)' and
'heavy'. In data collected for Harlow (1979), *katau* 'right' was recorded for
Tūhoe, Waikato, Taranaki and the South Island, while *matau* occurred in Ngāti
Tūwharetoa, Ngāpuhi, Te Aupōuri, Ngāti Porou, and Ngāti Kahungunu. For
'heavy', the preferred forms are *toimaha* in Waikato, *taimaha* in the remaining
western areas, and *taumaha* elsewhere.

Finally, it appears that the South Island dialect(s) had one or two sporadic processes which led to forms of some words which differed from cognates in the north. For instance, forms such as *poueru* 'widow' and *pounemu* 'greestone, jade' for North Island *pouaru* and *pounamu* respectively point to an assimilation process analogous to the much earlier (and thus much more widely attested) assimilation in PNP *fenua ~ fanua 'land' from PPN *fanua.[12]

Grammatical variation

There are one or two instances of morphological variation, which correlate with region. The distribution of the 'default' passive suffix is referred to in chapter 5, but beyond this there are variations, in part at least analogical in origin, to be found in prepositions, pronouns and determiners. The pairs of prepositions *kai ~ kei, hai ~ hei* 'at (present), at (future)' have been mentioned above. Otherwise, the only point at which there is real regional variation in the form of prepositions is a northern use of *ko* in lieu of *hei* 'at (future)', e.g. *ko reira* (P there(anaphoric)) 'will be there'.

In the personal pronouns, the eastern/western alternation in the plural suffix of the non-second-person pronouns (*-tau ~ -tou*) has already been mentioned. In addition, there are the following forms to note: in Northland, shortened unstressed forms of the non-second-person dual forms are found – *tao, mao, rao* for *tāua, māua, rāua* '1Incl.Du., 1Excl.Du., 3Du.' – while both Northland and the East Coast exhibit analogical change in the non-singular second-person forms. In most regions, inherited *kōrua* and *koutou* '2Du., 2Pl.' are preserved, while Northland has *kourua* and *koutou* against East Coast *kōrua* and *kōtou*.

Most regions preserve the inherited alternation in determiners: *t- ~ Ø-* for singular and plural, thus *tēnei* 'this'*~ ēnei* 'these', *tōku* 'Sg.of.1Sg., my (one thing)' *~ ōku* 'Pl.of.1Sg., my (several things)'. In the Waikato area, however, plural forms with prefixed *ng(e)* are common: *ngēnei, ng(e)ōku* created on the analogy of the specific article, *te ~ ngā*, the only determiner to show plural without the *t- ~ Ø-* alternation.

The final case to be mentioned here, but one which will be of interest in the matter of the origin of Māori dialect variation, is a range of possessive forms. Following the possessive prepositions *o* and *a*,[13] the singular pronouns have suffixal allomorphs, *-ku, -u, -na*. These prepositions form the basis for possessive determiners, as well as for the prepositional phrases: *o/a* +NP, *nō/nā* + NP, *mō/mā* + NP 'of, belongs to, for NP'. Thus, using the pronominal allomorphs, *nāku* 'belongs to me', *mōu* 'for you (Sg.)', *tāna* 'his/her', etc. In dialects of the East Coast, a set of expanded second-person forms also occurs: *tāhau/tōhou, nāhau, mōhou*, etc. There is some evidence from texts and other historical sources, that the dialect of the South Island also knew these forms, and in fact had extended them to the other persons as well: *tāhaku, nōhona, mōhoku*, etc.

Some regional variation in areas of syntax is also reported. Biggs (1989:71–2), for instance, gives a list of some twelve points where he had himself observed variation. However, some at least of the items he names are a matter of syntactic change, and the innovative and conservative variants are not distributed regionally. This notwithstanding, there are a few aspects of syntax to which one can point where there are at least regional preferences. For instance, while the verbal markers (see chapter 6) *e . . . ana* 'progressive' and *kei te* ∼ *i te* 'progressive (present* ∼ *past)*' are available in all dialects, the latter forms are preferred in the east. Similarly, *kīhai* 'negation (past)' is known in all dialects, but is nowadays used at all productively only in Northland. Northland too is the only region in which personal nouns can be used as the subject of a clause without the personal article (Biggs 1989:71): *Ka kī Moetara* (TA say M) 'Moetara said', whereas this would always be *Ka kī a Moetara* elsewhere. Conversely, examples are found in Taranaki of the use of personal pronouns after prepositions ending in *-i* without an intervening personal article: *ki rātou* 'to them', beside the *ki a rātou* of all other areas.

Bauer (1997:123) notes that in East Coast dialects, among others, habitual aspect can be indicated on a verb by the particle *ai* without any preposed tense/aspect marker – *Tuhituhi reta ai ia* (write letter *ai* 3Sg.) 'He writes letters' (Bauer's example 829) – but that northern dialects such as that of Te Aupōuri use instead *e . . . ana* for both habitual and progressive senses.

Lexical variation

Lexical variation which correlates with region is of three kinds. The first type, which has already been referred to above, is the existence of phonologically slightly different forms of what is obviously the same word, for instance *tipu* ∼ *tupu, taina* ∼ *teina* (see tables above). In other cases, a word-form is shared by several dialects, but with differing meanings – e.g. *kirikiri*, which in the west, as in PN languages generally, has the meaning 'gravel, small stones', but in the east means 'sand'. Similarly, *pakeke* occurs widely with the meaning of 'adult, grown up, age', but in Northland means 'hard (not soft), difficult'. Occasional examples of this type occur in the area of plant nomenclature.[14] For instance, *kahika* occurs in some eastern dialects in the sense '*Podocarpus excelsum*, a tree species' but in the Far North of the North Island as '*Metrosideros excelsa*' (a different tree species). Biggs (1989:73) provides another good example: *kererū*, the designation for the 'woodpigeon' in the east, means 'black stink-bug' in the north. Now, both woodpigeons and stink-bugs are known and named everywhere, so that in fact the distribution of terms occurs as shown in Table 3.6.

This state of affairs leads straight to the third and most extensive type of lexical variation; different dialects have quite unrelated word-forms for the

Table 3.6. *Distribution of terms for 'woodpigeon' and 'stink-bug' in two regions of the North Island*

	Northern	Eastern
woodpigeon	*kūkupa*	**kererū**
stink-bug	**kererū**	*kēkerengū*

same meaning. A number of examples of this type have appeared already in, for instance, Table 3.1, drawn from Rikihana (1976). Other examples include the following: 'smoke' in the west is *paoa* ~ *pawa*, in Ngāti Porou *kauruki*, elsewhere *auahi*; 'shell' is *kota* in Te Aupōuri, *mākoi* in the Waikato, *anga* elsewhere; 'fish' is *ngohi* in Te Aupōuri, *ika* elsewhere.

A special case of this type of variation occurs where some dialect preserves an indigenous word for some referent while another area now uses a borrowed word. Richard Benton has expressed the view (personal communication) that in fact differential borrowing accounts for much of the difference between dialects in modern Māori. This is borne out to some extent in the data collected and reported on in Harlow (1979), in which, for instance, western dialects reported *wai tote* (*wai* 'water', *tote* < 'salt') for the item 'saltwater', vs *waitai* (*tai* < PPN *tahi 'sea'), and in which the word lists elicited varied considerably in the number of loanwords included, the fewest being two and the most eighteen.

It is hard to gauge the full extent of these types of lexical variation in the absence of good dialect dictionaries or general research findings on Māori regional variation. Harlow (1979) does give some indication, though this study was restricted to basic vocabulary and thus did not deal with areas of the wider vocabulary, such as plant and bird names, which are particularly known to vary. As indicated above, this paper, as well as summarising phonological and grammatical aspects of regional variation, reported on a comparison of eight lists of basic vocabulary collected from native speakers from the North Island, plus two lists, of South Island Māori and Mōriori, compiled from published sources.

Two types of result were extracted from these lists. The first was a pairwise comparison of the lists collected to arrive at a table of the sort familiar from lexicostatistical studies in historical linguistics.[15] The point of this exercise was to obtain, in the absence of any previous research on the matter, a crude indication of the extent of lexical variation between Māori dialects. Table 3.7 (reduced from Table 3.1 of Harlow 1979:129)[16] shows the relative levels of shared basic vocabulary of the eight North Island dialects for which lists were elicited.

Table 3.7. *Percentages of shared basic vocabulary between eight North Island dialects of Māori*

	TUH	TWH	WAI	NPH	AUP	NPR	KAH
TWH	76.6						
WAI	75.4	76.1					
NPH	75.2	74.6	74.3				
AUP	75.4	73.4	75.0	84.9			
NPR	82.0	77.5	76.3	77.8	78.5		
KAH	80.1	73.1	73.7	74.4	76.4	79.6	
TAR	74.8	74.6	77.9	74.1	75.2	76.1	78.1

The first thing that strikes the eye perhaps about this table is the level of the figures. There is a convention in the literature on lexicostatistics which classifies speech forms with levels of shared vocabulary of 81 per cent or greater as dialects of a single language.[17] Lower figures point to distinct languages. On this basis, only the dialects of Te Aupōuri and Ngāpuhi on the one hand, and Tūhoe and Ngāti Porou on the other, would count as related to each other as dialects of a single language; all other pairings are distinct languages. However, quite apart from the issues surrounding the use of the terms 'dialect' and 'language' in the case of closely related speech forms (see, for instance, Chambers and Trudgill 1998:3–4) and the lack of match between the purely statistical criterion and the usual senses of the terms, any attempt to apply this criterion in the present instance does great injustice to the relationship between these speech forms. On all accounts, these speech forms are dialects of a single language; they are so regarded by their speakers, and mutual intelligibility is very high. Significantly too, much of this lexical difference between the dialects is a matter of preference rather than the presence/absence of similar words. That is, the words elicited in the lists are generally rather more widely known than in just the dialects where they are recorded.

Before turning to the other type of analysis reported in Harlow (1979), it is worth pointing out that these figures weakly support Biggs' eastern grouping of dialects (Tūhoe, Ngāti Porou, Kahungunu) in that for all three dialects, the other two are those with the highest level of shared vocabulary. Biggs' original classification was, however, based more on phonological and morphological criteria (see above).

As well as being compared globally, the lists were investigated to identify innovations shared by subsets of dialects. Examples include *kūiti* 'narrow' recorded in the lists for Waikato, Ngāpuhi and Taranaki, against *whāiti*[18] in other dialects; *kirikiri* in the sense of 'sand' in Tūhoe, Ngāti Porou and Kahungunu lists;[19] *mātenga* 'head' shared by Ngāpuhi and Te Aupōuri, etc. Again, the data as analysed in this fashion provide some weak support for Biggs' classification, though, as we shall see, some of the items adduced in this context turn out to be more complicated/interesting than Harlow (1979) claimed.

Wharehuia Milroy (1996), while emphasising that mutual intelligibility between Māori dialects is very high, points to a further and at least symbolically important type of variation, namely idiom, especially address forms and other expressions such as exclamations, which fall outside the sentence. To provide only a brief example of what Milroy refers to, three forms for the extra-sentential 'no', in answer to a polarity question, are heard: *ehē* is very characteristic of Tūhoe speakers, *nō* (obviously borrowed) is a clear mark of Northland speech, while *kāo* is the more general term.

The implication of regional variation in Māori

Apart from the simple fact of their existence, and therefore their place in any synchronic description of Māori, the variations to be found in the language are of interest from two other perspectives. One of these points to the past, the other to the future. The significance of regional variation in Māori for the present-day efforts to maintain and develop the language has already been mentioned in this chapter and will be taken up again in chapter 7. The extent to which dialect loyalty has the potential to impede the normalisation of Māori in modern New Zealand is not a negligible factor in these efforts.

The perspective which looks to the past is the question of the relevance of the variation found in Māori for the prehistory of New Zealand – in particular, for the matter of the settlement of the country by Eastern Polynesians. Much of the variation found in modern Māori has arisen within New Zealand. This variation is consistent with a model of settlement which posits a single, perhaps chance, arrival, bringing the EP speech form which became Māori and diverged over time. However, not only the orally transmitted history of the Māori, the 'canoe' traditions,[20] but also a range of other types of evidence,[21] suggest the possibility of multiple settlement, even of deliberate two-way voyaging. Thus, it is possible that, rather than there being just one single settlement which saw the arrival in New Zealand of a single Eastern Polynesian speech form, different parts of the country were initially settled or subsequently visited by groups speaking closely related but slightly different Eastern Polynesian 'dialects'.

The data on the dialects of Māori are relevant to this issue to the extent that, in many instances, varying forms within Māori have parallels elsewhere in the Pacific. If it can be shown that a form of restricted distribution is an innovation within Māori and is shared with some language outside New Zealand, an argument can be made for a historical connection between the dialect of Māori in which the form occurs and that language. In arguing in this way, one must proceed very carefully, so as to exclude shared retentions, and possible instances of convergence. That is, assuming the subgrouping relationships of Māori sketched in chapter 2, one would have to show in each individual case of a feature apparently shared by some dialect of Māori and some language or languages outside New Zealand that the feature was probably not present in Proto-Tahitic, and that it is unlikely that the feature could have arisen independently in Māori and the other language(s). Only when both of these conditions are satisfied, can one argue that the feature is suggestive of some contact between the dialect of Māori and the other languages concerned.

All three of the systematic phonological features are candidates.

(1) The similarity of Māori as spoken in the Taranaki region and the languages of the Southern Cook Islands, in that both have replaced an earlier /h/ with /ʔ/ is often remarked on. In fact though, not only does the same phenomenon occur also in Mangarevan at the far eastern end of French Polynesia, almost certainly independently, but in the Cooks the change can only have occurred after the merger of *f and *s. Māori has, however, preserved this distinction. On balance, it must be concluded that the shifts are instances of convergence, and not an indication of any sort of contact between Cook Islands languages and Taranaki Māori independently of the other dialects of Māori.

(2) A similar conclusion seems best in the case of the merger of *n and *ŋ to /n/ in parts of the Bay of Plenty. Similar mergers appear in southern dialects of Marquesan and Hawaiian, as well as two, possibly three, languages in the Outliers[22] (Takuu, Sikaiana, and probably Luangiua).

(3) In the case of the merger of *k and *ŋ in South Island Māori, one is probably on firmer ground. There is direct evidence of this merger in only one other Polynesian language, the northern dialects of Marquesan, though Green (1966:22) is probably right in suggesting that it also occurred in prehistoric Tahitian, where both *k and *ŋ appear as /ʔ/. The South Island Māori, however, shows a few other features suggestive of a connection with the Marquesas, which, coupled with the relative 'unnaturalness' of the merger, make it more plausible that this is not a case of convergence, but occurred only once.

In addition to these features, a number of the more idiosyncratic variations in individual lexical items have parallels in related languages. Thus, for instance, while western dialects preserve PCE *toke 'worm',[23] found also in Rarotongan, Hawaiian, Mangarevan, Tahitian, etc., eastern dialects use *noke*, evidently an innovation. However, cognates of *noke* are also found in northern dialects of Marquesan. The alternation *kōhatu* ~ *pōhatu* 'stone' referred to above is similar. This time, however, it is the (now retreating) eastern *pōhatu* which is the reflex of the PCE word, and has cognates in Hawaiian, Mangarevan, Tahitian, etc. The western (and now dominant) *kōhatu* seems to be an innovation, but one shared with Mangaian, a language of the Southern Cook Islands.

As a final example of this sort, the distribution of *matau* ~ *katau* 'right (not left)' is interesting. PPN *mataʔu is reconstructed for this meaning, while *katau is a Central Eastern Polynesian innovation.[24] Reflexes of *katau are the only forms in the Southern Cook Islands languages, Hawaiian, and other CE languages. Yet, in Māori, the CE *katau* and the apparently inherited *matau* both occur. Biggs (2000a: under *katau*) labels this latter form eastern. However, the distribution of the two forms is more complicated than that. *Katau* seems to be the only form used in South Island Māori, while in the north, the eastern dialects seem to use both forms in free variation, Northland dialects have only *matau*, and Waikato only *katau*.

Particularly striking is the distribution of the extended possessive forms of the second person singular, *tōhou*, *nāhau*, etc., for inherited *tōu*, *nāu*, etc. (see above). As already indicated, South Island Māori not only shares these forms with dialects of the East Coast, North Island, but also has extended possessive forms for the first and third person pronouns as well: *tōhoku*, *māhana*, etc. A very similar distribution of very similar forms occurs in the Cook Islands. Southern Cooks languages such as Rarotongan have second person forms *tōʻou*, *nāʻau*, etc.[25] Manihiki/Rakahanga, a language of the Northern Cook Islands, on the other hand, has these forms as well, and also a set of similarly extended forms parallel to those of South Island Māori: *tōhoku*, *nāhana*, etc.[26]

The question with all these (and similar) items with tantalising distributions is what to make of them. On the one hand, at least some of these items seem likely to be reflexes of a single innovation which has been somehow spread into those dialects of Māori and the language(s) outside New Zealand which know the item. On the other hand, if these distributions were due to contact of some specific kind between an individual area of New Zealand and the other languages concerned, one would expect rather more evidence than a single feature of the sort mentioned here. For while these items do indeed exist, they are not plentiful and do not conspire to point decisively to special relationships between certain dialects of Māori and other individual languages. Only in the case of the South Island can one find a few separate pieces of evidence which seem to point in the same direction. This is something to which we return below. It should perhaps be noted, however, that if the modern Eastern Polynesian languages were in their relative positions, but on a rather smaller landmass, instead of spread over thousands of kilometres of sea, these features would probably be regarded in much the same way as the more familiar innovations shared in an irregular pattern by the Indo-European languages.[27] These are features which are distributed across a number of subgroups of Indo-European in a way which defies an account relying solely on a 'family-tree' model of the divergence of the family. Rather they point to the spread of innovations among already divergent but closely related speech forms in a way characterised by the so-called 'wave theory' of the spread of change. To apply this approach to at least some of the dialect features of Māori which are apparently shared with some languages outside New Zealand entails positing at the very least some sort of contact which would allow the partial spread of innovations. Quite what this was like, we will probably never know in detail.

Whether or not Māori as we know it now was brought to New Zealand by a single group or was at least influenced in different areas by contact with other closely related languages, or indeed was the result of different CE languages arriving and settling at different times and places, the history of the language has seen numerous innovations which cover the entire language. Some of these, such as *ringa* 'hand' from *rima, are mentioned in chapter 2. In this connection, it is interesting to observe that the shifts of meaning in, for instance, names of trees provoked by arrival in an environment which differed markedly from the homeland are to a very high degree the same everywhere in New Zealand. If some of the regional variation in Māori were due to multiple settlement, one could anticipate that reapplication of names for trees not found in New Zealand to new species not encountered before would vary from place to place and thus dialect to dialect. With very few exceptions, this seems not to have happened. The only really good instance of the same inherited form being applied to different plants is the case of *kafika 'Malay apple', whose reflex *kahika* is used in the Far North of New Zealand for a plant '*Metrosideros excelsa*' called *pōhutukawa* elsewhere, but in the east of New Zealand for a different plant again, '*Podocarpus excelsum*, a pine'.

South Island Māori

South Island Māori is essentially an eastern dialect of Māori. This is shown not only in its sharing of many of the eastern features discussed above, but also in its scoring markedly higher proportions of shared basic vocabulary with Ngāti Porou and Kahungunu than with other dialects in Harlow's (1979) comparative lists.

Traditional history explains this connection in that at least most of the South Island was populated by three 'layers' of peoples: an 'indigenous' tribe called Waitaha, and successive incursions by people from the north, Ngāti Mamoe and Ngāi Tahu, whose genealogical connections are with the East Coast tribes.

At the same time, however, the South Island dialect as recorded in the variety of sources at our disposal shows a few features, especially in phonology and lexicon, which distinguish it from northern dialects of the language, and which at the same time show similarities with languages outside New Zealand. The merger of *k and *ŋ to /k/, to which reference was made above, is shared in exactly this way only with northern dialects of Marquesan. A few lexical items found in the south but apparently unknown in North Island varieties are clearly retentions from PCE. For instance *iwi* 'narrow' (Harlow 1987: under *iui*) seems unknown in the north, but has cognates in Tahitian, Tuamotuan (*ivi* 'thin'), Hawaiian (*iwiiwi* 'skinny') and Marquesan (*ivi* 'thin'). Likewise, *whiro* (Harlow 1987: under *firo*) 'twist into string' is parallelled in Rapanui, Mangarevan (*hiro*), Marquesan (*hi'o*), Hawaiian (*hilo*) and Rarotonga (*'iro*), all with the same meaning. In these and similar cases, nothing can be concluded except that South Island Māori has retained words lost in other varieties of Māori. In the case of four other items, however, a more positive link, again with Marquesan, can be argued for.

(1) *Rewa*, evidently the name of a fish, is attested in Harlow (1987: under *reua*). H. W. Williams (1971) records *rua* in this sense, but gives as his only example a South Island text. The only possible cognate for this word in Eastern Polynesian seems to be Marquesan *'eva* 'fish fatal to man'.[28]

(2) *Whakatekateka* 'pride' is an interesting case. The word is probably PPN, occurring in Fijian as *vakateqateqa* 'proudly' and Tongan *fakateketeka* 'keep aloof'.[29] However, Tahitic languages have innovated in this word, changing it to *fakatekoteko: Tahitian *fa'ate'ote'o* 'proud, haughty', Hawaiian *ke'oke'o* 'proud', Tuamotuan *fakatekoteko* 'display pride'. North Island dialects also have this innovative form as *whakatekoteko* 'make grimaces'. The occurrence of *whakatekateka* in South Island Māori can be explained only by its being brought there from tropical Polynesia either *before* the Tahitic innovation took place and was subsequently brought to northern New Zealand, or from a non-Tahitic language of Eastern Polynesia. A plausible candidate for this latter explanation is again Marquesan where *ha'atekateka* 'behave badly or in an inappropriate, unreasonable manner' is attested.

(3) *Kakahu* (< *ŋaŋahu) 'bite'. The history of the words for 'bite' in EP languages is complicated. Suffice it here to say that the occurrence of this form in South Island Māori is parallelled in Hawaiian (*nahu*), Mangarevan (*ŋaŋahu*), Marquesan (northern dialects *kakahu*, southern *nanahu*), all meaning 'bite', against North Island *ngau*, with cognates in Rarotongan (*ngau*), Tahitian (*'au*), Tuamotuan (*ŋau*).

(4) *Whakateki* 'children's quarrels' has cognates only in Marquesan (*ha'ateki* 'sulk, pretend not to hear') and Mangarevan (*teki* 'be silent, not answer').

Again, the question arises as to what to make of these features. Chance similarity cannot of course be excluded entirely, but becomes increasingly unlikely the more items there are which point in the same direction. When these few items are allied with archæological evidence which in itself is also only suggestive, but points in the same way to a South Island – Marquesan connection,[30] the most plausible account posits some kind of multiple settlement in the south involving perhaps a Marquesic substratum in that part of the country to which the northern incursions recorded in traditional history added the elements which are more characteristically Māori.

Mōriori

Similar, though harder, problems face the scholar with respect to Mōriori. This is the name now given to the indigenous population of the Chatham Islands, and to their language. The Chatham Islands form part of New Zealand and lie some 650 km off the East Coast of the South Island. The English name for the archipelago, Chatham Islands,[31] comes from the name of the ship which made the first recorded visit by Europeans in November 1791. At that time, it is estimated, there were some 2,000 Polynesians living there. However, contact with European diseases, due to frequent visits by whaling and sealing ships in the early years of the nineteenth century, depletion of food sources for the same reason, and especially the invasion and the enslavement of the inhabitants by Taranaki Māori in 1835, led to a severe reduction in the population and the weakening, not to say deliberate suppression, of their culture.[32]

The same developments led to the loss of the language by about the beginning of the twentieth century and we are dependent for our knowledge of it on a range of sources, all of disputable value and authenticity. Clark (1994 and 2000) provides the best discussion of these sources and summarises what can be elicited from them about the language. Very briefly, the major documentary sources derive ultimately from just two 'informants', a native speaker of Mōriori, Hirawanu Tapu, and William Baucke, who was the son of a missionary and the first European born in the Chathams. Tapu was the scribe of a manuscript (GNZMMSS 144) dating from 1862 held in the Auckland Public Library in which Mōriori elders petitioned Governor George Grey for the restoration of land. The MS also contains lists of names, some narrative and other material, often in parallel Māori and Mōriori versions. Tapu was also the main informant for a word list of Mōriori vocabulary published by Samuel Deighton in 1889, which has appeared as an appendix in King (1989:195–203), and was the main contributor to Alexander Shand's (1911) collection of texts.

William Baucke spent the first twenty-five or so years of his life in the Chathams, but it was only about fifty years later that he produced any written materials on the language (Baucke 1922, 1928). Baucke was highly critical of the earlier materials, especially Shand's. However, Clark (1994, 2000) has developed an ingenious argument for the position that the earlier materials are indeed authentic. One of the striking things about Mōriori as recorded in Shand's work is the existence of over twenty different forms of the definite article, contrasting starkly with the invariant *te* of Māori. Clark is able to show that this 'allomorphy' is rule-governed and is with a high degree of consistency dependent on the initial phoneme of the following word and on the presence and form of any preceding preposition. However, neither Shand himself nor subsequent work dependent upon Shand's texts identified the 'rule', but rather, to the extent that comment is provided at all, saw the phenomenon as random.

The only plausible explanation for this state of affairs is that Shand's texts unwittingly reflect accurately at least this aspect of the language.

Interpretation of the sources is made difficult by two main factors: the presence of interference from Māori, which had been spoken widely in the archipelago for nearly thirty years by the time of the earliest substantial source (Tapu was, for instance, fluent in both languages, but arguably literate only in Māori); and the lack of a conventional orthography in contrast to the contemporary state of affairs in Māori. Representations of Mōriori words are thus a combination of 'Māori-fied' and 'impressionistic' spellings.

Nonetheless, it is possible to derive a picture of sorts of this language, enough to allow a tentative answer to the question of its relationship to Māori. This is the question which Clark (1994) primarily addresses, by exploring the three possibilities presented by the clear evidence that Mōriori was a Central Eastern Polynesian language:[33]

(1) Māori and Mōriori are not specially related beyond both being Central Eastern languages

(2) Mōriori and Māori are distinct languages but belong to a common subgroup within Central Eastern

(3) Mōriori and Māori are the same language, i.e. Mōriori is just another Māori dialect (1994:130)

In order to attempt an answer, Clark (1994:130–1) tabulates two types of data: possible innovations exclusively shared by Māori and Mōriori; and possible innovations shared by all Māori dialects, but not Mōriori. The former features point to solutions (2) and (3) against (1), while the latter point to solution (2) against (3).

The possible shared innovations are largely lexical, and should at least in part be treated with caution, as it is not entirely clear how far the sources report a language influenced by the Māori of the invaders. Some confidence in the authenticity of some items can be gained from the fact that they seem to reflect some of the clear phonological differences between Mōriori and mainland Māori.[34] Thus, among the forms listed are Mōriori *hooriri* = Māori *hoariri* 'enemy', *ii* = *ia* 'current', etc. Clark points to a couple of possible grammatical innovations, e.g. the use of *ehara* to negate nominal sentences: Mōriori *E hari i tangata* = Māori *Ehara i te tangata* 'It's not a man', which incidentally also serves to illustrate the zero allomorph of the definite article in Mōriori.

All of the points at which Mōriori differs from all Māori dialects adduced by Clark are in fact instances of retention in Mōriori, so that the innovations supposedly shared by mainland Māori dialects are in fact all losses. Clark's conclusion is that (2) best characterises the relationship between Māori and Mōriori, but he rightly concedes that the distinction between (2) and (3) is not entirely clearcut.

I included a word list of Mōriori forms extracted from the documentary sources in my lexicostatistical comparison of Māori dialects (Harlow 1979).[35] It will be recalled from Table 3.7 above that all North Island dialects share pairwise between 73 and 85% of basic vocabulary. South Island Māori is more divergent, sharing between 65 (with Tūwharetoa) and 76% (with Kahungunu) with North Island dialects, and Mōriori shares between 57 and 68% with mainland dialects. The dialect with which Mōriori shares 68% is that of Taranaki, almost certainly a result of influence of the invaders' dialect on the Mōriori reflected in the sources. Otherwise, it is with South Island Māori that the Mōriori list shows the greatest affinity (66%). Strikingly, Mōriori also shares with South Island Māori the (sporadic) shift of *ŋ to /k/ – giving forms such as *tchakat* for Māori *tangata* – and a reflex of *ngahu 'bite', against North Island Māori *ngau* (see above).

The most plausible conclusion to be drawn from these data – though it must remain tentative, given the sketchy and, to quite a degree, unreliable nature of the data – is that the indigenous language of the Chatham Islands was an offshoot of New Zealand Māori after this language had already separated from its other close relations, and, more specifically, of a variety of this language spoken in the South Island.

Māori themselves are very much aware of the continued existence of variation within their language, despite the fact that speakers of all varieties have been mixing now for generations. As more and more speakers of Māori acquire their knowledge of the language through education rather than through intergenerational transmission (see chapter 7), it is to be expected that levelling of variation will increase. At the same time, given the dialect loyalty to which reference has been made, it is equally to be expected that a set of shibboleths characteristic of at least the broad dialect areas will become established. In general, this is an area in which far too little research has been carried out, and it may already be too late to record what may once have been significant differences between the dialects.

NOTES

1. Banks (1962 II:35f.). Banks' spelling is of course 'impressionistic', see chapter 4.
2. Only a handful of very introductory texts such as W. L. Williams (1862) and its several later editions do not draw attention to this variation, though even Williams (1862) mentions, *à propos* of the passive suffix, that usage varies in different parts of the country.
3. Letter of James Watkin to his colleague, Revd J. Buller, 14 September 1840, see Harlow (1987:vii). Watkin goes on to report that he read from a New Testament translation but that his effort was met by incomprehension.
4. Benton's codes for this example are: *Au = Te Aupōuri, *W = Waikato, *E = Eastern (including Tūhoe, Ngāti Porou, Ngāti Kahungunu). See Map 3.1 for the location of these areas.

5. The list used contained 228 items, and had been developed by Bruce Biggs for earlier lexicostatistical work in comparative PN linguistics.

6. This dialect of Māori is to all intents and purposes extinct, shift to English having occurred much earlier and much more thoroughly in the south than in most of the North Island. Some people affect a 'southern' dialect by colouring their speech with a few well-known markers such as the historical merger of *k and *ŋ to /k/ referred to below.

7. Taitokerau ('Northern Coast') is the Māori designation of the whole of Northland. At the time of writing, the dictionary can be found at: http://130.216.239.118/dictionary/dictionary-index.htm.

8. In historical times, the very northern parts of the South Island were inhabited by recent arrivals from the north.

9. To judge by early transcriptions and borrowed place names, see Harlow (1979:126).

10. In this instance, Taranaki dialects agree with eastern, rather than western, forms.

11. The alternation /h/ ~ /f/ seen in these forms is due to the prehistoric shift f > h before rounded vowels, on which see chapters 2 and 4.

12. See chapter 2 above, also Harlow (1987: under *poenemu* and *koekohi*) for other similar phenomena. In a similar way, assimilation of *a to /e/ in *tētahi* ~ *ētahi* to *(t)ētehi* 'a, a certain, some' creates a form characteristic of the Waikato region.

13. See chapter 6 on the distinction.

14. On this, see especially Biggs (1989, 1991, 1994b).

15. For critical discussion of this method and its uses, see Crowley (1997:171–86) and Campbell (1999:177–86).

16. Only the results of the comparison of North Island dialects are reported in the present table, because of the difference in the way the South Island and Mōriori lists were compiled. The abbreviations in this table are: TUH Tūhoe; TWH Ngāti Tūwharetoa; WAI Waikato; NPH Ngāpuhi; AUP Te Aupōuri; NPR Ngāti Porou; KAH Ngāti Kahungunu; TAR Taranaki. See Map 3.1 for the location of these varieties.

17. See Crowley (1997:173–84), where this convention is also rightly criticised.

18. Biggs reconstructs PPN *faaiti* 'narrow', see Biggs (2000a: under FAA-LASI).

19. In this case, the shared innovation is the shift of meaning from 'gravel'.

20. See especially Simmons (1976) for accounts of these, together with discussion of their sources and interpretation.

21. See papers in Sutton (1994). The papers in that volume which address the linguistic material relevant to the question are those by Biggs and Harlow. See also Green (1966).

22. Polynesian languages spoken in Melanesia and Micronesia. See references in chapter 2.

23. From PPN *toke 'sea-eel', a meaning shift in CE languages.

24. Most CE languages change PPN *mauī 'left' to reflexes of *kauī by analogy with *katau. Tahitian has both pairs *'atau* ~ *matau* and *'auī* ~ *mauī*, and Māori has no trace at all of a *kauī*.

25. In these languages, /ʔ/ is the regular correspondent to Māori /h/ and /f/. Most CE languages, but not Māori, have merged the inherited possessive series *n*- and *m*- to *n*-forms only.

26. The other Tahitic language of the Northern Cook Islands does not seem to know any of these extended forms, exhibiting only the inherited short ones: *tōu*, etc. The third Northern Cook Islands language, Pukapuka, is Samoic.
27. See, for instance, Anttila (1972:305) for discussion and a 'dialect map' of Indo-European.
28. Marquesan reflects PEP *r as glottal stop.
29. Fijian is PPN's closest relation outside Polynesia: <q> = /ŋg/ and corresponds to *k in PPN. Tongan shows the effects of a vowel assimilation process, whereby unaccented /a/ is attracted to neighbouring non-low vowels; hence the second <e> in the Tongan form, from earlier /a/.
30. See Green (1966:31).
31. The name in Māori is Wharekauri, and in Mōriori itself, Rēkohu.
32. Michael King's *Moriori: A People Rediscovered* (1989) is an excellent and thorough account of this unhappy history, as well as of the beginnings of a renaissance among descendants of the original inhabitants of the Chathams, in which they are trying to recover their identity, culture and language.
33. See chapter 2 on the subgrouping of Polynesian languages.
34. These include, in Mōriori, deletion of final short vowels, affrication of *t to <tch> – see especially Clark (2000:16–18).
35. See also Clark (1994:132), who gives a summary of the data from this study which relate to Mōriori.

Like most PN languages,[1] Māori has relatively few segmental phonemes, very simple phonotactics, and little in the way of phonological rules apart from the regularities of the phonetic detail of the phonemes. Nonetheless the phonology of Māori has some features which are not without interest and which raise questions of analysis.

What little morphophonemic alternation Māori exhibits, mostly between long and short vowels in processes such as reduplication and passive suffixation, and the literature on these phenomena, is dealt with in chapter 5. Accordingly, this chapter will restrict itself to the treatment of the phoneme inventory, the phonetics of the realisation of these phonemes, stress, and phonotactics. Included in phonotactics is the matter of which prosodic units are relevant to which later rules, and the relationship between such units.

The development of the writing system(s) now used for Māori parallels to quite a degree the growing awareness of the structure of the Māori sound system. An account of this representation of Māori concludes the chapter.

Phoneme inventory

The Māori system seems to have been relatively conservative, compared with its closest relations, and reflects the phonology of Proto-Central Eastern Polynesian fairly closely.[2] Most dialects of Māori[3] have ten consonant phonemes and five distinct vowel qualities. Sets of contrasting 'minimal decuplets' for consonants, and 'quintuplets' for vowel qualities are very easy to find. For instance, for the consonants, using standard orthography for the moment

> *pā* 'fortified town', *tā* 'print', *kā* 'burn', *mā* 'white', *nā* 'there by you',
> *ngā* 'the plural', *rā* 'sun', *wā* 'time', *whā* 'four', *hā* 'breathe'

where all these words are distinct in the majority dialects, and there are no other combinations of a consonant plus long /a/ in the language which both count as Māori words and are distinct from these ten. The phonemic labels usually encountered in the literature for this set are: /p, t, k, m, n,

Table 4.1. *The phonemes of Māori*

	labial	dental/alveolar	velar	glottal
stops	p	t	k	
nasals	m	n	ŋ	
fricatives	f			h
liquid		r		
semivowel	w			

	front	central	back
high	i		u
mid	e		o
low		a	

ŋ, r, w, f, h/. Similarly for monophthong vowel qualities, there are just five contrasts:

> *tā* 'print', *tē* 'not', *tī* 'tea', *tō* 'pull', *tū* 'stand'.

Further, /w/ and /u/, which are phonetically similar, can be shown to contrast in pairs such as: *taua* 'that (anaphoric, not demonstrative)' vs *tawa* 'a tree (sp.)'

Begging some questions as to the phonetic detail, these sounds can be set out in conventional articulatory terms as in Table 4.1. Apart from its size, which is in any case typical of PN languages, the only remarkable aspect of this inventory, as stated here, is the lack of a sibilant and, to a lesser extent, of a /j/; statistically, these are the most common fricative and semivowel, see Lass (1984:151 and 159). The vowels, as phonemes, constitute what is perhaps the most common system in the world, and the consonants, apart from the points referred to, present nothing unusual in terms of the manners and places of articulation occupied.

In addition to this sort of statement of the phoneme inventory, which can be found in any one of a number of discussions of Māori, there are a few analyses which essay either partial or complete accounts in terms of distinctive features. The earliest is shown in Table 4.2 from Hohepa (1967:7).

As does much contemporary work, this account assumes the Jakobsonian features, and argues for this distribution of features on acoustic grounds (1967:8). However, since the focus of his work is syntax, Hohepa provides no rules for Māori which use and thus justify this feature specification.

It is left to later work, in particular Kearns (1990) and de Lacy (1997), to argue for specific assignments of feature values based on phonological evidence. Kearns argues for the assignment of the feature [+high] to /h/. According to

Table 4.2. *Hohepa's (1967) assignment of feature specifications*

	p	t	k	r	f	h	w	m	n	ŋ	i	e	u	o	a
consonantal/non-cons.	+	+	+	+	+	+	+	+	+	+	−	−	−	−	−
interrupted/continuant	+	+	+	+	−	−	−	−	−	−	Ø	Ø	Ø	Ø	Ø
nasal/oral	−	−	−	−	−	−	−	+	+	+	Ø	Ø	Ø	Ø	Ø
voiced/unvoiced	−	−	−	+	−	−	+	Ø	Ø	Ø	Ø	Ø	Ø	Ø	Ø
compact/diffuse	−	−	+	−	Ø	−	+	Ø	−	−	+	−	±	−	±	+
grave/acute	+	−	Ø	Ø	Ø	Ø	Ø	+	−	Ø	−	−	+	+	Ø

contemporary views, /h/, if it is a glottal fricative, should have no supralaryngeal features. However, Kearns is able to point to aspects of the Māori treatment of loanwords which suggest that /h/ is able to spread the feature [+high] to neighbouring vowels. It will be recalled, from chapter 2, that loanwords into Māori undergo considerable change, because of the limited range of consonants available to 'represent' the much wider ranges of sounds of English, the major source language, and because of the phonotactics, which prohibit consonant clusters and final consonants. In consequence, Māori /h/ often appears in loans for English sibilants, and loanwords often acquire epenthetic vowels to expand clusters or cover a final consonant. The extent of the incidence of /i/ as such an epenthetic vowel next to /h/ in loans leads Kearns to the conclusion that /h/ is in fact underlyingly not a glottal fricative, but a [+high] fricative, an assignment which is consistent with Hohepa's remarks on the phonetics of /h/,[4] and with its history.[5]

De Lacy (1997), working in much later frameworks, proposes an underlying feature assignment exploiting more recent ideas in theoretical phonology such as underspecification and feature geometry.[6] De Lacy's article is an account of some co-occurrence restrictions in Māori phonotactics, to which we will return below, and operates with the feature tree in Figure 4.1 (1997:16, after Clements and Hume 1995).

[±F] are binary features, the others privative, and particular (classes of) sounds may lack certain nodes and their dependent features. Vocoids, for instance – that is, vowels and the semivowel /w/ – have the general feature structure shown in Figure 4.1, while non-vocoids have no V-Place or Vocalic nodes; C-Place immediately 'dominates' the place features.

On the basis of this feature set, de Lacy proposes an assignment of features for Māori phonemes, as in Table 4.3 (1997: 16–17). These features are 'licensed', a property important for the account that de Lacy proposes for the co-occurrence restrictions his paper deals with. Other features are required for full specification, but are predictable and 'filled in' by implications / redundancy rules, of which these are the main ones (1997:17):

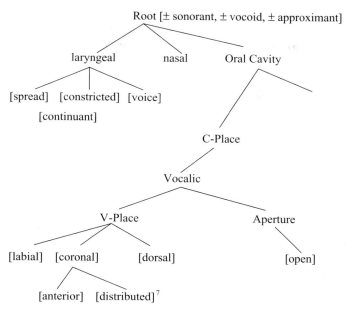

Figure 4.1 De Lacy's (1997) feature tree.

[α sonorant] → [α voice]
[α approximant] → [α continuant]
[vocoid, labial] → [dorsal]
[ ]_{Place} → [coronal]

/h/ and /a/ are distinguished from other related sounds in lacking a Place node altogether, and the height feature needed to distinguish /e/ ∼ /i/ and /o/ ∼ /u/ is ignored in this account, as it has no bearing on the particular purpose for which de Lacy uses this analysis. Finally, /w/ and /u/ are distinguished prosodically, in that though their feature composition is identical, /u/ is (at least underlyingly) associated with a mora (see below), while /w/ is not.

De Lacy (1997:18) points out that, apart from the nasals, /f/ is the only sound requiring two features, and that this state of affairs is avoided cross-linguistically. In the case of /f/, this fact plays a role in the issue which de Lacy is addressing, and assuming a similar feature specification for earlier stages of Māori, accords well with the 'fragility' of /f/ historically in Eastern Polynesian languages (see chapter 2). Similarly, the relatively 'marked' status of /ŋ/ in these terms correlates with the fact that it is the only phoneme to undergo mergers in the recent history of Māori (see chapter 3). However, the same consideration would predict that /m/ should be similarly vulnerable. This is decidedly not the

Table 4.3. *De Lacy's (1997) feature specifications*

Root	Phoneme	Labial	Coronal	Dorsal	Nasal	+*Continuant*
−Approx	p	✓				
−Sonorant	t					
−Vocoid	k			✓		
	f	✓				✓
	h					✓
−Approx	m	✓			✓	
+Sonorant	n				✓	
−Vocoid	ŋ			✓	✓	
	r					
+Approx	i					
+Sonorant	e					
+Vocoid	a					
	o	✓				
	u	✓				
	w	✓				

case, in fact *p and *m, quite unlike *f, are the most stable of PPN consonants, undergoing no change in any modern language.[8]

Vowel length

In addition to these phonemes, Māori has a range of phonetic diphthongs, to which we return below, and a distinction between long and short monophthongs. That is, there are very many minimal pairs where the only phonetic distinction is the length of a vowel. The following set illustrates this:

> *kēkē* 'armpit' ∼ *keke* 'cake'
> *kākā* 'bird species' ∼ *kaka* 'garment'
> *kōkō* 'tui, bird species' ∼ *koko* 'shovel'
> *kīkī* 'speak' ∼ *kiki* 'kick'
> *kūkū* 'pigeon' ∼ *kuku* 'mussel'

There are essentially two possible accounts of this state of affairs. Bauer (1993:543–5) presents the fullest account of the arguments for both positions, though the ideas go back to Biggs (1961). One could regard the ten vowels as contrasted in the above example as ten distinct phonemes, five of which are inherently long, and five short, in much the same way that presentations of English phonology frequently list /iː/, etc., as simply distinct from /ɪ/, etc. In favour of this approach is the observation that the pairs of vowels differ from each other not only in length, but to some extent also in quality. On this, see more below, but for the moment it can be noted that there is a tendency for the short vowels to be more centralised than the corresponding long ones.

The other approach, which is favoured by most writers, and is taken for granted by recent work on Māori phonology, such as de Lacy's (1997), is that the phonemically distinct long vowels are underlyingly successions of two like short vowels. The main arguments in favour of this analysis are, first, that there are phonetic long vowels which clearly are the result of the juxtaposition of like short vowels across morpheme and even word boundaries. As Bauer (1993) points out, forms such as *hāereere* (reduplication of *haere* 'go') have a range of pronunciations: [hɑːɛɾɛʔɛɾɛ] ∼ [hɑːɛɾɛ.ɛɾɛ]⁹ ∼ [hɑːɛɾɛːɾɛ]. The last of these is normal in casual fast speech, while the first two, if used at all, are found in more careful formal styles. Similarly, phrases such as *e waiata ana* (TA sing TA) 'is singing' are pronounced [ɛwɐiɐ'tɑːnɐ] in casual styles. The long vowels which arise in this fashion are indistinguishable from morpheme-internal long vowels both in quality and length and in their role with respect to stress assignment.

The second argument, which applies equally to diphthongs, and supports the analysis of these as successions of unlike simple vowels, is that long vowels pattern exactly like sequences of VCV with respect to rules which refer to the *mora*,[10] in particular, reduplication (on which see chapter 5) and the rules handling the allomorphy of the vocative and imperative markers. Both these markers have /e/ and zero as allomorphs, with the choice conditioned by the number of moræ in the stem or phrase which they introduce. The details need not concern us here, but as a rough characterisation of the condition suffice it to say that the /e/ allomorph of both particles occurs before bimoraic words, and the zero allomorph occurs before longer words. Thus, *e noho* (TA sit) 'sit down!', but *patua* (Ø strike-passive) 'hit it!',[11] and *e Rewi* (P Rewi) 'Rewi!', but *Mereana* (Ø Mereana) 'Mereana!' In this calculation, long vowels (and for that matter, diphthongs) pattern exactly like VCV sequences: *e tū* (TA stand) 'stand up!', but *kīa* (Ø say-passive) 'say it!', and *e Kā* (P Kā) 'Kā!', but *Hōne* (Ø Hōne) 'Hōne!'

Bauer (1993:537) tentatively proposes a third analysis. Drawing attention to the relatively very high frequency of [aː] when compared not only with other long vowels, but with all two-vowel combinations, she suggests that it may be necessary to identify six vowel phonemes for Māori: /a, e, i, o, u, aː/; however, the argument for this, apart from the matter of the frequency, is not developed. It will be seen below that there is at least one further way in which [aː] is different from the other long vowels; however, the very environments in which this phenomenon occurs necessitate the analysis as /aa/.[12]

Table 4.4. *Frequency of Māori phonemes*

phoneme	percentage	phoneme	percentage
a	18	p	1.8
aː	4.6	t	9.8
e	8.7	k	7.9
eː	0.8	m	3.7
i	11.3	n	3.4
iː	0.3	ŋ	2
o	5.7	f	1
oː	1.5	w	0.9
u	6.1	r	5.7
uː	0.4	h	4.5

Table 4.5. *Frequency of short vowels*

vowel	percentage
a	26.1
e	9.7
i	11.8
o	7.2
u	6.4

Distribution of phonemes

The ten consonants and ten vowels (assuming for the moment that diphthongs are a succession of simple vowels, and taking in the first instance the phonetically long vowels to be distinct phonemes) are by no means evenly distributed. As one would expect in a language which does not admit consonant clusters or closed syllables, and which allows onset-less syllables as well as a range of phonetic diphthongs, vowels account for appreciably more than half the tokens of phonemes in text. However, within both vowels and consonants, there are great differences in the extent of occurrence.

Table 4.4 presents rough results of a count of the phonemes in a Māori text of some 500,000 tokens. These data treat long and short vowels as distinct phonemes. If one applies the analysis that long vowels are a sequence of two like short vowels, then the figures for the five vowels emerge as in Table 4.5.

Vowels now account for over 61 per cent of the phonemes in the text studied, /a/ by itself making up over a quarter. This count agrees very well with Bauer's (1993:536), according to which /a, i, t, e, k, o, u/ in that order are the most frequently occurring sounds, as well as with her set of least frequent sounds: /iː, uː, eː, w, oː/ (in ascending order from least frequent).

Diphthongs

In addition to the ten consonant phonemes and five monophthongs, Māori has a range of diphthongs.[13] It is easy to find contrasting sets of monosyllabic morphemes such as: *tai* 'sea', *tae* 'arrive', *toi* 'art', *toe* 'be left over', *tao* 'spear', *tau* 'year', *tou* 'anus, tail of a bird' – all of which are distinct phonetically.[14] All combinations of a vowel plus a higher vowel can appear as diphthongs, plus at least /oe/.[15] On /io/ and /iu/, see further below. Other combinations always act as two syllables. For reasons similar to those advanced above *à propos* of the long vowels, diphthongs are analysed as sequences of unlike short vowels.[16] However, the issue immediately arises as to which sequences of short vowels constitute diphthongs and when. As is frequently pointed out in the literature, all possible pairs of unlike short vowels occur,[17] both within morphemes and across morpheme boundaries, but by no means all such pairs constitute diphthongs. Biggs (1969:131) and Williams (1971:xxxiii) hold superficially contrary, but in fact identical, and arguably equally erroneous, views on the question, the former treating all sequences of unlike vowels as diphthongs and the latter claiming the language has no diphthongs at all. Schütz (1985b) has a useful discussion of the issue, pointing out that some such sequences behave differently from others with respect to stress assignment.

The matter is further complicated by the fact that those sequences which do constitute diphthongs under some circumstances fail to do so on other occasions. The factors here seem to be a combination of the presence or otherwise of some morpheme boundary, style of speech – whether casual or more 'careful' – and simply speaker variation. We will have to return to this matter in more detail below. For the moment, suffice it to note that, as well as ten monophthongs, Māori has a range of diphthongs which appear as syllable peaks, including six 'long' diphthongs, all combinations of /aa/ and a higher vowel, plus /eei/ and /oou/.[18]

Phonotactics

Again, like other Polynesian languages, Māori has very simple phonotactics: all syllables are open, and syllable onsets contain at most one consonant. Possible surface syllables are thus zero or one of the consonants followed by one of the ten monophthongs or one of the diphthongs, giving a formula: $\$ = (C)V(V(V))$.[19] Not all such syllables actually occur; apart from some accidental gaps, there is a systematic restriction on the sequences: /fo/, /fu/, /wo/, /wu/. These occur only in a few words borrowed from English, such as *whutupōro* 'football', *wūru* 'wool', *whoroa* 'floor'. There is, however, one inherited word whose pronunciation by some speakers infringes this restriction: *hoatu* 'give (to 2nd or 3rd person)' is often heard as /foatu/, though the related *hōmai* 'give (to me/us)' is never so pronounced.

The absence of /fo/ and /fu/ in words which are not recent borrowings is due to the change mentioned in chapter 2, whereby PPN *f before rounded vowels merged with *s as /h/. The sequences *fo and *fu are widely attested in non-EP languages, and are thus easily reconstructible to PPN. With respect to the non-occurrence of /wo/ and /wu/, however, it is another matter. Other PN languages do indeed contain a few items with reflexes of PPN *w, followed by /u/ or /o/. However, there are never very many, and the few there are are often borrowings (e.g. Tongan *vuka* in *longovuka* 'rumour that is flying about' < Fijian *vuka* 'fly',[20] Tokelauan *volipolo* 'volleyball'), or otherwise marginal, e.g. possibly onomatopœic (Tokelauan *vovole* 'make a noise by talking, scolding', Tahitian *vovō* 'distant sound, for instance, distant thunder'). In any event, no items containing *wo or *wu have been reconstructed to PPN; POLLEX (Biggs 2000a) contains only one such item: *wiwo 'flute' with reflexes in the Cook Islands and French Polynesia, so PCE.

It seems likely that this avoidance of *wo and *wu goes further back as well. For instance, no items containing these strings are reconstructed in Ross *et al.* (1998 and 2003).[21]

In any event, the lack of inherited words in Māori containing the sequences /fo/, /fu/, /wo/, /wu/ is due to the convergence of two quite distinct historical events or states of affairs, and the presence of loanwords, otherwise fully adapted to Māori phonology, which do contain these sequences, suggests that the phonotactics of the modern language do not in fact contain a restriction against them. De Lacy (1997) argues that the language contains not only this particular restriction as part of its synchronic grammar, but related ones as well. He identifies four such restrictions (1997:12): *w{o,u}, *wh{o,u}, *{o,u}w and *uo. The third of these he derives from the apparent loss of /w/ between a back vowel and a non-back vowel, seen in doublets such as *tauwehe* ~ *tauehe* 'separate (intr.)'. In this and many similar cases, the /w/ is etymological, this word being a derivative of *wehe* 'divide, separate (tr.)'. However, not only are there many instances where there is no doublet, e.g. *kūwata* 'desire', but there are even cases of doublets where the /w/ is intrusive, e.g. *kōwanu* ~ *kōanu* 'cold' (cf. *anuanu* 'cold'). Further, it is not clear that there is any difference in pronunciation between the members of those doublet pairs which are attested. It is possible to see the phenomenon mentioned by de Lacy not as a change (loss of /w/) motivated by a restriction of the sort he identifies, but rather as the sporadic capture in spelling of the spontaneous bilabial glide which arises at the transition between /u/ or /o/ and a following non-back vowel. Inherited /w/ in this position is not phonetically distinct.

The fourth of de Lacy's restrictions depends on there being something odd about the sequence /uo/. It is true that, unlike all other combinations of like or unlike short vowels, /uo/ does not occur in bimoraic morphemes. Bauer's (1993:545) table illustrating the combinations shows this up clearly. All other combinations are given in actual words of the form CVV, in most cases the C being /h/; /uo/, however, is illustrated in the form *tuota* 'a type of charm', there being no word of the form /Cuo/. De Lacy is probably right that many, if not all, cases of /uo/ in modern Māori, apart from loanwords, are historically polymorphemic, with the /u/ and /o/ separated by a morpheme boundary. However, it would be very hard to show that this analysis is valid synchronically.

De Lacy's article is a very thorough and cogent account within the framework of modern theoretical phonology, and exploiting underspecification, multi-tiered feature geometry, and Optimality Theory. The specific constraints he proposes, especially those which account for *{w,f}{o,u}, provide also explanations for the changes in EP languages (see chapter 2) by which *f and *s (partially) merge, and the observed avoidance of *wu and *wo throughout the family.

Furthermore, the formulation of these restrictions as Optimality Theory constraints also allows for the occurrence of these sequences in loanwords, where the constraints are outranked by faithfulness conditions.

Chapter 5 contains some remarks on possible word shapes, and we will have to return to some issues of phonotactics below – in particular, the matter of diphthongs alluded to above. The fact that all syllables are open, and consonants occur only singly, as well as the size of the inventory of both vowels and consonants, entail that borrowed vocabulary undergoes quite far-reaching adaptation, as sketched in chapter 2.

Syllables and moræ

It was asserted above that the syllable shape in Māori is (C)V(V(V)), taking the long monophthongs and both long and short diphthongs to be sequences of short vowels. Syllables thus defined play a role in some rules; in particular, stress assignment needs to refer to them. However, there are other rules which refer to a smaller unit. Since Bauer (1981b) first discussed this issue, this smaller unit is referred to as a *mora*, and consists of a single short vowel plus any consonant which may precede it: (C)V. It is to this unit that the patterns of reduplication refer, as well as the allomorphy of the vocative and imperative particles, as sketched above. Further, there is evidence that it plays a role in a metrical principle of Māori poetry.[22]

Both units can be accommodated in a grammar of Māori by assuming that underlying representations are all structured in terms of the smaller unit, the mora, and undergo a process of syllabification to form the units which are of relevance to stress assignment, and, as we shall also see, to the phonetics of Māori. That is, taking a word such as *kaumātua* 'respected elder', I assume an underlying form of six moræ (/ka.u.ma.a.tu.a/), but a surface form of four syllables (/kau.maa.tu.a/), which results from the combination of some, but not all, adjacent vowels to form long vowels or diphthongs. The process of syllabification is thus an account of the occurrence of long vowels, as opposed to rearticulated adjacent short vowels, and of the circumstances under which unlike vowels form a phonetic syllable. To put it yet another way, it is an attempt to answer the question as to when the following takes place:[23]

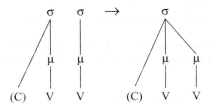

Clearly, given the existence of long diphthongs, syllabification of three adjacent moræ also occurs, that is

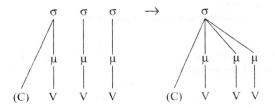

though this section will deal only with the bimoraic cases.

It turns out that at least three factors determine the operation or not of this syllabification process: the identity of V_1 and V_2; the presence or not of morphological boundaries; the style, whether formal and careful or allegro. Even then there are cases where particular constellations of these factors do not uniquely determine an outcome; there is simply variable behaviour on the part of speakers.

Biggs (1961) and Hohepa (1967) both deal with the issue of syllabification,[24] but the principal work in this area is Bauer (1993:548–53) who discusses the earlier contributions and provides considerable data on the question. This section will not repeat her findings and level of detail, but will approach the issue by reporting the results of a small study on the question stated above.

In determining whether a pair of vowels constitute a single syllable or not, we will follow a suggestion by Schütz (1985b:19), who draws attention to the difference in stress patterns between diphthongs and heterosyllabic vowel sequences.

The following example illustrates: *akoako*, the reduplication of *ako* 'learn', is stressed in the same way as, for instance, *katakata*, the reduplication of *kata* 'laugh', with primary stress on the first mora. On the other hand, *ohooho*, reduplication of *oho* 'wake up', is often pronounced [oˈhoːho] with stress on the vowel following the first /h/. This difference in stress pattern is taken to indicate that the /oa/ of *akoako* is a sequence of short vowels, while the /oo/ of *ohooho* is a single syllable peak.[25]

Schütz (1985b) uses a similar argument to show that /au/ in *maunga* 'mountain' is a diphthong, while /oa/ in *moana* 'sea' is not. He contrasts:[26]

> *te móana#   te moána nui#*   vs   *te máunga#   te máunga nui#*

Vowels find themselves adjacent, and thus potentially subject to the resyllabification diagrammed above, in a number of positions within a phrase.[27]

(1) Many morphemes contain non-initial moræ consisting of just a vowel, so that this vowel is adjacent to the vowel of the preceding mora.

(2) Reduplications of vowel-initial stems, such as *akoako* and *ohooho* mentioned above, bring vowels into contact.

(3) Prefixation to vowel-initial stems, such as *whakaako* 'teach' from *whaka-* 'CAUSE' and *ako* 'learn'. To all intents and purposes, only *whaka-* is of interest under this heading. The other productive prefixes (see chapter 5) either are generally of a shape that prevents any chance of syllabification with a following vowel,[28] or act like particles rather than prefixes. For instance, *toko-*, a prefix added to some numerals where human beings are being counted, never combines, e.g. *tokoono* 'six (human beings)' is always /to.ko.ˈo.no/.

(4) There are three productive vowel-initial suffixes, all allomorphs of {passive}: *-a*, *-ia* and *-ina*. Clearly, suffixation of these brings vowels together, as all verb stems have final vowels.

(5) A few particles which typically follow the head of the phrase in which they occur begin with vowels, so that the sequence base + particle can lead to the situation under discussion.

(6) Finally, the sequence of preposed particle plus vowel-initial base occasionally show the effects of resyllabification.

It is in environment (1), within morphemes, that the highest degree of uniformity and of resyllabification can be observed; all pairs of like vowels in this environment regularly surface as a single long vowel, and all combinations of unlike vowels which can form a single syllable peak do so.[29]

It is in the array of other contexts that syllabification shows considerable variation in its application. In this respect there are three hierarchies, although, as mentioned, variability between individual speakers[30] is a fourth factor:

(1) where syllabification is possible, it is more likely to occur in faster, more casual speech than in more careful speech;

(2) syllabification is increasingly less likely to occur as one progresses through the hierarchy of contexts: reduplication, affixation, a sequence of base plus particle, a sequence of particle plus base;

(3) syllabification is increasingly less likely to occur as one progresses through the hierarchy of candidate pairs: /aa/,[31] other /V_1V_1/, /a+V/, other eligible sequences (e.g. /oi/, /ei/, etc.).

The pair **/aa/** is phonetically a long monophthong in reduplications, e.g. *ataata* 'video' (/a.'taa.ta/, from *ata* 'shadow'); in passive of verbs with stem-final /a/ and suffix -*a*, e.g. *hangaa* ~ *hangā* 'be built' (/ha.'ŋaa/); very frequently in words derived by affixation of *whaka*- 'C A U S E' to a stem with initial /a/, e.g. *whakaako* 'teach'; in sequences of base with final /a/ and particle with initial /a/, e.g. *karanga atu* 'call out' (/ka.ra.'ŋaa.tu/); and often also in instances of particle plus base, e.g. *ka aroha* (TA love) 'loves' (/'kaa.ro.ha/).

/V_1V_1/ can appear phonetically as a long monophthong in reduplications, e.g. see above on the pronunciations of *hāereere*, also *iriiri* 'baptise' (both /'i.ri.i.ri/ and /i.'rii.ri/ are heard); in sequences of base plus particle, e.g. *muri iho* (behind downwards) 'afterwards' (both /mu.ri.'i.ho/ and /mu.'rii.ho/); but never in the case of particle plus base, thus *te ekenga* 'the descent' is always /te.'e.ke.ŋa/.

The pair **/a+V/** can be realised as a diphthong in reduplications, e.g. *pāinaina* 'bask' (and similar cases) is variously pronounced /paai.'nai.na/ and /paa.'i.na.i.na/, and similarly *uaua* 'difficulty' is heard as both /u.'au.a/ and /'u.a.u.a/; further, /ai/ is always a diphthong where the /i/ is the initial phoneme of the passive suffix, e.g. *arohaina* 'be loved' (/a.ro.'hai.na/). The sequence /a+V/ is less likely to be a diphthong where the /a/ is the final phoneme of the prefix *whaka*-; however, the extent to which the word so derived has been lexicalised, that is, the extent to which the speaker is aware of a morpheme break, plays a role. Biggs (1961:12) draws attention to the difference in pronunciation of *whakairo* 'carved pattern' (/fa.'kai.ro/) and *whakairi* (C A U S E hang) 'hang up (tr.)' (fa.ka.'i.ri/). Nonetheless, this is a point where variable behaviour is observable, and while *whakairo* is never pronounced as a tetrasyllable, forms like *whakairi* or *whakaeke* 'attack, approach' are encountered with trisyllabic realisations. As for sequences of /a+V/ at junctures of bases and particles, in either order, diphthongs are rarely if ever formed. An exception is the greeting *kia ora* (TA healthy), which is usually pronounced /ki.'ao.ra/. However, the same phrase used as a predicate meaning 'that (someone) should be healthy' is always /ki.a.'o.ra/, just as *tōna ingoa* 'his/her name' is /too.na.'i.ŋo.a/ for all speakers and styles.

Table 4.6. *Merger of adjacent short vowels to form phonetically long vowels and diphthongs*

	Reduplication	*whaka-*	Base + particle	*tua-, toko-, taki-*[32]	Particle + base
/aa/	✓	✓	✓	NA	✓/x
/ee/, /ii/, /oo/, /uu/	✓	NA	✓/x	x	x
/a+V/	✓	✓/x	x	x	x
/oi/, /ou/, etc.	✓/x	NA	x	x	x
/ea/, /oa/, /eu/[33]	x	NA	x	x	x

For the pair $/V_1V_2/$ (V_1 not /a/) diphthongisation of the eligible sequences of this shape is really restricted to morpheme-internal environments. There is some variation within reduplications, giving alternate pronunciations like /'u.to.u.to/ ~ /u.'tou.to/ for *utouto* 'use vindictively' (from *uto* 'revenge').

Table 4.6 summarises this short account. In the table, ✓ means formation of a single heavy syllable peak is possible, while ✓/x means the same, though bisyllabic pronunciation is the more common.

The phonetics of Māori

Many of the introductory textbooks of Māori provide rough and ready guidelines on the pronunciation of Māori, usually by referring to supposedly similar sounds in English. Only Biggs (1961:9–11) and, in considerably greater detail, Bauer (1993:530–42) attempt to give accounts of the phonetics of Māori in 'language-neutral' terms. The summary presented here will draw on both these works, but also on preliminary observations made in the context of the MAONZE research programme referred to in chapter 2. This project[34] involves the detailed analysis, both auditory and acoustic, of a group of male Māori speakers recorded in the 1940s by the Mobile Unit of Radio New Zealand, and the comparison of these interviews with two other groups, elders (aged sixty-five and older) alive today, and younger speakers (aged between fifteen and thirty-five). The purpose of the research is in the first instance to track changes in the pronunciation of Māori over the three groups and to investigate the influence of English in the process, as well as any detectable influence of Māori on the English pronunciation of these informants.

In the pronunciation of the sounds of Māori considerable variation can be observed, quite apart from the variable behaviour with respect to long vowel and diphthong formation referred to above. The actual realisation of many phonemes exhibits wide ranges of phonetic values within the speech of individuals, between individuals, over time, across registers, and to some extent in differing phonological environments, to the point where there is some overlap of allophones, especially of the short vowels and to a lesser extent some obstruents. It will be impossible to go fully into all these phenomena here. However, a brief characterisation of the 'cardinal' realisations of the phonemes is appropiate, as well as some illustration of the types of variation. As mentioned, more detail is available in Biggs' and Bauer's work (1961 and 1993, respectively).

Voice is not distinctive in Māori and, as one would expect under these circumstances, obstruents are inherently voiceless, and are clearly so phonetically in careful speech, while sonorant consonants and vowels are inherently voiced. Nonetheless, there is some systematic reversing of [±vce] values. Phrase-final vowels, especially short vowels, are often voiceless. In faster speech, this extends to long vowels and diphthongs and even to whole post-stress syllable sequences, producing occasionally voiceless allophones of sonorants. Conversely, /h/ and the fricative allophones of /t, k/ (see below) can be voiced in unstressed environments in fast speech. The labial obstruents /p, f/ seem never to be voiced.

Consonants

The stops, /p, t, k/, are respectively bilabial, dental/alveolar and velar. Both /t/ and /k/ show some variation, depending on the following vowel, with /k/ ranging from almost palatal to retracted velar, and /t/ showing affrication before /i/ and /u/, especially when these are in final position and voiceless. In extreme, though not thereby 'non-native', pronunciations, a word such as *tamaiti* 'child' can sound like [tɐ'mɐitʃ]. Reference has already been made in chapter 2 to the matter of the increasing aspiration of these voiceless stops since the late nineteenth century. Modern speakers vary markedly in the extent to which they aspirate these sounds, but they are never as aspirated as the corresponding sounds in English. In fast speech, /t/ and /k/ can be heard as fricatives; indeed, unstressed *te* 'the' can be found pronounced [ðə], very like English 'the'! Similarly, voicing of /k/ as [ɣ] can be encountered in unstressed positions, e.g. particles, in faster speech.

The place of articulation of /h/ varies according to the following vowel. Thus *hī* 'fish with a line', /hii/ = [çiː], while in a word such as *hoa* 'friend' the pronunciation of the /h/ entails not only a back tongue position, but also lip-rounding.

The phoneme /f/, spelt <wh> (see below, this chapter), is both the most varied in its pronunciation and the most controversial; it is the only phoneme whose realisation from time to time excites correspondence with the editors of national newspapers and journals. The majority of modern speakers of Māori, both native speakers and second-language speakers, use [f] for this phoneme. However, the facts that it is <wh> and not <f> which is used to spell this sound and that it was the last phoneme to acquire a distinct spelling show that historically at least this was not always so. Details on the past and present pronunciations, and how these vary regionally, can be found in chapters 2 and 3, as well as below in the section on the writing system.

The phoneme /w/ is a bilabial semivowel.

The Māori /r/ is usually realised as an alveolar flap [ɾ]. As indicated in chapter 3, lateral pronunciations are also encountered; nineteenth-century texts and borrowed placenames show that this was particularly so in the South Island, but this phenomenon is not restricted to that dialect and can be found sporadically in the speech of North Islanders as well. In faster speech, and particularly in successions of more than one instance of /r/ with intervening short unstressed vowels, e.g. in *kōrero* 'speech, speak', actual tongue-tip contact may not occur, so that realisations as [ɹ] can be heard. Outside these contexts, however, continuant pronunciations of /r/ are clear cases of interference from New Zealand English, and can be heard in the speech of language learners and L2 speakers.

The majority of Māori dialects (see chapter 3) distinguish three nasals, /m, n, ŋ/, with /n/ and /ŋ/ showing a similar spread in place of articulation to the corresponding stops.

Vowels

It is perhaps in the vowels that the greatest variation within idiolects, between speakers, and over time is to be seen. The fullest account of the phonetics of the Māori vowel system is to be found in Bauer (1993:534–42), and will not be repeated here in any detail. Rather, some general points about the vowel system will be made, and some data becoming available from the MAONZE project on the pronunciation of Māori, to which reference has been made above, will be reported.

As one might expect in a system which distinguishes only five vowel qualities, each vowel quality exhibits quite a range of realisations. Figure 4.2, which reports the analysis of thirty tokens each of both the long and the short vowels from one speaker born in the 1880s, shows typical central values for the vowels. The graph shows two noteworthy features of the Māori vowels: the peripherality of the long vowels compared with the corresponding short ones; the relative frontness of both /u/ and /uu/. As will be seen, both features have been subject to change within recent decades.

Figures 4.3 and 4.4 show the distribution of, respectively, the long and short vowel tokens for the same speaker, and serve to illustrate the point just made about the range of each vowel.

Bauer (1993:537) reports similar variation in the speakers whose speech she analyses for her own account, adding that it occurs 'without any apparent

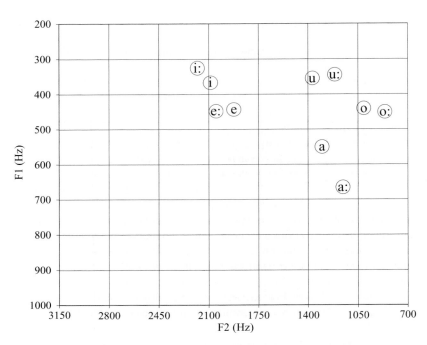

Figure 4.2 Mean format frequencies for the long and short vowels of a speaker born in the 1880s.

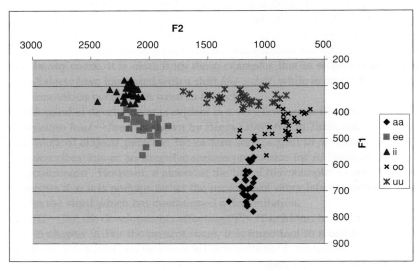

Figure 4.3 Formant frequencies of the long vowels of a speaker born in the 1880s.

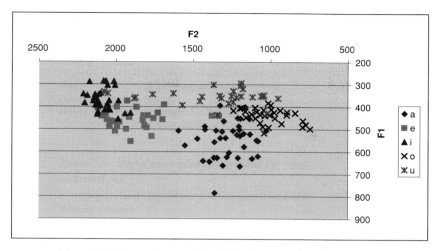

Figure 4.4 Formant frequencies of the short vowels of a speaker born in the 1880s.

conditioning factor'. This is true also of the speaker whose values are shown here, with the exception that there is noticeable fronting of /u/ and /uu/ following /t/.

As noted above, and mentioned also by Bauer (1993), there is noticeable variation between comparable speakers as well as within idiolects. Figure 4.5 shows the mean values of formant frequencies of a second speaker born in the same part of New Zealand as the first speaker, also in the 1880s.

Despite these differences, and taking these speakers to be typical,[35] the following general points can be made about the pronunciation of monophthongs in L1 speakers of Māori from this earlier period:

- the long and short vowels are distinct in both quality and quantity; as noted by both Bauer (1993) and Biggs (1961), the long vowels are more peripheral than the corresponding short vowels; measurements of some thirty tokens of each vowel for these two speakers give mean lengths of 140 and 70 ms respectively.
- /u/ and /uu/ are further forward than cardinal [u]. This is a tendency which has increased in more recent speakers, as will be seen.
- the diphthongs /ai/, /ae/, /ao/, /au/, /ou/ are all clearly distinct at this stage of the language; the starting point for /ae/ and /ao/ is lower than /a/ or the starting point of /ai/ and /au/. The diphthongs /ai/ and /au/ do not yet show the marked centralisation of their starting points characteristic particularly of modern younger speakers. Contrary to Bauer (1993:540), the starting point for /ao/ is not markedly further back than that of any of the other diphthongs.

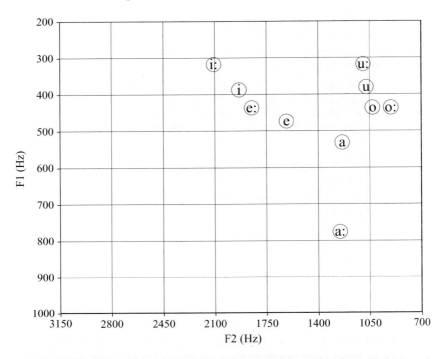

Figure 4.5 Mean formant frequencies for the long and short vowels of a second speaker born in the 1880s.

Such data as already exist for more modern speakers show the same kind of spread of realisations for each sound within an idiolect, as well as divergence between speakers. What is also observable though is that there are numerous shifts of detail in comparison with the earlier data.[36]

Figure 4.6 shows the comparable data for monophthongs in the speech of a pair of younger (aged 25 and 32) speakers recorded recently. Comparison of this graph with the corresponding graph for the older speakers reveals a number of differences. Most strikingly, both /u/ and /uu/ are further forward – indeed, are very similar to the New Zealand English vowel of words such as 'boot'; the difference in quality between short and corresponding long vowels is now much smaller. Measurements of the length of monophthongs in these speakers' speech show a similar reduction in the difference in quantity as well. At the same time, the starting point for both /ai/ and more especially /au/ has become centralised, so that such pronunciations of the latter as [əu] are normal. For many speakers, even some elderly native speakers, /au/ and /ou/ are no longer distinct, the latter having shifted from having a back rounded starting point to a much more centralised one.

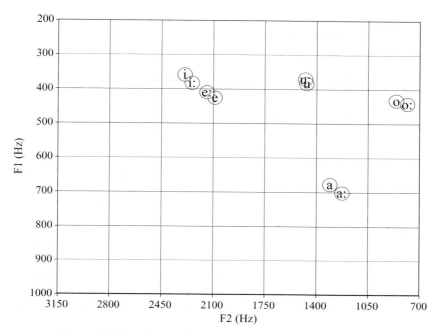

Figure 4.6 Mean formant frequencies for the long and short vowels of two speakers born in the 1970s.

Before concluding this summary of vocalic articulations, there is one final point to mention. Such pairs of unlike vowels as form diphthongs systematically are all stressed on the first element. However, especially in faster speech, the /i/ of /io/, /iu/ and to a lesser extent /ia/ can be heard as [j]. The resultant sequence of [jV] is not appreciably longer than short vowels generally, unlike the rising diphthongs, which correspond in length to the phonetically long monophthongs.

Stress

Stress placement is perhaps the feature which auditorily most sets Māori apart from its fellow PN languages. Other PN languages tend generally to assign stress to the penultimate mora of a word, and lower levels of stress to even-numbered morae towards the beginning of the word.[37] Schütz (1985b), for instance, begins with the remark: 'One of the first impressions that Māori makes on someone familiar with other Oceanic languages is that its accent patterns seem out of step.' The description of stress in Māori has, like other aspects of the language,

Table 4.7. *Differing stress assignment*
according to Hohepa's and Biggs' rules

Hohepa's rule	Biggs' rule	
/ma'rae/	/'marae/	'marae'
/ma'mae/	/'mamae/	'pain'
/ma'tau/	/'matau/	'right (not left)'

been the subject of developing discussion.[38] Earlier textbooks have very brief accounts; for instance: 'Maori words are generally accented on the first syllable; but compound words have a secondary accent on the second portion of the word . . . When a word begins with the form *whaka* accentuate the third syllable, e.g. whaka-*re*-warewa' (A. T. Ngata 1926:8).

Biggs' doctoral thesis (published as Biggs 1961) contains the first account of any sophistication. He claims that primary stress is phonemic, adducing 'minimal pairs' such as /kaa káa/ (TA burn) 'burns' vs /he káakaa/ (Det. parrot) 'a parrot', though he concedes that 'in no case is a stress difference a minimal distinction between base morphemes' (Biggs 1961:11). Hohepa (1967:13) points out that Biggs' minimal pairs are always comparisons of a word and a phrase, and, claiming, in opposition to Biggs, that stress is predictable, proposes a set of rules for the assignment of word stress (1967:10). Subsequently, in his influential textbook (1969:132–3), Biggs implicitly accepts Hohepa's reasoning and adopts a version of his rules. To quote Bauer's summary of these:

The rules for primary stress invoke a hierarchy of syllable types:

$$(C)V_iV_i > (C)V_iV_k > (C)V$$

i.e., syllables with long vowels (or geminate clusters) take precedence over syllables with diphthongs, which in turn take precedence over syllables with single/short vowels. The basic stress rule is this:

> In a monomorphemic form, the syllable type highest on the hierarchy receives primary stress, and if more than one syllable of the same hierarchic status occurs, the first will be stressed. (Bauer 1993:557, see also 1981b:31–2)

This formulation correctly assigns word stress as in the following examples: /'ra.ŋa.ti.ra/ 'chief', /ma.'taa/ 'flint, bullet', /'koo.kaa/ 'aunt', /'tau.ra/ 'rope', etc. However, Biggs' and Hohepa's versions of these rules differ, as Bauer (1981b) points out, in that, for Biggs, word-final instances of the syllable type $(C)V_iV_k$ do not outrank short syllables. For a certain class of word, therefore, stress is assigned to different syllables (see Table 4.7).

Bauer (1981b:31, 1993:557) attributes this phenomenon to a dialect difference, Biggs' account matching eastern dialects, and Hohepa's, western dialects. However, these alternations, along with others which seem to represent departure from either version of these rules, can be due to the interaction of intonation and stress. Biggs (1969:133, see also 1971:471–2) points out that, in non-final phrases, 'phrase stress' falls on the second last mora,[39] so that: 'the same word may be stressed differently according to its position in the sentence, e.g. *marae* and *rangatira* in the following examples: *Ko te rangatíra, o teenei márae* [the chief of this marae] *Ko te maráe, o teenei rángatira* [the marae of this chief]'.

A particularly nice example is furnished by one of the early speakers being analysed in the MAONZE project. The first of those speakers whose vowels were graphed above produces the following at an early part of his discussion of Māori mythology and religion:

> *Te wāhi tuatahi ko Io-matua. Ko Io-matua te tīmatanga . . .* (the place first P Io-matua. P Io-matua the beginning) 'The first "place" is Io-matua. Io-matua is the beginning . . .'[40]

In the first sentence, the phrase *ko Io-matua* is final, and the stress falls on the first /a/ of the name, where it is realised as greater intensity and higher F0 than its counterpart in the second sentence. In the second sentence, the same phrase is predicative and non-final, and it is the /u/ which bears the stress, again realised as greater intensity and higher F0, plus in this case markedly greater length then the /u/ in the first sentence. We return to this matter below in the context of de Lacy's (msb.) account of sentence intonation.

These rules apply to morphologically simple words. As it turns out they also apply to words derived by means of the productive passive and nominalisation suffixes: *ka'ranga-tia* 'call.passive' (< *'karanga* 'call'),[41] *ranga'tira-tanga* 'chiefly status' (< *'rangatira* 'chief'). However, reduplicated forms and forms derived by means of prefixes, esp. *whaka-*, require further clauses in the rules. In particular: 'In reduplicated words, stress the first syllable of both reduplicated portions, but put heaviest stress on the first reduplication: e.g. *aanĭwanĭwa*' (Biggs 1969:133).

This extra clause applies to forms containing or consisting of the complete reduplication of a bimoraic root, as in this example ('rainbow'), and Biggs' other ones. As noted above, some pairs of vowels brought together by reduplication can variably form long vowels or diphthongs. In such cases, the heavy syllable formed in this way bears the word stress: *u'aua* vs *'uaua* 'difficult', *hāę'reęre* vs *hā.'ere.ere* 'go about'.[42]

In partially reduplicated forms of such roots, however, the stress can be heard occurring either on the first mora of the root: *pa'paki* 'slap', or in a position in accordance with the rules for simple forms, *'papaki*. Word stress never falls on the prefix *whaka-*; however, if its second /a/ forms a long vowel or diphthong with the initial vowel of the root to which it is prefixed, then the heavy syllable thus formed is stressed: *whaka'puta* 'cause to emerge, publish', *wha'kaako* 'teach'.

Schütz (1985b) rightly points out that many otherwise fully adapted loanwords from English do not follow these rules. Indeed, since some of them are longer than four moræ,[43] and are not susceptible to any morphological analysis, the rules cannot apply to them at all. He observes that some of these loanwords with apparently similar syllable structure have stress on different syllables, e.g. *'konotaraka* 'contract' vs *pe'rehitini* 'president'. He goes on to propose the existence of a phonological unit which he calls a measure, between the syllable and the phonological phrase. There are three types of measure: (1) a single heavy syllable; (2) a syllable, heavy or light, followed by a short unaccented syllable; (3) either of the first two patterns preceded by a single short syllable. All utterances can be segmented into such measures, and each measure has a stressed peak; in (1) it is the only syllable, in (2) it is the first of the two syllables, irrespective of length; and in (3) it is the second syllable. This system accords with the Biggs–Hohepa approach in always assigning stress to a heavy syllable. However, for strings of short syllables, Schütz's system does not provide an algorithm for the distribution of measures: a string of, say, CVCVCVCV could be CV'CVCV.'CVCV or 'CVCV.CV'CVCV. The measure structure of a word or indeed of a phrase of this sort is not predictable. But this is Schütz's point, as illustrated in the loanwords cited above. It must be conceded that, with respect to loanwords, which in very large part follow the stress pattern of their source, this is so; however, the unpredictability entailed in Schütz's proposals does not extend to the placement of word stress in the vast majority of cases, where it is sufficient to know the grammatical structure; a unit such as Schütz's measure, which is independent of grammatical structure, is not required.

Reference has been made to the interaction of stress and position in the sentence. Biggs (1969:133) discusses this in terms of sentence-final and non-final phrase stress. Others, especially de Lacy (2003b, msb.), deal with the same phenomenon within discussion of intonation. De Lacy identifies four intonation patterns in Māori which occur in his Phonological Phrases.[44] A 'default' tune consists of a high tone on the stressed syllable of the last 'prosodic word' (essentially lexical word or postposed particle) and a following low at the end of the phrase. In de Lacy's data, this pattern, which most closely corresponds to Biggs' final phrase stress, and indeed is the only pattern in the final phrases of declarative sentences, can also occur in non-final phrases. A continuation rise, which may occur in non-final phrases, consists in the occurrence of a low tone on the final stressed syllable, followed by a high tone at the right edge of the Phonological Phrase. De Lacy does not deal with intensity or length differences in his paper; however, this late occurrence of a high tone in a non-final phrase corresponds to the example quoted above from the MAONZE speaker.

The two tunes, default and continuation rise, are the only ones to occur in neutral declarative sentences. An imperative tune is found in sentences expressing commands, and consists in the placement of a high tone at the lefthand edge of the verb phrase, lowering to low tone at the end of that phrase. Any other phrases in the imperative sentence bear default tunes. Finally, there is also an interrogative tune, which de Lacy describes as involving a low-high tune on the last Phonological Phrase. In his data, this pattern is seen in all questions, whether yes–no or wh-questions. Bauer's (1993:2–19) very full examples and discussion show that in wh-questions the normal pattern is a rise on the phrase containing the wh-word, with the rest of the sentence progressively lowering.

Finally, Bauer (1991) points to an intonational difference between sentences in which the first element is the predicate or focussed, and those where a topic occurs in initial position. In pragmatically neutral sentences, the main intonational and stress peak lies on the predicate phrase, which is very typically first. Such predicates may also bear a greater level of emphatic stress. Older speakers do not shift stress from this position to some other constituent in order to focus it, as one might in English,[45] rather there is a range of constructions which can move material into initial position, where it can receive emphatic stress.[46] In sentences where a constituent occurs in initial position because it is a topic, the main sentence stress remains on the predicate, which is now the second phrase. Bauer (1991:4–5) contrasts

> *Ko Rewi e 'whāngai ana i   te   kūao   kau.*
> P   Rewi TA feed   TA Obj. Det. young(animal) cow
> '(As for) Rewi(, he) is feeding the calf.' (my glosses and translation)

and

> *Ko "Rewi e whāngai ana i te kūao kau.*
> 'It is Rewi who is feeding the calf.'

Though there have been a number of valuable contributions to the description of Māori stress and intonation, the fact that most writers mention the existence of considerable variation highlights that there is much more to be done. The MAONZE project intends to try to address this issue as it progresses.

The Māori writing system

With a phonology superficially as transparent as the one sketched above, it is a wonder that modern Māori does not enjoy a single, universally agreed and consistently used writing system. However, instead, considerable divergence of usage is observable in the range of documents in Māori produced in recent decades.

The representation of the consonants has been in place since the 1840s, and is in fact used by all writers. As the reader will have had ample opportunity to observe, the ten consonant phonemes /p, t, k, m, n, ŋ, w, f, r, h/ are represented by the letters <p, t, k, m, n, ng, w, wh, r, h>. The only divergence from this system is to be found in attempts by some writers to represent orthographically the few phonemic differences between dialects. This is seen most consistently in some writers from the South Island, whose historical dialect lacked /ŋ/ through merger with /k/. The practice has developed of writing <k> for the merged sound, but underlining those <k> which correspond to original /ŋ/: thus, leaving aside the issue of vowel symbols for the moment, <k̲ākau> for North Island *ngākau* 'seat of emotions'.

Similar uniformity is found in the orthographic representation of vowel qualities, and, in particular, the short vowel phonemes and diphthongs: <a, e, i, o, u> and combinations of these being used for these sounds. It is the representation of the long vowels which defines three 'families' of spelling systems.

(1) No distinct representation of long vowels: thus <kaka> could represent any one of /kaka, kaaka, kakaa, kaakaa/, all of which are distinct items: 'clothing', 'bittern', 'red hot', 'parrot'. This was the standard usage for all writers and publications until quite recently, and is still widely used. All Bible translations use this convention, except a very recent reissue of St Luke's gospel and the projected reprint of the whole Bible, which will be using the second convention.

(2) Designation of morpheme-internal long vowels by means of a so-called macron. This is the convention used in this book, and the closest thing to a standard in that the Māori Language Commission prescribes its use in their 'Orthographic Conventions'.[47] It is used by most universities, in government publications, in recent editions of traditional literature, and in most educational material. The four words listed in the previous paragraph are thus distinguished in this system as: <kaka, kāka, kakā, kākā>.

(3) Designation of long vowels by doubling the vowel letter, e.g. <kaka, kaaka, kakaa, kaakaa>. This convention was argued for strongly by Bruce Biggs at the University of Auckland, and as a result is found mostly in Biggs' own publications, including his language course and dictionaries (especially 1969, 1981, 1990a), and in publications and signage produced by his students. Biggs' arguments for this convention are partly theoretical and partly practical; it reflects the analysis of long vowels as sequences of two like short vowels presented above, and involves the use of no diacritics, a feature especially useful in the age of typing, and only slightly less so now in the computer age, when the macron symbols are not yet standardised across fonts and platforms. A further argument that could be

made is that 'double-vowel' spelling changes the appearance of text to an extent where, once one is used to it, it is more difficult to misspell than in the corresponding 'macronised' convention, where the diacritic is too easily seen as an optional extra, not a true part of the spelling of a text. This last conspicuous property of the 'double-vowel' spelling, however, is what led to sometimes vehement opposition to it from people used to 'single-vowel' representation.[48]

In fact, neither of these conventions for the representation of long vowels is modern. What is recent is the attempt to make them rigorous and consistent. As early as 1842, Maunsell uses macrons in the paragraphs where he draws attention to the significance of vowel length. This practice is also followed, for instance, in W. L. Williams' *First Lessons in Maori* (1862 and subsequent editions), but neither author then continues to use the macron as part of the spelling of words in the rest of their books. The earliest editions of the W. L. Williams' dictionary (first edition 1844) do not indicate vowel length, but mark word stress by means of an acute. However, from 1871 on, vowel length is marked by means of a macron, though in a haphazard and unreliable way. Consistency and accuracy improve with later editions, but even in the most recent edition (H. W. Williams 1971), where the marking of headwords in this way is very good (though not perfect), the macron is still implicitly simply a guide to pronunciation, analogous to the IPA representation of items in English dictionaries, in that all Māori text other than headwords is unmarked for vowel length.

'Double-vowel' spelling of long vowels is similarly found from the nineteenth century on, though sporadically. In the case of one or two words, idiosyncratic 'double-vowel' spellings have achieved almost standard status for many writers, no matter which convention they are following. Thus, for instance, /roopuu/ 'group' is frequently found spelt <roopu> in texts of all kinds instead of the 'correct' <ropu, rōpū, roopuu> which the various conventions would require.

All three conventions agree in spelling long vowels which arise over morpheme boundaries by doubling the vowel letter. This occurs in affixation, reduplication and compounding, e.g. <whakaako> 'teach' = /fakaako/ = [fa'ka:ko] from *whaka-* 'CAUSE' + *ako* 'learn';[49] <ohooho> 'awake' = /ohooho/ = [o'ho:ho] from *oho*; <ātaahua> (<ataahua>, <aataahua>) 'beautiful' = /aataahua/ = [a:'ta:hua] from *āta* 'gently' and *āhua* 'appearance'.

Two further factors lead to other variation within the written image of Māori. The first of these is differing practices with respect to word division, including the use of hyphens. Space precludes the presentation of more than two or three examples, but they are by no means untypical:

(1) the prefix *kai-*, which derives agent nouns from agentive verbs (see chapter 5), is often encountered written as a separate word: *kai kōrero* ~ *kaikōrero* 'speaker';

(2) some pairings of particles which have idiosyncratic meaning are frequently encountered written together, thus *noiho* for *noa iho* 'only, just';

(3) the Māori Language Commission prescribes spellings of placenames with hyphens dividing the component morphemes in many cases where most writers' practice is to write a single word: *Ngongo-tahā* ~ *Ngongotahā*.

A second factor which is so prevalent that it must almost be regarded as a feature of modern written Māori is individual inconsistency and inaccuracy. It is the author's impression that the level of misspelling in modern Māori, even in published documents, is considerably higher than one would encounter in the writing of New Zealand English. This state of affairs is probably due to two factors.

One is the fact that many people who write in Māori either have not themselves received much in the way of literacy training in that language, their schooling having been primarily in English, or have been taught by other people of whom this is true. More detail of this will be given in chapter 7, but for now it should be noted that, in general, education using Māori as the language of tuition, and the teaching of Māori as a second language in schools and universities, to any wide extent, are activities only of recent decades.

The other factor is more speculative, and has to do with attitudes to the language. Chapter 7 will discuss wider aspects of the language attitudes affecting Māori, but one which is of relevance here is the often heard claim that 'Māori is an oral language.' This slogan, empty of content at one level, since virtually all languages are oral, is intended to emphasise that historically Māori was not written, and that writing is a recent and foreign import. Thus, it is implied and sometimes explicitly argued that any written forms of Māori are of far less significance, are less truly Māori, than spoken forms. It is certainly true that to this day oral genres, especially rhetoric, song and story telling including traditional history, are very important in Māori culture. This has, however, led to an unfortunate downgrading of writing and of written Māori in the minds of many.

The development of written Māori

As is of course only to be expected, word lists and other transcriptions stemming from the very early period of contact between Europeans and Māori show very 'impressionistic' spelling.[50] Not only was there no model to follow, but until the appearance in 1820 of Kendall's second book on Māori, no one with anything like a linguistic approach to the matter had been involved. Even after the appearance of this book and the continual development towards the modern system, at least for the consonants, examples are found of documents whose writers have struggled to represent what they thought they heard by some adaptation of an orthography they knew, usually English. The result is often a text

Table 4.8. *Some examples of items in Boultbee's word list*

Boultbee's item	Boultbee's gloss	modern spelling
madōōa wahēīne	'mother'	*matua wahine*
goòree	'dog'	*kurī*
èka	'fish'	*ika*
tŏoparbuk	'corpse'	*tūpāpaku*
rĕdi	'angry'	*riri*
cārditti	'angry'	*ka riri*
gìrook	'up'	*ki runga*[53]
toūra	'rope'	*taura*
ràkkoo	'tree'	*rákau*

which is hard to interpret; even in the case of words known from later sources or the modern language, there is sometimes difficulty in identifying some items.

A word list left by John Boultbee will serve to illustrate the sort of spelling used in this early period, as well as the occasional difficulty in interpretation.[51] Boultbee, born in 1799 in Nottinghamshire, led an adventurous life, in the course of which he spent nearly two years (1826–8) in the Far South of New Zealand, engaged in sealing. In his journal he left a word list of nearly 220 items along with a couple of unintelligible song texts and some names. Most of the items in the list are readily identifiable with words known from the modern language or other sources written in more transparent orthography.[52] Table 4.8 (based on Starke 1986:109–14) sets out a number of the items in Boultbee's list along with the equivalent spellings in modern Māori. The two systems are by no means isomorphic – on the contrary, Boultbee often uses different characters for what we know now to be a single phoneme, and also the same characters to represent now one phoneme, now another.

Boultbee's use of <t, d> for /t/, <p, b> for /p/, and <k, g> for /k/ is typical of this period and reflects the relative lack of aspiration in the pronunciation of these consonants. Similarly the rendition of /r/ variously as <l, r, d> reflects variation in its pronunciation, sometimes a lateral, but more frequently an apical, flap.[54] The list contains some items which show a feature of southern Māori which is present to some extent in all varieties, but seems to have been more pronounced in the south. This is the devoicing/deletion of short final vowels, seen in Table 4.8 in <tŏoparbuk> and <gìrook> (see further Harlow 1987:xiv).

These difficulties of interpretation are compounded by the occasional ambiguity of the handwriting found in this and other manuscripts. That is, it is sometimes hard to be sure quite what letter is intended, let alone the sound that letter is supposed to represent. This leads to differing transcriptions, as seen in Table 4.9.

Table 4.9. *Examples of differences in
editors' transcription of Boultbee's list*

Begg and Begg	Starke	Boultbee's gloss
tuīnow	tāīnow	'cousin'
ēētoomatta	eēloomatta	'long since'

Table 4.10. *Examples of Kendall's (1815)
orthography*

Kendall's spelling	gloss	modern spelling
Kapi	'is good'	*ka pai*
kodooa	'you two'	*kōrua*
Tuakunna	'elder sibling'	*tuakana*
nue	'great'	*nui*
wanhoungha	'friend'	*whanaunga* ('relation')

Not only early manuscripts show this type of spelling: the first published book
in Māori, Kendall's (1815) *A korao no New Zealand*, shows similar impressionistic, though more consistent, use of an English-based system, with forms as in
Table 4.10.

It is not until the appearance in 1820 of Kendall's second book, which benefit-
ted from the expertise of Professor Samuel Lee of Cambridge, that a systematic
approach to Māori based on continental vowel values is adopted. In this publication, there is still some variation and inaccuracy, for instance /r/ is variously
<r> and <d>, /ou/ and /u/ both appear as <u>, and /h/ is sometimes written
and sometimes omitted. Nonetheless, the spelling system used marks a considerable advance on earlier attempts. Table 4.11 contains a few lines from the
Lord's Prayer (Kendall 1820:130).

However, while this represents a considerable step in the direction to the modern system, it was not a smooth road from there. Kendall's system was opposed
by a number of other missionaries, who wanted a system using English values for vowel symbols.[57] The controversy around this matter may have been
fuelled by considerable personal difficulties which obtained between Kendall
and some of the most influential of the missionaries. However, with progressive further refining, it was the Kendall–Lee system which prevailed, so that
documents – such as biblical translations – produced in the late 1830s and early
1840s, including the Treaty of Waitangi,[58] are written in an orthography which
closely resembles modern writing using convention (1) for long vowels, with
the exception that /f/ and /w/ are both written <w>.[59]

Table 4.11. *Part of the Lord's Prayer in Kendall (1820)*

Kendall's text	my translation[55]	modern spelling
To tátu Matúa, kei te Aó tóu noho wánga nei,	'Our Father, Your dwelling place is in heaven'	*Tō tātou*[56] *Matua, kei te ao tōu nohoanga nei,*
Kía pai ra óki tóu Ingóa	'May Your name be good'	*Kia pai rā hoki tōu ingoa*
Me waka róngo te tángata o te wénua nei ki á koe, me te tíni ánga o dúnga o te rángi ka róngo.	'The people of this earth should listen to You, as the host of heaven above hears'	*Me whakarongo te tāngata o te whenua nei ki a koe, me te tini hanga o runga o te rangi ka rongo.*

Maunsell (1842) was aware that there were two distinct sounds, which he describes by saying (1842:9): 'w has two sounds, one simple, as in wind &c, . . . an aspirated *w* as in when, where &c. whai "follow", whare "house".' In this passage he uses the digraph <wh> for his 'aspirated' sound, but does not do so at all consistently from then on, writing always <ware> for 'house' and variously <whangai> ~ <wangai> for 'feed'; <wanautanga> 'birth', but <whanau> 'be born'; and so on. However, from very shortly after this time, the use of <wh> to spell this sound becomes very consistent.

That it was <wh>, and not for instance <f>, which became the norm, is due to the pronunciation of this phoneme in the region in which most missionary activity took place at this early period: Northland. Further south, spellings are found in which <f> is used for this sound. Both John Boultbee and James Watkin, the first missionary (1840–4) in the Otago area, use this spelling (Harlow 1987), though in neither case is it the only representation of /f/: Boultbee, for instance, has <fettoo> 'star' (*whetū*), but <werri> 'house' (*whare*), <aoeto> 'seven' (*whitu*); and Watkin uses a similar diversity, settling on <wh> only towards the end of his list, by which time this spelling was becoming standard (Harlow 1987:xiii).[60]

The other feature of spelling which took a little longer to settle to the present set of conventions was word division. This is seen especially in the juxtaposition of preposed particles and lexical word-forms within phrases, and to a lesser extent of prefixes and stems.[61] Thus, for instance, the 1837 edition of the New Testament has *kai-*, which forms agentive nouns, as a separate word (*kai wakawa* for modern *kaiwhakawā* 'judge'), but writes *erima* for modern *e rima* (TA 5), and *ekore* for modern *e kore* (TA not). By and large, however, the modern patterns were in place by about 1848.

With the exception of the matter of the long vowels, the modern spelling system was essentially in place by this time. However, an interesting proposal, which appeared in some printed texts, but which enjoyed only very limited success, should be noted. On the basis that /f/ and /ŋ/ are single sounds, as are, say, /t, n/, etc., it was proposed that there should be one letter also for these phonemes. Herbert Williams makes this case in his article in the June 1908 issue (No. 123) of the newspaper *Te Pipiwharauroa*,[62] and from this issue until No. 165 for February 1912 this paper printed <ŋ> for /ŋ/ instead of <ng>, and <ʋh> for /f/ instead of <wh>, with larger versions for upper-case.

The Māori spelling system is arguably one of the best to be found anywhere, especially if phonemic vowel length is indicated accurately. However, to return to the point made at the beginning of this section, it is striking what variation can be seen in its actual use by writers. Increased use of Māori as a language of tuition and wider use of correctly spelt Māori in the public domain may well tend to reduce this and accord the language in both spoken and written form the same prestige and cultivation.

NOTES

1. Compared with 'triangular' PN languages like Māori, some of the Outliers have rather more elaborate inventories, largely due to contact with non-PN languages.
2. The languages of the Tuamotu Archipelago, of Manihiki-Rakahanga and of Tonga-reva (these latter islands in the Northern Cook Islands) are very similar to Māori in this respect. Other CE languages have variously undergone shifts and mergers in their phonological history. See especially Biggs (1978).
3. See chapter 3 for the two cases of a reduced inventory due to historical mergers.
4. See below. Hohepa (1967:5) attributes 'palatal through glottal' allophones to /h/.
5. See chapter 2. Māori /h/ is from PPN *f and *s, and, at least in Northland, some /h/ seem to have had some sort of sibilant pronunciation well into the nineteenth century.
6. See, for instance, Gussenhoven and Jacobs (1998) for an introduction to these ideas.
7. De Lacy treats [coronal] as a terminal feature, because [anterior] and [distributed] are not contrastive in Māori.
8. See chapter 2 and especially Biggs (1978:708–9).
9. In this and similar cases, there is a syllable boundary realised as 'a new input of energy' (Bauer 1993:534), a increase in intensity, see below.
10. On this unit, which consists of (C)V, see further below.
11. The imperative of verbs with an (not necessarily explicit) object take passive morphology, see chapter 6.
12. This is a difference in the sandhi phenomena where like vowels meet across word and morpheme boundaries; see below.
13. Bauer (1993:544–54) provides a detailed discussion of the issues surrounding these.
14. At least for many speakers. There is a tendency in the modern language towards a merger of /au/ and /ou/, and to a lesser extent of /oe/ ~ /oi/ and /ai/ ~ /ae/.
15. For the reasons why it is hard to be precise in this area, see Bauer (1993:544–54).
16. In contrast to many treatments of, say, English, in which the dipthongs are listed as distinct unit phonemes.
17. See for instance Biggs (1961:12) and Bauer (1993:544). De Lacy (1997:17–18), see further below, disputes this, claiming that there is a restriction against /uo/ within

morphemes, and pointing out that the sequence is rare, and seems to occur only in items where, at least historically, a morpheme boundary intervened. Synchronically, however, there is no denying the existence of this sequence alongside all the others.

18. *Kāinga* 'home' ~ *kainga* 'eat.passive', *hāunga* 'besides' ~ *haunga* 'stink', and *teina* ~ *tēina* 'younger sibling same sex as EGO, singular ~ plural' illustrate the phonemic distinction between the long and short diphthongs.

19. Assuming the analysis of long vowels and diphthongs as sequences of short vowels. Of course not all sequences of VV(V) are possible here, as noted above; many such sequences constitute separate syllables.

20. Fijian /v/ is from POC *p (Tongan /f/), while Tongan /v/ (= Fijian /w/) is from POC *w.

21. Lynch *et al.* (2002) do not mention such a restriction, but elsewhere Lynch (2002) draws attention to the scarcity (marginality?) of POC 'labiovelars' ($*p^w$, $*b^w$, $*m^w$) followed by *o or *u. The present observation may be related.

22. On all these phenomena which refer to the mora see Bauer (1981b), and references there, especially Biggs (1980). See further, on the metrical principle concerned, McLean (1981).

23. The word 'mora' is used with systematic ambiguity, designating both the unit of phonological weight (the μ in this diagram – see, for instance, Gussenhoven and Jacobs 1998:160–4), and the unit (C)V, as proposed by Bauer (1981b). σ is used here both for this latter 'mora' and for the syllable as underlying and surface units.

24. As does de Lacy msa., where it is asserted that the Prosodic Word (very roughly = morpheme) is the domain of syllabification, implying that no syllabification occurs across the edges of these units. The paper demonstrates that this is indeed so for some candidate pairs and in the context particle plus base.

25. In fact, *ohooho* illustrates well the type of variation observable in this area of pronunciation. Recall Bauer's (1993:543–5) observation that words of this type have several pronunciations, in this case [oho?oho], [oho.oho], [oho:ho], depending on speaker, style and speed. The first two pronunciations are stressed like *katakata*.

26. He uses # to designate the end of a sentence. As will be seen below, phrase stress, which interacts with word stress, differs depending on whether the phrase is sentence-final or not.

27. With one exception, this 'resyllabification' never operates across phrase boundaries. The exception is the sequence *ana au* (TA]$_{PHRASE}$[1Sg.), which bridges a phrase barrier, yet is normally pronounced [ɐ'nɑːu]. On phrases as a unit of Māori grammar, see chapter 6.

28. E.g. *kai-* 'agent', must form a syllable of its own. Even when attached to a stem beginning with /i/, e.g. *iriiri* 'baptise', a syllable boundary falls after the /ai/. Thus *kaiiriiri* 'Baptist' (as in 'John the . . .') is either /kai.i.'rii.ri/ or /kai.'i.ri.i.ri/.

29. Again, the reader is referred to Bauer (1993) for detailed discussion on quite which these are. For the present summary, suffice it to say that all combinations of a vowel and a higher vowel, plus /oe/, are candidates, but on the criterion used here, combinations such as /ea/, /oa/, /ue/ are not. However, see below on the phonetics of sequences involving /i/ plus a lower vowel.

30. To some extent this idiolect variation correlates with the fluency of the speaker; L2 learners are more likely not to syllabify than L1 speakers. However, this is not hard

and fast, and it is possible to hear very fluent first-language speakers of Māori say, for instance, [feke'ʔeko] for *whakaako* 'teach'.

31. The markedly greater propensity for /aa/ to syllabify to [aː] than for other /VV/ pairs to become [Vː] is a second feature, besides its much higher frequency, which marks it as *sui generis*. However, this same feature militates against the tentative suggestion of Bauer (1993:537) that [aː] might best be regarded as a sixth vowel phoneme beside the five short vowels.

32. Although these forms are usually treated as prefixes – see chapter 5 – they behave in the present respect more like particles, and belong with the rightmost column. The prefix *tua-* never occurs before a root beginning with /a/.

33. I.e. the VV sequences which never form diphthongs, even within morphemes.

34. Supported by the Marsden Fund, administered for the government by the Royal Society of New Zealand.

35. See Maclagan *et al.* (2005).

36. See especially Harlow *et al.* (2004).

37. This brief statement greatly simplifies the situation, ignoring for instance what happens in reduplications and other derived forms, and the interaction of word stress with phrase and sentence intonation. However, it is largely true for simple words in isolation in other languages. See Biggs (1971:469); also, for instance, Peltzer (1996:24) for Tahitian, and Elbert and Pukui (1979:18) for Hawaiian.

38. As with much else in the phonology of Māori, the fullest account of stress and intonation is to be found in Bauer (1993:555–63, 574–7; pp. 2–19 contain a detailed discussion of question intonation). Schütz (1985b:5–13) also presents a very useful summary and discussion of the treatment of stress up to Hohepa's work, before proposing his own account.

39. His actual formulation refers to the 'last syllable if it is long . . . the penultimate syllable if the last syllable is short' (1971:471).

40. Io, with many epithets, appears in a range of mythological texts as the single supreme divinity, creator and first parent.

41. In fact, there is some variation in forms like this one; Bauer (1993:575), for instance, reports ˈkaranga-ˈtia.

42. It is in the context of these word stress rules that the distinction between those adjacent unlike vowels which form diphthongs and those which do not becomes important. For instance, while *uaua* has the two pronunciations given above, ˈakoako 'learn, practise' is always stressed like ˈkatakata 'laugh'. Both Biggs and Hohepa, however, treat any pair of unlike vowels as equivalent with respect to their stress rules.

43. The rules for stress placement in simple words apply only to the last four moræ. However, any 'indigenous' Māori word longer than four moræ is, at least historically, complex, and is treated as such by stress placement. See Biggs (1969:132) and Bauer (1993:557).

44. These are like what are called Prosodic Phrases in de Lacy (msa); see also the beginning of chapter 6 below. Prosodic/Phonological Phrases correspond closely with grammatical phrases, the only major exception being that an unstressed subject pronoun, though a separate grammatical phrase, is often cliticised to the preceding predicate phrase.

45. Bauer herself notes what is a rather widespread phenomenon in modern Māori, and that is that younger speakers, for many of whom Māori is L2, do borrow the English pattern and thus can focus phrases *in situ*.

46. De Lacy (msa) deals with this by claiming that in sentences with initial focus, only the focussed phrase constitutes a Prosodic Phrase; the rest of the sentence remains unparsed prosodically.

47. Available at the URL: www.tetaurawhiri.govt.nz/english/pub_e/conventions.shtml.

48. See Pawley (1981:21). Biggs was once accused by a bishop of 'murdering the Māori language' through his suggested spelling convention.

49. The Māori Language Commission's conventions contain an inconsistency at this point in *allowing* the use of the macron to indicate the long vowel which results from the affixation of passive -*a* to a stem ending in /a/: *hangā* 'be built' from *hanga* as well as *hangaa*.

50. See also Schütz (1990:351–63).

51. On Boultbee's travels, see Begg and Begg (1979) and Starke (1986). Boultbee spent time in Asia as well, and his journal also contains a Malay word list.

52. In the case of Boultbee's list, these include the word list prepared by James Watkin some fifteen years later – see Harlow (1987).

53. Since the dialect Boultbee was transcribing was from the Far South, the actual form used would have been *ruka* (Southern merger of *ŋ and *k to /k/). Strikingly, Boultbee has *tóngata* for North Island *tangata* 'man'.

54. It appears from other evidence that a lateral pronunciation of this phoneme was more common in the south than elsewhere.

55. Kendall's 'translation' is the English version known from the Authorised Version of the Bible.

56. Notice that Kendall inadvertently uses the first person plural *inclusive* possessive determiner to address God, thus calling Him His own father!

57. See Parkinson (2001a, 2001b, 2003, 2004) for a very detailed account of this period in the development of the orthography.

58. See chapter 7 for the significance of this document.

59. The Wesleyan Press was the first to use <wh> consistently, all publications from 1841 showing this spelling. See H. W. Williams (1924: item 68).

60. See also Maclagan and King (2002) for an account of the progress to a consistent spelling for /f/.

61. See chapters 5 and 6 for these, and for phrase structure.

62. This and many other Māori language newspapers can be consulted (both in transcription and as images) at: www.nzdl.org/cgi-bin/niupepalibrary?a=p&p=about&c=niupepa&l=mi&nw=utf-8.

5   The morphology of Māori

Parts of speech

As in all languages, the words of Māori do not all behave the same way either morphologically or syntactically; there are word classes, grouping together those items which share privileges of occurrence and/or can undergo the same morphological processes. On this, all writers on Māori would agree, but from that point on there is a bewildering diversity in the analyses proposed. This state of affairs is partly due to the range of paradigms within which descriptions of Māori have been composed. Partly, however, it is due to the fact that in Māori, as also in other Polynesian languages, there is relatively little in the way of inflectional morphology which would contribute to class assignment, while very many lexical items can appear systematically in a variety of syntactic environments.

To take the former point first, 'prior to 1960, all published grammars of Polynesian languages were "traditional" grammars, sometimes referred to as Latinate' (Mutu 1989:399). While this brief summary glosses over some useful discussion by earlier individual writers, it is essentially correct in that early accounts of, say, Māori grammar rely heavily and largely uncritically on the parts of speech, and the criteria for assignment of words to them, familiar from traditional European grammars. Even Maunsell (1842), who 'would . . . insist in reply to those who would bind him down to the model of some of the European grammars, that Maori, like Hebrew, is altogether different from those languages in structure' (1842:xii), uses noun, adjective, verb, adverb and preposition as the categories under which he discusses morphology and syntax. He himself admits difficulty in the classification of some words using this set of categories.

To take just one other example from the period 'prior to 1960', Kirkham (1917), whose work, though brief, is by no means untypical, quite uncritically uses the same set, assigning Maori words to these categories on the basis of the part of speech of the usual English gloss.

The significance of the date 1960 in Mutu's statement is that by then Bruce Biggs had completed his doctoral thesis in Indiana, and had returned to Auckland, where he exerted a tremendous influence on the study not only of Māori but of Polynesian languages generally until his death in 2000. The thesis, a structuralist grammar of the phrase in Māori, appeared as Biggs (1961) and the analysis in it formed the basis of his (1969) influential textbook of Māori.

In this work, Biggs rejected the traditional set of lexical categories as used in earlier descriptions of Māori and in Williams' dictionary (most recent edition, H. W. Williams 1971). As mentioned above and as will be discussed more fully below, many Māori words can occur in a variety of syntactic environments. Use of the 'traditional' parts of speech thus led to the state of affairs exemplified by Biggs (1969:51, glosses added): '*raakau* ['tree']¹ is a noun, *tangi* ['mourn'] a verb-noun, *pai* ['good'] an adjective-noun-neuter-verb and transitive verb . . . And there is *no way of knowing how many parts of speech a given word embraces* without consulting all of its definitions in the dictionary' (Biggs' italics). Biggs' solution was to propose two major classes of words, particles and bases, with five subdivisions of the latter. Particles are those words which occupy the peripheries of phrases and fulfil such functions as case marking, tense/aspect marking, directionality, deixis, and so on. We return to these more fully below (especially in chapter 6). Bases are those words which occupy the nucleus of phrases – in particular, they can head phrases – and provide the lexical content. Biggs (e.g. 1969:51ff.) divides these into non-overlapping classes on the basis of compatibility with passive morphology and with various subtypes of particle.

His definitions (with my additions in [ ]) are (Biggs 1969):

A NOUN is any word which can take a definite article but which cannot occur as the nucleus of a verbal phrase [i.e. a phrase marked by tense/aspect particles].

Thus *te raakau* 'the tree', but not **e raakau ana* 'is treeing / is being a tree, or some such' and so on.²

A UNIVERSAL is any word which may be used passively.

Thus, *inu* 'drink' with passive *inumia* 'drink-pass.' is a universal.

A STATIVE is any base which can be used verbally but not passively.

Ora 'healthy, well, alive' can occur for instance in the phrase *kua ora* 'has recovered, has got well (again)', but not as *oratia*.

A LOCATIVE is any base which can follow the locative particle [preposition] *ki* ['to'] directly [i.e. without a determiner].

The class of locatives thus includes not only place names, *ki Aotearoa* 'to New Zealand', but also a set of 'relator' nouns, such as *runga* 'on, top surface, space above', *mua* 'front, space before'.

A PERSONAL is any base which takes the personal article *a* after the locative particle *ki*.

Personal names, along with names of tribes, and, for some speakers, the names of months belong to this class: *ki a Rei* 'to Ray', *ki a Ngāitai* 'to Ngāitai (a tribe of the eastern Bay of Plenty)', *ki a Hūrae* 'to July'. Biggs claims that there is a unique class assignment for every base under this system, and that this assignment provides all necessary information about the constructions in which a word may occur. His work has been invaluable in breaking with the 'Latinate' model used previously, in drawing attention to the problems in the issue of parts of speech not only for Māori, but for Polynesian languages more generally, and thus providing the basis for further research. Biggs' classes of noun, locative and personal have largely stood the test of time; however, it was not long before modifications in the other two classes were introduced. Hohepa's (1969b) significant article on negation in Māori provided further evidence for the existence of the class Biggs called statives, but proposed splitting this class into two sub-classes, which he called stative verbs and stative adjectives.

Somewhat later again, Reedy's (1979:21–4) doctoral thesis contained a brief discussion of verb classes and proposed five classes covering Biggs' statives and universals on the basis of the complements and oblique phrases which typically accompany them. Intransitives are divided into stative verbs, adjectival verbs and 'experience' verbs; the other two classes are transitives and di-transitives.

The year 1978 saw the publication of Chung's doctoral thesis on Polynesian syntax. Chung, whose primary interest is in clause structure and case marking, distinguished four classes of verb, not including adjectives: canonical transitives, 'middle' verbs,[3] intransitive, and stative verbs (Chung 1978:29, 47, 143–4). In the same vein, Bauer (1983) makes a very good argument for the recognition in Māori of a class of 'experience' verbs, which corresponds to Chung's 'middle'. Bauer provides a range of syntactic arguments, to which we return below, for distinguishing these from other transitive verbs. Finally in this brief survey of published views, work within the recent generative framework assumes the lexical categories which are standard within that framework. Waite (1994:59–61) discusses the issue and his own treatment in the context of earlier discussion, especially Biggs' position. In particular, he deals with the observation that many words seem systematically to be able to appear in a variety of syntactic environments not by positing parts of speech which somehow encode this range of environments, but by arguing that functional categories such as I(nflection) and D(eterminer) can take any of a number of different categories of phrase as their complements. Thus, for example (1994:61):

$[_{DP} [_{D'} \text{ Det. XP]]}$, where X $= \{V, N, A\}$

The insight expressed in this way, that for instance *pai* 'good' is not a noun in the expression *te pai* ('the good') 'goodness', or a verb in the expression *e pai ana* (TA 'good' TA) 'is/was good', will be maintained in this chapter, as will Waite's position that zero-derivation, especially of verbs to nouns, plays a significant role in Māori. Waite further makes the point that the basic assignment of a part of speech is, in his word, 'intuitive'. That is, using the present example, to say that *pai* is an adjective used variously to modify nouns, head a nominal phrase and head a verbal phrase (or in Waite's terms, head the complements of a DP or IP respectively), rather than saying that the word is a noun which, like other nouns, can also be used to modify and to head a verbal phrase, verges on the arbitrary. It is, however, possible to give a reasoned basis for assigning *pai* to a class we could usefully call 'adjective'; *pai* has certain privileges of occurrence which will be sketched below and belongs to a group of words which can be used with certain particles in comparative and superlative senses.

The position I take here is indebted to this discussion and especially to the work of Bauer (1997:70ff.), who provides a good account of the whole issue. For reasons of space, it will be impossible to present all the detail, especially of placement and functions of the particles, and readers are referred to the fuller descriptions in Bauer (1993, 1997) and Harlow (2001).

Particles vs bases

Much of the discussion of Māori syntax in the next chapter will depend on the notion of the 'phrase' and the role and structure of this important unit will be dealt with there. Some mention of phrase structure and of phrasal categories is, however, required at this point as these are among the criteria used in word class assignment. Biggs' (1961, 1969) model, which will be followed for the moment, trisects the phrase into three slots: a nucleus, which contains lexical material (bases), and two peripheries, which contain particles. Each of the peripheries has paradigms of particles peculiar to it, and a (relatively) fixed order for these paradigms in the event that more than one is represented. The paradigms of particles which occur in the so-called preposed periphery are typically grammatical in function, expressing categories like tense/aspect and case, and including determiners. Those which follow the nucleus are more modifying in nature, with sets of 'manner', directional and deictic particles, among others. Thus, the following are Māori phrases.

> [[*me i*]   [*haere wawe*]   [*mai*]]
> if   TA go   quick   Dir.
> 'if . . . had come quickly'

[[*ki te*]   [*whare wānanga*] [*nei hoki*]]
P   Det. house   learning   Loc. also
'to this university as well'

In this second example, [*ki te*] is the preposed periphery and contains members of the paradigms of prepositions and determiners, [*whare wānanga*] is the nucleus containing two bases, and [*nei hoki*] is the postposed periphery.

This account of the phrase allows the differentiation of types of phrase and the distinction between particles and bases. Biggs (1961 and 1969) distinguishes nominal and verbal phrases depending on the presence in the preposed periphery of prepositions/determiners on the one hand and of tense/aspect particles on the other. I will be making the further distinction between nominal phrases, those whose first element is a determiner, and prepositional phrases, those which are initiated by one of the prepositions.

The distinction between base and particle created by this analysis will also be maintained, and the rest of the discussion will be about the subdivisions of bases. However, it is necessary also to point out that there is a certain arbitrariness about the particle/base divide.

(1) A property of phrases generally is that the nucleus at least must have material in it, must have a lexical head. The converse of this is that particles cannot occur alone, without lexical material either following or preceding in the same phrase. Counterexamples to this generalisation are an idiomatic use of the postposed particle *atu* to mean 'further to, apart from' and the systematic use of some determiners without lexical heads.

[Ø Ø *atu*][4] [*i a   ia*]
        Dir.   P Pers. 3Sg.
'apart from him/her'

[*He waka*] [*tēnei* Ø Ø].
Det. car   Det.
'This is a car.'

(2) Other particles, though unable to stand alone as a phrase, behave in other ways like bases used as modifiers. In particular, Māori exhibits a peculiar type of agreement between the head of a phrase and a lexical modifier; if the former is marked passive, then so must be the latter. Indeed, it is possible to omit the passive marking from the head but not from the modifier.

Kai-nga mata-tia ai ngā   kai.
eat-Pass. raw-Pass. TA Det.Pl. food
'Food used to be eaten raw.'

In this example, the suffix can be omitted on *kai*, but not on *mata*. A certain class of particles, usually referred to as manner particles, which if present in a phrase immediately follow the lexical material, similarly undergoes passive agreement.

> *Kei te waiata-tia tonu-tia   ngā   mōteatea tawhito.*
> TA   sing-Pass. still-Pass. Det.Pl. songs   ancient
> 'The ancient songs are still being sung.'

(3) As will be seen in more detail in chapter 6, Māori is a 'head-first' language. Thus, basic word order is VSO, full NP possessors follow the possessum, relative clauses follow their antecedents. To a very large extent, it is true also within phrases. In particular, if two or more lexical items occur in sequence within a phrase, then the leftmost is the head of the lexical phrase and the others modify the item immediately to their left. Thus in the phrase:

> *te   hunga tito   waiata*
> Det.   people compose song
> 'composers, people who compose songs'

waiata is the incorporated object of *tito*, and that construction modifies *hunga*. Exceptions to this very general pattern are a small and closed set of words which stand before the item they modify, e.g.[5]

> *he   wahine tino   ātaahua*
> Det. woman   very   beautiful
> 'a very beautiful woman'

In this case, *tino* modifies *ātaahua*, and that expression modifies *wahine*. Similarly, in *me āta haere* (TA carefully go) 'one should go carefully', *āta* modifies the head *haere*. It seems pointless to call some of these words particles and the others bases, yet some of them can also occur either as lexical head of a phrase or as following modifiers, like bases, while others are unable to appear except in this premodifying position.

A further problem with 'particle' is the wide range of functions these words fulfil, ranging from tense/aspect and case markers, through determiners to modifiers and deictics. As a result, researchers working on Māori within a generative framework treat Biggs' particles in quite different ways. Determiners and tense/aspect markers are heads respectively of DP and IP; other particles head PPs, while yet others with similar distributions are regarded as case markers. Deictic particles are treated in ways parallel to possessors and number expressions.[6]

These points notwithstanding, it will be convenient to maintain Biggs' distinction and to concentrate here on the issue of the classes of bases, leaving the particles and their functions in large part for chapter 6. As noted, it will be necessary to refer to some of the subclasses of particles – in particular, tense/aspect markers, determiners and some prepositions – and to the three types of phrase whose definition these allow: verbal, nominal and prepositional.

A recurring problem for discussion of parts of speech in Māori, as has been said, is the observation that very many bases can occur not only in both verbal and nominal phrases, but also as modifiers to other bases. It is this state of affairs which led Biggs to propose his scheme, sketched above. What will be proposed here follows much more closely the work of Bauer (see especially 1997:70ff.) with reference to a number of phenomena in Māori word formation and syntax. These are as follows.

(1) Any clause whose predicate is a verbal phrase headed by a verb[7] can be nominalised by replacing the tense/aspect marker by *te* 'the', or by a singular possessive determiner encoding one of the arguments. The head of the predicate phrase and any other arguments and/or obliques remain unchanged. This gives the appearance of a verb also being a noun. For instance,

> *E   kōrero ana rātou i   te   reo   Māori.*
> TA speak TA   3Pl. Obj. Det. language Māori
> 'They are speaking Māori.'

can be nominalised as:

> *tā.rātou kōrero i   te   reo   Māori*
> their   speak Obj. Det. language Māori
> 'Their speaking Māori'

For cases like this, I subscribe to Waite's (1994:61) analysis, mentioned above, that this is an instance of a VP acting as complement to a determiner.

(2) Producing superficially similar constructions in many cases is productive application of zero derivation, which relates numerous nouns to verbal stems. Thus, beside *kōrero*, a verb meaning 'speak', and its zero nominalisation as exemplified in the previous paragraph, there is a noun *kōrero* 'talk, story, discourse, speech'. Similarly, from *waiata* 'sing' is derived *waiata* 'song'. An expression like *tā rātou waiata* is thus ambiguous as between 'their singing' (the nominalisation) and 'their song' (the deverbal noun). However, with most other determiners and with plurals of the definite article or possessive determiner, only the deverbal noun in the sense of 'song' appears. Thus, *ā rātou waiata* can only mean 'their songs', while the expression

tā.rātou waiata i   tā.rātou waiata
their   sing   Obj. their   song
'their singing of their song'

illustrates both uses of the ambiguous singular.

(3) As mentioned above, there is considerable freedom for words to occur in a variety of phrase types. Particular instances of this freedom will become plain in the account of the parts of speech below. For now, here are just a few examples of nouns which are free to appear as heads of verbal phrases. The meaning expressed in such phrases is of course related to that of the noun, but not entirely in predictable ways. Thus, *ngaru* 'wave' can be used in sentences like:

E   ngaru ana te   moana.
TA wave TA   Det. sea
'The sea is choppy.'

Rākau 'tree' can similarly appear in a verbal phrase such as *Kua rākau* (TA tree) meaning 'has become covered with trees'.

In other cases though, the verbal phrase headed by a noun in this way conveys the meaning of 'become an N' and occurs primarily with non-progressive tense markers. This is particularly, but not exclusively, so of nouns designating human beings. For instance, the compound noun *tangata whenua* (person land) 'a person/people of the land' refers to a person or group of people who are at home in a given area and thus enjoy certain rights as well as the obligation to act towards visitors as hosts. After formal welcoming ceremonies, this distinction is neutralised and the visitors are said to have 'become locals': *kua tangata whenua* (TA person land).

A further group of nouns designating periods of time have verbal uses meaning 'to pass that period of time' or 'to be that period of time'. That is, the verbal phrases can be impersonal or have personal subjects. Thus *kua pō* (TA night) 'It has become night', but also:

Ø   Pō   mai tāua   ki Fiji.
TA night Dir. 1Du.Incl. P Fiji
'We spent the night in Fiji.'

An argument in favour of regarding such expressions as having the shape 'TA + noun' rather than 'TA + denominal verb' is the fact that the zero nominalisation mentioned under (1) above is not available for verbal phrases of this sort.

(4) Apart from a handful of systematic restrictions, a very general phenomenon is that any base may follow any other as a modifier. Thus not only

adjectives, but also verbs and other nouns can be found modifying nouns in this
way: *he tangata pai* (Det. + N + A) 'a good person', *he whare kōhatu* (Det. +
N + N) 'a stone house', *he rōpū waiata* (Det. + N + V) 'a singing group'.
Similarly, verbs may be modified by nouns (object incorporation), adjectives,
and (in a restricted fashion) by other verbs: *ka whakaputa whakaaro* (TA + V +
N, TA express thought) 'expresses thoughts', *ka tae wawe* (TA + V + A, TA
arrive quick) 'arrives quickly', *ka tangi haere* (TA + V + V, TA weep go) 'goes
weeping'.

These aspects of Māori grammar render some of the criteria traditionally associated with particular parts of speech unusable. Compatibility with tense/aspect
markers does not single out a single class of word, nor does use with *te*, or ability to modify nouns within a phrase. The same is true of one of Biggs' criteria
mentioned above. One of the very few suffixes used in Māori forms passives.
Words derived this way are clearly verbs,[8] but it is not so clear that only verbs
may be made passive by application of the suffix. On the contrary, quite apart
from manifestations of passive agreement, whereby bases and some particles
which modify a passive head are themselves suffixed, other items may take the
suffix apart from verbs (see below, section on passive suffix). Similarly, those
bases derived by means of the nominalising suffix, on which see further below,
are nouns, yet a variety of types of word, not just verbs, may be nominalised in
this way.

Despite these points, it is possible to identify criteria which usefully provide
a basis for the assignment of bases to a number of parts of speech. Numerals and
pronouns are special cases, respectively, of verbs and personal nouns and will
be described further below. Apart from these though, bases fall into two large
groups, verbs and nouns, each category having a number of subdivisions. This
primary division is based on the stereotypical role of some bases as heading
arguments and adjunct phrases, while others head predicates. Nothing of significance rides on this division; it is the subdivisions, five in the case of verbs, and
three in the case of nouns, which are the grammatically important categories.

Verbs

Stereotypically, these words head phrases marked for tense/aspect. The five subcategories differ from each other in argument structure, privileges of occurrence
with particles, and other grammatical features.

(1) **Transitive verbs** are those which take two arguments, an agent and
a patient. Unique among verbs, transitive verbs can occur in three sentence
types: active, in which the agent is subject and the patient an object marked
with (usually) the preposition *i*; passive, in which the patient is subject and
the agent an oblique marked with the preposition *e*; actor emphatic, in which

the patient is again subject while the agent is initial, marked with a possessive preposition. These three constructions are exemplified using again the example from chapter 2:

Active

> *Ka hoko te matua i ngā tīkiti.*
> TA buy Det. parent Obj. Det.Pl. ticket
> 'The parent buys the tickets.'

Passive

> *Ka hoko-na ngā tīkiti e te matua.*
> TA buy-Pass. Det.Pl. ticket Agt. Det. parent
> 'The tickets are bought by the parent.'

Actor Emphatic

> *Nā te matua ngā tīkiti i hoko.*
> P Det. parent Det.Pl. ticket TA buy
> 'It was the parent who bought the tickets.'

A further property of transitive verbs which serves to distinguish them from middle verbs, but which they share with some intransitives, is that when nominalised their active subjects become possessors marked with *a*.[9] In fact, transitive verbs show two patterns of nominalisation:

> *Te patu-nga a Hēmi i te poaka*
> Det. kill-Nom. of H Obj. Det. pig
> 'Hēmi's killing of the pig'

> *Te patu-nga o Hēmi e te hoariri*
> Det. kill-Nom. of H Agt. Det. enemy
> 'Hēmi's being killed by the enemy'

(2) **Middle verbs**, like transitives, take two arguments. However, Bauer (1983), who calls these bases 'experience verbs', presents a number of characteristics in which these two classes differ. In the first instance, there is a semantic difference in the roles of the arguments – the middle verbs, being in large part verbs of perception and mental attitude – liking, wanting, remembering – take an experiencer as subject when active, and the second argument, the thing or person seen, wanted, loved, is usually marked with *ki*. Like transitives, middle verbs can be made passive, but are not used in the Actor Emphatic construction. The reader is referred to Bauer's (1983) article for the full discussion, but it is possible here to point to one or two of the features which distinguish these two classes of verb.

As will be seen in chapter 6, one of the relativisation strategies of Māori is deletion. This strategy is available for all subjects, for possessors and for objects of middle verbs, but not objects of transitive verbs. In nominalisations of middle verbs, subjects are regularly encoded as *o*-category possessives, in contrast to those of transitives, whose agents/subjects are *a*-category possessives.

(3) **Intransitive verbs** take only one argument, but may of course be modified by adjuncts of place, goal, time, etc. Many, particularly verbs of motion, may also take an 'internal object' or 'cognate accusative', and can then be made passive. Typical intransitive verbs in Māori, as in most languages, are verbs of motion, bodily states and activities, mental states, etc.

> *kua oma-kia   tōku oma-nga.*
> TA   run-Pass. my   run-Nom
> 'I have finished my course.'
>   (2 Timothy 4:7)

When nominalised, intransitive verbs do not show consistent marking of their subjects. Some, idiosyncratically, take *a*-category marking: *tā rātou noho* (Sg.-of 3Pl. stay) 'their stay(ing)'; in other cases, marking varies according to the degree of agency of the subject and/or pragmatic factors such as focus. Thus, zero-nominalisations of *haere* 'go' normally have *o*-category marking of inanimate subjects, such as vehicles, but may have *a*-category marking of animate subjects.

(4) **Neuter verbs** similarly take one argument, but are distinguishable from intransitives in a number of ways. The category has been recognised in writings on Māori grammar for quite some time. W. L. Williams in the fifth edition (1904) of his *First Lessons in Maori* (first edition 1862) refers to them, calling them variously neuter verbs, participles or verbal adjectives. They belong to Biggs' stative class, but an important article of Hohepa's (1969b) showed that a distinction must be made in Biggs' stative class between what are here called neuter verbs and adjectives. The class of neuter verbs is not large but contains some items of high frequency. Attempts have been made to list this class exhaustively, but such lists do not coincide. Bauer (1997:75f., 490ff.) provides a comparison of these attempts and makes the point that the differences between these lists is due at least in part to variation among speakers as to the ways in which some particular verbs are used. While the class may not be closed in that there is no definitive list of members, it remains very largely true, as Bauer points out (1997:491), that 'no newly created words are added to the class'. The present writer is, however, aware of two borrowings from English which, at least for some speakers, have become neuter verbs. These are *pīti* 'to beat' and *wini* 'to win', which are constructed according to the neuter verb pattern.

The single argument of a neuter verb is its patient. If an agent is expressed with such a verb, it is an oblique phrase marked with the preposition *i*. In Māori, neuter verbs are often the more usual way of expressing some meanings, which in other languages, like English, are encoded as transitive verbs.

> *I pakaru te wini i a Hōne.*
> TA break Det. window P Pers. H
> 'Hōne broke the window.'

Similarly with *mau* 'catch', *ngaro* 'lose', *pau* 'use up', *riro* 'take, acquire', etc.

Among the ways in which neuter verbs are distinguished from intransitives and other classes of verb are:

(i) their behaviour in complement clauses – Māori has two complementisers for forming object noun clauses and some final clauses, *kia* and *ki te*. The latter is available if the subjects of both the higher and the lower clauses are identical, and the lower verb is not passive *or neuter*.[10]

> *Kāore au i te hiahia **ki te** haere ki reira.*
> Neg. 1Sg. TA want Comp. go P there
> 'I don't want to go there.'   (Same subject)

> *Kāore au i te hiahia **kia** haere ia ki reira.*
> Neg. 1Sg. TA want Comp. go 3Sg. P there
> 'I don't want him to go there.' (Different subjects)

> *Kāore au i te hiahia **kia** wareware i a koe.*
> Neg. 1Sg. TA want Comp. forget P Pers. 2Sg.
> 'I don't want you to forget me', lit. 'I don't want to be forgotten by you.' (Same subject)

(ii) in nominalisations, their subjects are always possessives in the *o*-category. This follows from the semantic role of the subjects; they are always patients.

(iii) transitives and intransitives form imperatives by means of a particle *e*/Ø.[11] Middle verbs, neuter verbs and adjectives on the other hand can be used as commands or wishes only with a jussive particle *kia*.

(iv) neuter verbs are not used to modify adjectives, though the converse does occur. Hohepa (1969b:14) was the first to remark on this, giving among his examples

> *I mahue mokemoke te kuia.*
> TA left(neut.) lonely(adj.) Det. old.woman
> 'The old woman was left lonely.'

> *I mākū tika te māra.*
> TA wet(adj.) correct(adj.) Det. garden
> 'The garden was wetted properly.'

Table 5.1. *Properties of verbal subcategories*

	Number of arguments	*a-/o-*	Imperative	Can modify	Can take passive suffix	Occurs in Actor Emphatic
transitive	2	*a-*	*e/Ø*	y	y	y
middle	2	*o-*	*kia*	y	y	n
intr.	1	*a-/o-*	*e/Ø*	y	y	y/n
neuter	1	*o-*	*kia*	n	n	n
adjective	1	*o-*	*kia*	y	n	n

but not:

> **I   mākū   ea   te   māra.*
> TA   wet(adj.)   suffice(neut.)   Det.   garden
> 'The garden was wetted sufficiently.'

(5) **Adjectives** are classed here as a subcategory of verb because in fact their syntactic behaviour is very similar to that of neuter verbs. Biggs (1969) classes both as statives, that is, as those bases which are compatible with tense/aspect markers, but not with the passive suffix. Adjectives in Māori, when used predicatively, can be combined with such particles: *e pai ana* (TA good TA) 'is good', etc. Their most typical distribution is, however, as modifiers within a phrase – *he whakaaro pai* (Det. thought good) 'a good idea' – and in predicates introduced by *he* 'a': *he pai te whakaaro* (Det. good Det. thought) 'The idea is good.'[12]

Adjectives may also head a nominal phrase introduced by *te* (or a singular possessive determiner). Such phrases name the *extent* to which something has the property named by the adjective, rather than the *fact* of its having the property. Thus *te roa o te taura* (Det. long P Det. rope) means 'the length of the rope', not 'the rope's being long', and can be quantified: *100 mita te roa o te taura* 'The rope is 100m long.'

The properties of these five subcategories of verb can be summed up in Table 5.1. In this table, *a-/o-* refers to the possessive marking on the subject of these verbs when nominalised; the column for the passive suffix refers to the base's behaviour when head of its own phrase – adjectives can of course take the passive suffix when modifying a passive head; the y/n marking for intransitives under occurrence in the Actor Emphatic reflects the variability of native speaker judgements at this point – for some speakers, agentive intransitives such as *haere* 'go' can be used in this way.

While this classification attempts to identify the subcategories of those words primarily used as heads of predicates in ways relevant to the syntax of Māori, it must be pointed out that it 'leaks' in two respects.[13] On the one hand, many verbs in Māori, as in other languages, can belong to more than one subcategory, often with differences of meaning, and, on the other, a few verbs have properties which seem to fall between these subcategories.

Numerous verbs can be used both as transitives and as intransitives. In the case of verbs such as *kai* 'eat', *inu* 'drink', it is simply a matter of whether a specific object is envisaged or not. In others such as *noho* 'sit, remain in a place, inhabit, dwell', the degree of affectedness of the place sat upon, stayed in, leads to encoding variously as an object or locative adjunct. Thus, *noho* can take an object of the place inhabited, and, for instance, the horse ridden, but an adjunct of the place in which one remains instead of leaving, or sits instead of lying or standing. In yet others, there is a distinct though recognisably related meaning in transitive and intransitive usages: *moe* 'sleep' is intransitive, though it may have an internal object such as *te moenga roa* (Det. sleep-Nom. long) 'the long sleep (death)' or *te pō* (Det. night) 'the night', but as a transitive it means 'to marry'.

Pai 'good' is an adjective, but is also used as a middle verb meaning 'to like'. *Wareware* is constructed both as a neuter verb and as a middle verb. Thus, both the following patterns occur:

> *Kua wareware i a   au   tana ingoa.* (neuter)
> TA   forget   P Pers. 1Sg. his   name
>
> *Kua wareware au   ki tana ingoa.* (middle)
> TA   forget   1Sg. P   his   name
> 'I have forgotten his name.'

In her article (1983) on middle ('experience') verbs, Bauer deals in detail with the verb *tūtaki* 'meet', and shows that it shares properties with middle, transitive and intransitive verbs. The solutions she proposes both for the behaviour of the words she calls experience verbs and for cases such as *tūtaki* are:

(1) that there is a 'transitivity cline' from canonical transitives such as *patu* 'strike' to intransitives such as *oma* 'run'. 'Experience' verbs and cases such as *tūtaki* lie at different points along this cline and thus share features of the verbs at the end-points. While this idea accounts for some of the phenomena involved, others such as the imperative marking are not in accord with such an approach.

(2) the 'verb-feature' hypothesis; that a variety of features such as degree of agentivity of subject, and degree of affectedness of any second argument, play a role in determining a verb's behaviour.

(3) the 'separate class' hypothesis; that there is a class of middle verbs distinct from both transitive and intransitive. Bauer herself points to the 'fuzziness' of the class as a problem for this solution.

The approach taken here is that the features identified by Bauer as marking off middle verbs justify a separate class, as above, and that the fuzziness Bauer draws attention to involves not just middle verbs, but indeed all subcategories. At least in part, this fuzziness correlates with exactly the sort of features mentioned in Bauer's second hypothesis; the possessive marking of the subject of a nominalised intransitive, for instance, varies according to the salience and agentivity of that subject; the distribution of imperative marking over the five subcategories proposed again accords with agentivity; *noho, kai, inu* mentioned above show transitive vs intransitive behaviours depending on the specificity and/or affectedness of an object/location. This conclusion accords both with Bauer's insight of a cline and with Hopper and Thompson's (1980) position that the transitivity of a clause is a matter of degree.

Nouns

The three subcategories of noun are far more straightforward with respect to the criteria, though even here there is some 'cross-membership' and variation of assignment.

Far and away the majority of nouns are **common nouns**, and head nominal phrases introduced by a determiner such as *ngā* 'the.Pl.' Common nouns *par excellence* are those derived by means of the 'nominalising suffix' to be described below. However, large numbers of other items, both simple and compound, belong to this class.

Locative nouns are those which, when heading the complement of the preposition *ki* 'to',[14] admit no determiner: *ki Aotearoa* 'to New Zealand', *ki mua* 'to the front, forwards'. This class consists of place names, the question word *(w)hea* 'where',[15] and a set of nouns indicating relative position, such as *runga* 'above', *mua* 'front', *tua* 'beyond'. Because Māori uses these to express locations for which English has specific prepositions, earlier accounts of Māori grammar often deal with them under the heading 'complex prepositions':

> *ki runga i te   tēpu*
> P   top   P Det. table
> 'onto the table', lit. 'to top of the table'

Personal nouns are those which, when they head the complement of the preposition *ki* 'to', are preceded by the 'personal article' *a*:[16] *ki a Rei* 'to Ray', *ki a wai* 'to whom?' The class includes names of people, names of tribes, the question word *wai* 'who', and, for many speakers, the names of the months.[17] Pronouns (see below) are a subclass of personals in that (in most dialects) they too take the personal article after prepositions like *ki*; however, they are rarely marked this way when subject of a clause.

There is some freedom to use nouns of one subcategory in constructions proper to another. A personal name used to designate the class of people of that name is treated as a common noun:

> *Koinā   te   Hōne   i   kōrero   nā   au.*
> That.is Det. H   TA speak   Loc. 1Sg.
> 'That's the Hōne I was speaking about.'

The common nouns *tangata* 'person' and *wāhi* 'place', when marked with the particle *kē* meaning, in this instance, 'other', are, respectively, a personal and a locative: *ki a tangata kē* 'to someone else', *ki wāhi kē* 'to somewhere else'.

Pronouns

As indicated, pronouns in Māori are a subclass of personal nouns, in that, after prepositions of the class represented by *ki*, they are preceded by the personal article *a*: *ki a tātou* 'to us'. Unlike personal nouns, however, they do not as a rule take the personal article when standing as the subject of a clause.

Māori pronouns distinguish three numbers – singular, dual and plural – and in the first person non-singular forms, exclusive and inclusive. On the other hand, there is no gender system in Māori. As noted in chapter 2, non-Eastern PN languages have different sets of pronouns for the different positions they can occupy: clitic subject, full, possessive. In Eastern PN languages, the clitic subject pronouns are lost, and the dual and plural forms are invariant whatever position they occupy. The singular pronouns show distinct allomorphs: *-ku, -u, -na*, which occur after possessive prepositions – thus *nōku, māu, āna* ('belongs to me', 'for you', 'of him/her') – beside *ki a au, i a koe, e ia* ('to me', 'at/with you', 'by him/her').

The dual and plural forms contain reflexes of PPN *rua 'two' and *tolu 'three', and are cognate with, for instance, the Fijian dual and paucal forms, the original plurals retained in Fijian being lost in all PN languages. These reflexes are odd in that PPN *l and *r are usually reflected in Māori as /r/. However, their loss in (most of) these forms is very old, being shared by all NP languages.[18]

The third person pronouns cannot be used anaphorically for all nominal phrases. Stereotypically, these pronouns can relate back only to phrases referring to human beings; others are represented either by zero or by a full phrase repeating the noun but often introduced by the anaphoric determiner *taua* ~ *aua* 'the aforementioned, Sg.~ Pl.'. This is, however, a 'rule' with fuzzy boundaries, and uses of these pronouns, especially in the singular, are also found for referents some way down the human/animacy scale. Pets, and personified objects, especially those of value, can be referred to in this way, and the singular,

Table 5.2. *Māori personal pronouns*

	singular	dual	plural
1st inclusive		*tāua*	*tātou*
1st exclusive	*au*	*māua*	*mātou*
2nd	*koe*	*kōrua*	*koutou*
3rd	*ia*	*rāua*	*rātou*

primarily in its form as a possessive determiner, can be used for referents as vague as 'the relevant situation': *ā tōna wā* (P Sg.-of-3Sg. time) 'in due course'.

Numerals, both cardinal and ordinal, also form a closed set with its own peculiar syntax. Space precludes treatment in detail here and the reader is directed to the reference grammars available.[19]

The modern Māori numeral system is decimal, though there is some evidence that in the past there was a vigesimal system and also separate systems for the counting of particular objects (see Best 1906). The basic numerals from 1 to 10 are: *tahi, rua, toru, whā, rima, ono, whitu, waru, iwa, tekau*. The numbers to 99 are constructed according to the formula: *X tekau (mā Y)*[20] 'X tens (and Y)', where X ranges over *rua . . . iwa*, and Y over *tahi . . . iwa*. The numbers 11–19 have the form *tekau mā Y*. Similarly, numbers greater than 100 are formed using *rau, mano* 'hundred', 'thousand', as illustrated in:

> E   rua mano e   rima rau e   whā tekau mā   ono
> TA   2   1000 TA   5   100 TA   4   10   and 6
> '2546'

The only general feature of numerals to mention here is also illustrated in the above example: numerals are verb-like in that they regularly occur with tense/aspect markers, usually *e*, and are characteristically used as relative clauses to modify nouns, or as predicates:

> *ōku*   *whare* [*e*   *rua*]RELATIVE CLAUSE
> Pl.-of-1Sg. house   TA   two
> 'my two houses', 'my houses which are two (in number)'

> [*E*   *rua*]PREDICATE   *ōku*   *whare*.
> TA   two   Pl.-of-1Sg. house
> 'I have two houses', lit. 'My houses are two in number.'

Ordinal numerals, on which see further below, are adjectives and can be used to modify the head of a noun phrase. However, cardinal numerals occur within noun phrases only if the head of the phrase is some sort of unit of measurement, in which case the numeral precedes and modifies:

> mō   te   rua wiki
> P   Det.   2   week
> 'for two weeks'

Word shape

All Māori words, be they particles or bases, are of course subject to the phonotactic constraints discussed in chapter 4: a syllable shape of (C)V(V(V)), and
an avoidance, at least in inherited words, of moræ of the shapes: */f,w/ + /o,u/.
There are, however, a few points beyond these that can be made in general about
word shape. Krupa (1966; see also the useful summary in Krupa 1968:38–60)[21]
provides an exhaustive statistical analysis of the matter, taking in turn the composition of what he identifies as morphemes and the combination of these to
form words. He stipulates that the basic shape of a root morpheme is (C)V(C)V,
which requires his analysing tri- and quadrimoraic words as complex, formed
by a combination of devices such as reduplication and affixation. While reduplication and some affixation are productive devices in Māori (on which see
below), Krupa's approach entails the postulation of a large number of 'prefixes'
and (to a lesser extent) 'suffixes', many of which may have been productive
in the past, but which cannot plausibly be analysed in this way in modern
Māori. Stipulation of (C)V(C)V as the basic morpheme shape allows Krupa to
investigate precisely the relationship between possible morpheme shapes and
actually occurring morpheme shapes. Given that there are ten consonants and
five vowels, the total number of possible items of the form (C)V(C)V is 3,025
(11*5*11*5). Of these, Krupa reports that 1,258 occur, and is able to identify a
variety of classes of possible shape which do not. For instance, 424 do not occur
because they would infringe the constraint against the moræ /f,w/ + rounded
vowel mentioned in chapter 4. Further, shapes involving $V_1 = $ /u/ and $V_2 = $ /o/,
as well as those having different labial consonants in the two C positions, are
strongly dispreferred.

A difficulty of Krupa's approach, of which he is himself aware, is that quite
distinct analyses are forced upon words which are clearly related. Krupa himself
(1966:33) reports the case of *patapatai* and *pātaitai*, which are both reduplicated
forms (with frequentative meaning) of *pātai* 'ask (a question)'. *Patapatai* is
analysed as the reduplication of the 'morpheme' *pata* followed by a 'suffix' *-i*,
while *pātaitai* is the reduplication of *tai* with prefix *pā-*.

As mentioned, Krupa's work identifies a range of affixes, many of which may
have been productive in the past. This is clearest in pairs of words like: *roku*
'grow weak, decline, wane (of moon)' and *wheroku* 'become faint, weaken',
in which there is obviously a similarity of meaning. However, very few such

affixes are at all productive today, or can even be associated with a consistent meaning. Thus, most of the words which are complex for Krupa are regarded here as simple lexical items, whatever their origin may have been. The same applies to a few items which are obviously historical compounds, but which now act as single items. *Ātaahua* 'beautiful' seems to be a compound of elements *ata* 'carefully, deliberately' and *āhua* 'form, shape, appearance', but not only is the meaning not (or no longer) derivable at all from that of the parts, the word functions to all intents and purposes as a single lexical item.

Only a handful of particles, like *ki* 'to', *e* 'by (agent of passive)', are shorter than two moræ. All bases and many particles thus consist of at least two moræ. As discovered by Krupa, there do seem to be some combinations of two moræ which are not instantiated, though a number of the shapes he identifies as non-occurring morpheme shapes in fact do occur as names (*Wano*), in loans (*whika* < 'figure'), or as substrings within longer words (**nanga* but *rūnanga* 'council').

Many of the bases longer than two moræ are indeed derived by affixation and/or reduplication, though there are many where such an analysis is warranted neither syn- nor diachronically: *tangata* 'human being, man', *wahine* 'woman' and very many others. One constraint on word shape to be added to Krupa's findings is the observation that words of the shape CV_1V_1CV are very rare. Among the very few examples are *māra* 'garden', *kāti* (< *ka oti* TA complete) 'well!', 'stop!' Finally, a small class of trimoraic verbs continue the PN suffix **-Ci*, which is no longer productive in Māori: *takahi* 'step, trample', *ārahi* 'lead', *rumaki* 'immerse'.

In the remainder of this chapter, I will discuss and illustrate those morphological devices which are at all productive in Māori, or at least show some degree of regularity of form and meaning, assuming the existence of simplex forms of various lengths up to as many as six moræ.[22]

Inflection

Use of morphological devices for what would normally be regarded as inflection is limited, with many of the categories often expressed this way in other languages being handled by means of particles. In particular, case and tense/aspect are so expressed; only number and verbal voice have morphological reflexes.

Number

As mentioned above, person pronouns distinguish singular, dual and plural. To the extent that number is distinguished at all elsewhere, it is a binary category: singular/plural.

Some eight nouns, all of them designating human beings, and all but one of them being kinships terms, have distinct plural forms, as in Table 5.3.

Table 5.3. *Māori nouns with distinct plural forms*

singular	plural	meaning
wahine	wāhine	'woman, wife'
tangata	tāngata	'person, human being'
matua	mātua	'parent'
tuahine	tuāhine	'sister of man'
tuakana	tuākana	'elder sibling same sex'
teina	tēina	'younger sibling same sex'
tipuna/tupuna[23]	tīpuna/tūpuna	'grandparent, ancestor'
tamaiti	tamariki	'child'

The word for 'child' and its plural are compounds of *tama*, which also occurs in the meaning 'son', and two adjectives meaning 'small'. The lexicalisation of these compounds as respectively singular and plural is old and has reflexes throughout the PN family. Similarly old is the pattern shown in the other forms in the table, in which the antepenultimate vowel is lengthened in the plural form. On the other hand, no two PN languages have exactly the same list of words showing this phenomenon.[24]

Apart from these cases, nouns are invariant for number. However, number is routinely indicated in the nominal phrase by the determiner. Unlike many other PN languages, which have distinct plural particles,[25] Māori has distinct singular and plural forms of almost all determiners. In the case of the specific article, there are non-cognate forms *te ~ ngā*, but all other determiners which show the distinction do so by the alternation *t- ~ Ø-*: *tēnei ~ ēnei* 'this ~ these'. This device is also very old, and occurs widely within the Nuclear Polynesian subgroup, though in many languages it is an archaism.

A few short and common adjectives form optional plural forms by partial reduplication, thus: *pai ~ papai* 'good', *nui ~ nunui* 'big'. Finally, complete reduplication is available for verbs to express a 'distributive' plural of the subject in the case of intransitives, or object in the case of two-argument verbs. Thus, *hokihoki* 'return' is used with a plural subject, if the members of the subject are each returning to a different place.

Passive

The only other category to be expressed inflectionally in Māori is voice; passive forms involve the use of a suffix. The suffix, usually referred to in literature on PN languages as –*Cia*,[26] has seventeen allomorphs, all ending -*a*, and many of the form 'thematic consonant + -*ia*'. Thus, *inu-mia* 'drink-Pass.', *hopu-kia* 'grasp-Pass.', *tangi-hia* 'mourn-Pass.', and so on. The allomorphs are extremely unevenly distributed in modern Māori; some occur with one or two stems, while others have become very productive, far beyond their etymological origin. The reason for 'the current mess'[27] is the loss of word-final consonants in many Oceanic languages referred to in chapter 2. As a result of this loss, earlier regular pairs such as *inum ~ inum-ia,[28] in which the 'thematic' consonant is present in both suffixed and unsuffixed forms, became irregular. The present state of affairs, its origins and the appropriate way to describe it have figured widely in the linguistic literature, making this aspect of Māori grammar perhaps the most discussed and best-known feature of any Polynesian language.[29] Much of this discussion uses the Māori passive as a case study in arguing for different types of analysis. Its usefulness in this area is that it is *prima facie* susceptible of two quite different types of analysis: a 'phonological' one, which posits underlying forms in which a final consonant is represented, plus a rule of final consonant deletion, thus mirroring the actual history; and a rather more superficial 'morphological' one, which assigns words to as many 'conjugations' as there are allomorphs of the suffix. More recently, Blevins (1994) provides a good discussion of the earlier contributions and analyses, and then proceeds to suggest an account within the framework of Autosegmental Phonology. Briefly, she posits that many Māori words have a final consonant on one tier, but that the skeletal tier admits only final vowels. Thus, in the unsuffixed form, there is no association possible between the 'final' consonant and the skeletal tier, so it does not surface. On the other hand the passive suffix[30] has the skeletal shape CVV, of which only the VV are associated with features, i.e., *-ia*. In the passive forms, the final stem consonant associates with the C of the suffix and thus surfaces. In the passive of stems with no final consonant, the C of the suffix is filled by *-t-*. This last point is particularly important, because, although the present state of affairs is, to use Lass' term again, a 'mess', it is by no means as much of a mess as it would have been, had the distribution of the allomorphs simply followed the etymological thematic consonants. In fact, two processes have been occurring in Māori, which tend to regularise again the formation of these passive forms.

(1) Throughout the discussion, cognisance is taken of the existence of 'default' suffixes. Certain suffixes have assumed a distribution far wider than their etymological one. In most of the country, *-tia* enjoys this status, though in some parts, especially in the east of the North Island, *-hia* and *-ngia* fulfil these functions. In particular, *-tia* (or one of the other 'default' forms) is the suffix used:

(i) in 'passive agreement', that is, as mentioned above, when certain modifiers of passive verbs are themselves marked passive;

(ii) on stems other than verbs – see below;

(iii) on polysyllabic loans, e.g. *puruma-tia* 'sweep' (< 'broom');

Table 5.4. *Examples of verbs with stem changes in passive*

Active	Passive	Meaning
ako	ākona	'learn, teach'
huti, huhuti	hūtia	'hoist, haul up'
kume, kukume	kūmea	'pull, drag'
mea	meinga, meatia	'cause, do, say'
noho	nōhia, nohoia	'sit, inhabit'
papaki	pākia	'to slap'
poki, popoki, pokipoki	pōkia	'cover over'
pupuhi	pūhia	'to blow or shoot'
riri	rīria	'be angry', the passive means 'to have someone be angry at one'
rongo	rangona, rongona	'hear'
tatari	tāria	'wait'[31]
tiki	tīkina	'fetch'
whai	whāia	'follow'

(iv) on transitive verbs derived by means of the prefix *whaka-* from stems which themselves have no passive, e.g. *whaka-māori-tia* (caus.- Māori-Pass.) 'translate into Māori;

(v) increasingly also on indigenous, simple polysyllabic stems, e.g. *kōrero-tia*'speak', *waiata-tia* 'sing'.

Other closely related PN languages have followed the same path as Māori and indeed gone further in generalising and making productive one of the inherited allomorphs. Hawaiian has, for instance, generalised -*'ia* (< *-kia), Tahitian -*hia*, and Rarotongan -*'ia* (< *-hia). In Māori many frequently occurring verbs retain lexically conditioned allomorphs, but in the modern language the use of the productive forms is spreading at the expense of these.

(2) Some subregularities have developed: -*nga* is used only after words ending in -*ai*, thus *kai-nga* 'be eaten', *hāpai-nga* 'be lifted'; -*ina* is used only after words ending in -*a*, thus *hua-ina* 'be named', *aroha-ina* 'be loved'; and -*mia* is used only after -*o* or -*u*, e.g. *whakangaro-mia* 'be made to disappear', *inu-mia* 'be drunk' (Moorfield 1988:66).

Most stems are made passive simply through the addition of one of these suffixes. In a number of cases, though, modifications to the stem also occur. In most cases, a vowel which is short in the active form is lengthened when the suffix is added. Table 5.4 (adapted from Harlow 2001:129) shows typical examples of this lengthening, along with the very few cases (*mea*, *rongo*) of idiosyncratic variation in the stem.

In 1991, I attempted (Harlow 1991b) to connect the long vowel of some of these forms, namely those where the active is usually reduplicated, with

Table 5.5. *Tableau on derivation of*
mahuetia *from de Lacy (2003a)*

/mahue+ia/	*FT	LAPSE_FT	DEP-C
☞ a. {(máhu)e}{(tía)}			*
b. {mahu(éi)a}		*!	
c. {(máhu)(èa)}	*!		

other instances in Māori morphology of a long ∼ short alternation and with a
handful of other cases of allomorphy.[32] De Lacy, however, working on these
same phenomena within modern theoretical phonology, proposes an explanation involving the notion of minimal word (in Māori two moræ) and a postulated
suffix of the shape: $+\sigma_\mu[\sigma[a]]$. By this is meant a monomoraic syllable CV,
where the C is assumed to be 'determined by the stem', plus a second light syllable /a/. In the case of stems which determine such a consonant, it is assumed
that /i/ will fill any free slot, as it is 'the most common epenthetic vowel in
Polynesian languages'.[33] With those stems, however, which determine no C,
the CV of the suffix is associated with the final CV of the stem, leaving, in the
case, for instance, of *kume* ∼ *kūmea*, only the *ku* as stem. Stems must, however,
be minimal words, so the vowel is lengthened to fit this requirement.

In more recent work still, de Lacy (2003a) proposes a complete account of
passive formation in Māori within the framework of Optimality Theory, and
appealing to the notion of Maximal Prosodic Word (PrWd). The length of the
Maximal PrWd of Māori is four moræ, and it contains one trochaic foot, and
no unfooted footable material. Thus, quadrimoraic roots such as *tamaiti* (=
{ta(mái)ti}) 'child', *kōrero* (={(kó:re)ro}) 'speak' are possible, because these
analyses postulate one foot (the internal material in brackets), and the remaining
material is too short to form a further foot. However, this approach entails that
rangatira 'chief' is not a possible root, and would be forced to treat this word
as a succession of two PrWds.

As for passive, de Lacy adopts the phonological answer, that (some) stems
have underlying final consonants which survive in suffixed forms, but are deleted
when word-final. He postulates that the passive suffix is *-ia*, which is sometimes
truncated to *-a* in order that the resultant suffixed form should not infringe the
PrWd constraint. On other occasions, it is appended to the thematic consonant,
and forms with it a second PrWd of its own. In yet other cases, those where trun-
cation will not produce an admissible PrWd, and there is no thematic consonant,
the default *-t-* is added to the suffix and forms a PrWd. See Table 5.5, where
just one example is used to illustrate this approach (de Lacy 2003a:504).[34]

The other major area of interest with respect to the passive suffix, apart from
its form, is the matter of what sorts of words can take it. It will be recalled that

ability to take the passive suffix was Biggs' criterion for assignment of a word to his Universal class. However, as will be seen, this is a property of a wide range of words which differ from each other in their semantic and syntactic characteristics. In all cases, the result is a verb of a class most like neuter verbs in general behaviour, though when there is an explicit agent, this is marked with *e*, not *i*.

Least spectacularly, transitive and middle verbs may be made passive. This results in the changes of case marking for the verbs' arguments familiar from passives in very many languages. The example from chapter 2 is repeated here:

> *Ka hoko te matua i ngā tīkiti.*
> TA buy Det. parent Obj. Det.Pl. ticket
> 'The parent buys the tickets.'

> *Ka hoko-na ngā tīkiti e te matua.*
> TA buy-Pass. Det.Pl. ticket Agt. Det. parent
> 'The tickets are bought by the parent.'

Intransitive verbs will also occasionally be found with passive morphology. *Haere* 'go', for instance, can be made passive, and means in these cases 'be gone over' or 'be gone for':

> *Koia tēnei ko te tangata e haere-a nei e tāua.*
> This.is Det. Foc. Det. man TA go-Pass. Loc. Agt. 1Du.Incl.
> 'So this is the man on account of whom we have come.'

> *te whenua e haere-a ana e Te Ponga mā*
> Det. land TA go-Pass. TA Agt. Te P others
> 'the land which was being traversed by Te Ponga and his party'

As mentioned above, intransitives taking an internal or cognate accusative can also be used in the passive.

Nouns are also encountered with passive suffixes deriving a verb meaning 'become a N'.

> *I kōhatu-ngia a Pānia.*[35]
> TA stone-Pass. Pers. P
> 'Pania turned into stone.'

Similarly, in a metaphor used in reference to the departed, one can talk about:

>nga   mātua-tīpuna   kua whetū-rangi-tia
>Det.Pl. parent-ancestor.Pl. TA   star-heaven-Pass.
>'the ancestors who have become stars of the heavens'

Rarely, but nonetheless idiomatically and grammatically, even names can be made passive:

>Koinei i   Ngā-Pōtiki-hia ai   aua   whenua.
>This.is TA   N-P-Pass.   Aph. Det.Pl.   land
>'This is why those lands become Ngā Pōtiki's.'[36]

Finally, and most bizarrely, certain whole phrases may be the unit to which the passive suffix is attached. As mentioned in chapter 2, Māori retains a very few traces of a phenomenon much better preserved in, for instance, Tongan; the head of a verb phrase may be itself a prepositional phrase. In Māori isolated examples occur where such phrases not only head a verb phrase, but are made passive. The most famous case is:

>[Mā te   matapihi]tia   mai.
>[P   Det. window]-Pass. Dir.
>'Pass (it) in through the window.'[37]

The phrase *mā te matapihi* means 'by way of the window'. Here it is treated as a verb meaning 'convey by way of the window' and made passive in accordance with the requirement (see chapter 6 and remarks in chapter 4) that the imperative of transitive verbs with (not necessarily explicit) objects are passive.

A similar example occurs in the Bible:

>Kei [rā runga]tia   mai tātou   e   Hātana:
>TA   [P   above]-Pass. Dir. 1Pl.Incl. Agt. Satan
>'Lest Satan should get an advantage of us:'
>   (2 Cor. 2:11)

Rā runga 'by way of above, over' is a prepositional phrase which could be followed by an oblique phrase dependent on *runga* stating 'above what', thus *rā runga i a tātou* 'by way of above us, over us'. It is this construction which is treated as if it were a verb plus object, rather than PP with adjunct, and made passive. Literally, the example means 'lest we be "gone over" by Satan'.

A final example of this rare type is taken from one of the many newspapers published in Māori in the nineteenth century:

>Ko te   waka i   [na runga]tia   mai ai ko   Aotea.
>Top. Det. canoe TA   [P above]-Pass. Dir. Aph. Pred. A
>'The canoe on which he (Turi, the captain of Aotea canoe) came here was Aotea.'
>   (*Te Waka Maori o Niu Tirani*, 2 October 1872)

Derivation

In contrast to the paucity of inflectional morphology, Māori makes use of a number of morphological devices for derivation, primarily prefixes and reduplication. There are relics of what may have been productive suffixes at some stage, but these are now fossilised. *Moemoeā* 'dream' and (*whai*)*whaiā* 'bewitch, witchcraft' show etymological connection with *moe* 'sleep' and *whai,* one of whose meanings is a type of spell.[38] A number of verbs show the remains of a suffix *-Ci*, used productively in, for instance, Tongan for deriving transitive verbs, but now unanalysable in Māori. Krupa (1966:54) provides a list of such forms connecting them with probably cognate unsuffixed forms in Māori – thus for instance: *ārahi* 'lead' ~ *ara* 'way', *horomi* 'swallow' ~ *horo, pēhi* 'crush, press' ~ *pē* 'crushed', etc. To Krupa's list can be added a couple of forms with unsuffixed cognates elsewhere: POLLEX connects *rumaki* 'immerse' and *takahi* 'tread' with PPN *loma* 'flood' and *taka* 'sandal' respectively. It is conceded that some of these etymologies are not very convincing, but a further argument which suggests that the final *-Ci* of these words was originally a suffix is that it is lost when the nominalisation suffix, to which we turn directly, is added: *arahanga, pēhanga, rumakanga, takahanga.*[39]

Nominalisation

The only other suffix, apart from the passive, used productively in modern Māori is of the general form *-Canga* and derives nouns. Mention has already been made of zero-nominalisation of verbs and adjectives, and a brief account of the difference between zero-derived nouns and those derived by means of the suffix will be given below. Like the passive suffix, and for the same reason historically, this suffix has a number of allomorphs. In particular, for certain classes of word it takes the form *-nga*, while in all other cases, the allomorphs have a 'thematic' consonant plus *-anga*.[40] Again, as with the passive suffix, certain of the allomorphs, especially *-tanga*, and to a lesser extent *-hanga*, have become the most productive forms. In general, there is agreement between the thematic vowels of the passive suffix and the nominalisation suffix when added to a stem. Thus, *inu* ~ *inumia* ~ *inumanga* 'drink ~ passive ~ occasion of drinking', *tangi* ~ *tangihia* ~ *tangihanga* 'mourn ~ passive ~ occasion of mourning', *whakaatu* ~ *whakaaturia* ~ *whakaaturanga* 'show ~ passive ~ exhibition'. Verbs whose passive suffix is *-a* usually take *-nga*: *patu* ~ *patua* ~ *patunga* 'strike ~ passive ~ a striking'. Verbs which now take one of the productive passive suffixes (see above, *-tia, -ngia, -hia*) take the parallel *-Canga* suffix:[41] *kōrero* ~ *kōrerotia* ~ *kōrerotanga* 'speak ~ passive ~ a speaking'.

Words other than those which routinely take the passive have nouns derived from them by means of this suffix. Neuter verbs regularly take the allomorph *-nga* – *oti* ~ *otinga* 'be complete ~ completion'[42] – as do a few adjectives:

roa ~ *roanga* 'long ~ length, extension'.[43] Finally, a number of nouns are found with *-tanga* used to derive an abstract noun meaning 'the property of being a . . .': *Māoritanga* 'Māori culture, "Māoriness" ', *rangatiratanga* 'chiefliness'.

In form then, this suffix parallels the only other productive suffix: where the passive has a thematic consonant, whether etymological, or the result of the spread of the default forms, so does the nominalisation suffix; on short stems, the default form is *-nga* parallel to passive *-a*, extending to cases where no passive occurs. A further parallellism can be observed in agreement; in a way similar to the passive agreement referred to often above, a word modifying the derived noun may take the suffix itself, usually *-tanga*:

> *taku   hinga-nga   tīraha-tanga*
> Sg.of.1Sg. fall-Nom.   lie-Nom.
> 'my falling prostrate'

> *taku   tae-nga   tuatahi-tanga*
> Sg.of.1Sg. arrive-Nom. first-Nom.
> 'my first arrival', 'the first time I went (to . . .)'

This rule seems, however, never to have been obligatory, and this usage is quickly vanishing in modern Māori.

The nouns derived in this way have a variety of meanings. Deverbal nouns usually designate 'an occurrence of V'. Thus, these nominalisations are frequently encountered in adjuncts of time:

> *nō tō.rātou hoki-nga   mai*
> P   their   return-Nom. Dir.
> 'on their return, when they returned'

Others designate the product of V – *tuhinga* 'a writing' – or the place where V occurs: *moenga* (sleep-Nom.) 'bed'.

There is some overlap in usage of the zero-nominalisations and those with *-Canga*; however, if a particular occurrence is being referred to, the suffixed form is preferred, whereas the zero-form is used for general references to the state or event of the verb. Contrast

> *Kei.te pīrangi a   Mere kia mutu   te   patu tohorā.*
> TA   want   Pers. M   TA   cease Det. kill whale
> 'Mere wants the killing of whales to stop.'

with:

> *Nā te   patunga   a Kae i   tana tohorā ka   riri*
> P   Det. kill-Nom. P K   Obj. his   whale   TA   angry

a   *Tinirau*
Pers. T
'Because Kae killed his whale, Tinirau became angry.'[44]

The first sentence refers generally to the killing of whales (*patu* 'kill' with incorporated object *tohorā* 'whale'); the second is about a specific occasion of killing a specific whale.

Prefixes

Krupa's (1966) work shows that Māori retains relics of a wide range of derivative prefixes; there are very many pairs of lexical items of related meaning where one is clearly derived from the other by some prefix. Thus, taking some of his examples randomly: *hīrori* 'stagger' ∼ *rori* 'giddy, staggering', *kongene* 'wrinkled, withered' ∼ *ngene* 'wrinkle, fold', *pātata* 'near' ∼ *tata*, *mōnehu* 'ferndust' ∼ *nehu* 'fine powder, dust', *whekoki* 'crooked' ∼ *koki* 'bent'. While such pairs abound, very few of these prefixes show any kind of consistent meaning, and even fewer are productive. Three which have discernible meanings, but which are not productive, are:

(1)   the remnants of the POC prefix *ma- (Lynch *et al.* 2002:82), which derives intransitives. A number of instances of this survive in Māori with this sense, but no new pairs are created, e.g.: *wehe* 'divide (tr.)' ∼ *mawehe* 'be divided (state)', *riringi* (passive: *ringihia*) 'spill (tr.)' ∼ *maringi* 'be spilt'.

(2)   in a number of words, the prefix *tau-* (often with reduplication) expresses reciprocity. In this and related senses, it has cognates in several other PN languages, such as Rarotongan, Niuean, Emae, Rennellese (see POLLEX – Biggs 2000a – under TAU.7). E.g. *patu* 'strike' ∼ *taupatu(patu)* 'be in conflict'; *whawhai* 'fight' ∼ *tauwhawhai* 'contend with one another'; *tito* 'compose (songs)' ∼ *tautitotito* 'sing songs in response to one another'.

(3)   *pū-* can be prefixed to three names for colours: *mā* 'white', *whero* 'red' and *pango* 'black' deriving adjectives meaning 'whitish, reddish, livid' respectively.[45]

A small set of prefixes occurs regularly with lower numerals, subsets of 1–10: *toko-* is prefixed to numerals counting human beings – *Tokorua aku tuāhine* (2 my sisters) 'I have two sisters' ∼ *E rua aku waka* (TA 2 my car) 'I have two cars'; *taki-N* means 'N at a time' and is primarily used as a modifier in a verbal phrase – *i haere takitoru rātou* (TA go *taki*-3 3Pl.) 'They went in groups of three'; and *tua-* forms ordinals which can be used either attributively (*te rā tuatahi* 'the first day') or as a noun with a partitive expression (*te tuarua o ngā rā* 'the second (one) of the days'). Beyond these few cases, there are three derivative prefixes which are productive.

kai-   This forms agent nouns from verbs.[46] Generally, only verbs with agentive subjects have agent nouns derived in this way: transitives, and agentive intransitives, but not middle verbs,[47] neuter verbs or non-agentive intransitives. There is thus considerable similarity between the set of verbs which take *a*-possessive marking on the subject of their nominalisations and those with derived agent nouns – for example, *kaimahi* 'worker', *kaiwaiata* 'singer', *kaiwhakahaere* (*kai*-caus.-go) 'administrator, organiser', *kainoho* 'inhabitant' (from *noho* 'inhabit'), but not *kainoho* with the meaning 'one who sits, "stayer"'. These agent nouns frequently have an incorporated object as a modifier: *kaitito waiata* (*kai*-compose song) 'songwriter', both *kaipatu* and *kaipatu tangata* (*kai*-strike person) for 'murderer', *kaipatu ōkena* (*kai*-strike organ) 'organist'.

Recently, the Māori Language Commission[48] has proposed some neologisms involving this prefix in order to create terms for people involved in some activity, including the various branches of science: *kaitōrangapū* (*kai*-politics) 'politician', *kaiahupūngao* 'physicist'.

ā-   This prefix derives denominal adjectives which can be used only attributively. The convention in writing such forms is to hyphenate both this prefix to the noun-stem and the whole derived adjective to the base (usually a noun or verb) it modifies. As a result, these sequences of <base-ā-noun> are often regarded as a type of compound. I prefer to regard such strings as base plus derived adjective for three reasons.

(1) Unlike many compounds, the meaning of such strings is entirely predictable from the meaning of the two bases involved. In particular, the *ā*- prefix derives adjectives meaning 'in the manner of . . . , by means of, as a . . .'; *waiata-ā-ringa* 'action song, song with hand movements';[49] *tae-ā-tinana* 'be physically present, "arrive by means of the body"'.

(2) In passive clauses, both the words are suffixed:

> *ngā   tāngata   e   whakamātautautia   ā-tuhitia   ana*
> Det.   people   TA   examine-Pass.   *ā*-write-Pass.   TA
> 'the people sitting written examinations', lit. 'who are being examined by means of writing';

(3) The 'word' formed in this way may be coordinated:

> *whakamāori-ā-waha,   ā-tuhi*[50]   *hoki*
> caus.-Māori-*ā*-mouth,   *ā*-write   also
> 'translate and interpret', lit. 'make Māori by means of the mouth, and by means of writing'

whaka-   By far the most important derivational prefix in Māori is *whaka*-. Not only is it the most frequent prefix in text, it can be used on a wide range of base types, produces a range of base types on affixation, and carries a number of meanings. The form itself is a reflex of POC *paka- 'causative' (Pawley 1973:130), and has in Māori, and a number of related languages (see POLLEX under FAA-), an allomorph *whā-*. Elsewhere (Harlow 1991b), I have tried to connect this allomorph with the irregular process of consonant deletion mentioned above in connection with sporadic lengthening of vowels in some passive forms. In particular, I suggested that the allomorph *whā-* is due to the irregular deletion of /k/ before stems beginning with /k/ at some point in the history of Māori. It is perhaps of interest in this connection that in the only two related languages in which cognates of *whā-* are at all regular, Hawaiian and Fijian, they occur respectively before /ʔ/ (< PPN *k) and before velars: Hawaiian *hō'ike* 'show', beside *ho'o-* elsewhere, and Fijian *vākedru* 'cause to snore' but *vakaoti* 'finish, complete'.[51]

Whatever its origin, this allomorph is not productive in Māori, but does occur with a number of stems, usually with causative meaning, the etymological and synchronically primary meaning of the prefix. In one or two cases, the choice is used to 'disambiguate' homophonous bases: *whākuru* < *kuru* (both meaning 'pelt'), but *whakakuru* < *kuru* (both meaning 'weary (tr.)').

As mentioned, the primary meaning of *whaka-* is to form causatives, that is, to form transitive verbs from adjectives, neuter verbs and intransitives meaning 'to cause to be . . . , or do . . .':[52] e.g. *whakaroa* 'lengthen' (*roa* (adj.) 'long'), *whakaoti* 'bring to completion' (*oti* (neuter verb) 'be completed'), *whakahaere* (*haere* (intr.) 'go') 'make go, organise, run (tr.)'. Its use with middle and transitive verbs is highly restricted. Two transitives with which it occurs are: *inu* 'drink' giving *whakainu* (also *whāinu* in the same sense) 'to give to drink', with the person who is to drink as object and the liquid as an indirect object with the preposition *ki* 'to'; *ako* 'learn' giving *whakaako* 'teach', again with two objects, marked respectively *i* 'Obj.' and *ki* 'to', though both orders of pupil and material taught occur: *whakaako i te tamaiti ki te reo Māori* and *whakaako i te reo Māori ki te tamaiti* (teach, Māori language, child).

Middle verbs which can take *whaka-* are: *kite* 'see', *mōhio* 'know' and *rongo* 'hear'. *Whakarongo* has the idiosyncratic meaning 'listen' and does not mean 'cause to hear'. The other two cases are causatives meaning 'show' and 'inform'. These few examples exhaust the cases where a two-place verb has a monoclausal causative. It is interesting to see how far Māori follows the pattern observed frequently in other languages with respect to the treatment of the arguments of the simple verb. Song (2001:263–8) provides an accessible summary of Bernard Comrie's work in this area. Briefly, it is a matter of what becomes of the subject of the simple verb (the causee NP) when a causer NP is introduced as the subject of the derived causative. Essentially, the causee NP is 'demoted' to the highest available slot on a Case Hierarchy of the shape: Subject > Object > Indirect Object > Oblique. Where the simple predicate has only one argument (its subject, the causee), this becomes the object of the causative. Where the simple predicate has two arguments, the causee cannot become the object of the causative; that slot is occupied by the second argument of the simplex; the causee is 'demoted' further to be the indirect object of the causative.

This pattern is largely followed in Māori; it is without exception the case with one-argument predicates. Among the few instances of two-argument verbs which can take *whaka-*, it is true also of *whakakite* 'show' (the subject of 'see' is the indirect object of the causative, and the thing seen or shown is the object of both *kite* 'see' and *whakakite*). However, *whakamōhio* 'inform'[53] and *whakaako* 'teach' have two constructions, one which follows this pattern where the material known/taught (the object of *mōhio* 'know' / *ako* 'learn') remains the object of the causative and the knower/learner (the causee, the subject of *mōhio/ako*) is its indirect object. In the other, equally grammatical pattern, however, the material is demoted to indirect object, and the causee becomes the object of the causative. Further, *whakainu* 'to give to drink' seems to have only this second possibility; the liquid is oblique (marked as instrument by *ki*) and the causee the direct object of the causative.

Whaka- also occurs, though far less productively, in verbs derived from words of other classes. *Whakaae* (Pass. *-tia*) 'agree to' is from *āe* 'yes', which can itself be used as a verb meaning 'agree', but is most common as the affirmative answer to polarity questions. *Whakaatu* (Pass. *-ria*) 'show' is from the particle *atu* 'away from the speaker'. *Whaka-* is also found deriving verbs from nouns: *whakatan-gata* 'become a man (intr.), make into a man (tr.)', similarly, *whakakōhatu* 'become stone, make into stone'. In other instances, the derived verb has an idiosyncratic meaning, e.g. *whakaingoa* (*ingoa* 'name') 'to name, nominate', *whakaahua* (*āhua* 'form, shape, appearance') 'make an image of, a picture'.

Finally, *whaka-* occurs also with locative nouns and with common noun phrases forming a set of words with directional meaning and a unique distribution. Such expressions are used, on the one hand, as attributive bases within verb and noun phrases, and on the other, as adjuncts to verb phrases in a manner parallel to prepositional phrases –

> *te   tai whaka-runga*
> Det. sea *whaka-*above (i.e. south)
> 'the south coast'

but

> *I   haere tonu rātou whaka-te-moana.*
> TA go   still 3Pl.   *whaka-*Det.-sea
> 'They went on towards the sea.'

This usage is the only reflex in Māori of a use of cognates of *whaka-* in related languages to form attributes meaning 'in the manner of . . .', e.g. Samoan: *fa'aSāmoa* 'in a Samoan way', *fa'apua'a* 'vulgar, like a pig' (*pua'a* 'pig').[54]

Reduplication

A morphological device of which Māori and Polynesian languages generally make great use is reduplication. This has already been referred to above in discussion of plural in Māori, but the forms and meanings of reduplication are far wider than the few examples given there. The existence of this device in Māori has been remarked on since the earliest descriptions of Māori started to appear.[55] Partial accounts occur in a range of more recent works whose main goal is wider than just this feature. Biggs (1961:28–9), for instance, which deals with phrase structure generally, identifies three types of reduplication: partial, as in *kikimo* 'close one eye' from *kimo* 'blink'; complete, as in *pakipaki* 'applaud by clapping' from *paki* 'pat'; internal, which reduplicates the first vowel of a base, as in *wāhine* 'women' from *wahine* 'woman'. Calling this last phenomenon reduplication allows Biggs to handle in a consistent way a feature of many reduplications in Māori, a vowel lengthening accompanying the copying of part of the stem. The only really productive pattern of reduplication for trimoraic stems, to which we return below, is illustrated in the pair: *haere* 'go' and *hāereere* 'wander about'. Biggs describes this pattern as reduplication of the three or four last phonemes along with 'reduplication' of the first vowel.

Krupa (1966) is the only author before the 1990s to deal at all fully with this important aspect of Māori morphology; however, his analysis, especially of cases like the one just mentioned, is constrained by his view, already referred to above, that the basic root shape in Māori is bimoraic. He identifies partial and complete reduplication of bimoraic stems along the lines of Biggs (1961), but, since he regards words such as *haere* as already complex (prefix *ha-* plus root *-ere*), has to regard the reduplication as complete reduplication of the root with the prefix *hā-*.

In contrast with the entire previous history of concern with Māori grammar, the 1990s saw significant progress in the treatment of reduplication in Māori, culminating in Keegan (1996). The principal thrust of this work has been accounting for the range of reduplication patterns attested, especially for stems longer than two moræ. Harlow (1991b:122) identified a number of such patterns as part of a wider discussion on length alternations.[56] This paper drew attention to the occurrence not only of the simple partial and complete reduplications illustrated above, but also of the following four types for longer stems:
(1) reduplication of the first mora: $\sigma_1\sigma_1\sigma_2\sigma_3$: *hohoata* < *hoata* both meaning 'the moon on the third day, pale, colourless'; *ānini* (= *a-anini*) < *anini* both meaning 'giddy, aching (of the head)'.
(2) reduplication of the first two moræ separately: $\sigma_1\sigma_1\sigma_2\sigma_2\sigma_3$ (with deletion of the repeated consonant in $\sigma_1\sigma_1$): *tāweweke* 'slow, dilatory' < *taweke* 'linger'; *mānenei* < *manei* (both meaning 'reach out to').

(3) reduplication of the first two moræ as a unit: $\sigma_1\sigma_2\sigma_1\sigma_2\sigma_3$: *takatakai* 'wind round and round' < *takai* 'wrap up'; *riariaki* < *riaki* (both 'raise').

(4) reduplication of all three moræ: $\sigma_1\sigma_1\sigma_2\sigma_3\sigma_2\sigma_3$ (with deletion of the repeated consonant in $\sigma_1\sigma_1$): *pākarukaru* 'break in pieces (tr.)' < *pakaru* 'broken'; *pāhūhū* 'pop, crackle' < *pahū* 'explode', i.e. *pa-a-hu-u-hu-u* < *pa-hu-u*.

What will be noticed here is the occurrence of a long vowel in the first syllable of the reduplicated forms in patterns 2 and 4. I attempted to account for this by appealing to a process of deletion of a repeated consonant under certain circumstances. However, later work is rightly sceptical of this explanation. Both Meyerhoff and Reynolds (1996) and de Lacy (1996), working independently, analyse the range of patterns mentioned, along with others I had not referred to, in similar but not identical ways within the framework of Optimality Theory. Essentially, in both accounts, vowel lengthening occurs in order to avoid infringement of prosodic constraints in Māori which are ordered ahead of some faithfulness constraints.

Finally, Keegan (1996) reviews all earlier accounts of reduplication, identifies yet further patterns found in Māori, and presents a discussion of the meanings expressed by this device. This matter is as complex as that of the forms encountered. It will not be possible here to go into this thoroughly and the reader is referred to Keegan (1996) for detail.[57] This section will restrict itself to the more productive uses.

Meanings of partial reduplication   As has been mentioned above, a number of common adjectives have partially reduplicated forms which can optionally be used with plural nouns, e.g. *pai* 'good' > *papai* as in *ngā tāngata papai* 'the good people' (*ngā tāngata pai* is also grammatical). These partially reduplicated adjectives may be used with an intensive meaning: e.g. *papai* 'good' and *nunui* 'big', as well as being used with plurals, can also be used with a singular to mean 'very good/big'. Oddly, the partially reduplicated form of some colour adjectives involves a weakening of the meaning of the simple form, e.g. *papango* 'somewhat black' < *pango* 'black', *whewhero* 'reddish' < *whero* 'red'.

In verbs, partial reduplication typically shows two types of meaning: reciprocity, e.g. *pipiri* 'cling together' from *piri* 'stick, cling', *papatu* 'strike together (e.g. weapons), beat each other (of people)' from *patu* 'strike', *totohe* 'contend with one another' from *tohe* 'persist, be urgent'; intensive, e.g. *kikimo* 'keep the eyes firmly closed' from *kimo* 'blink', *papaki* 'slap' from *paki* 'slap, pat' (cf. below *pakipaki* 'clap, i.e. applaud, or slap frequently'), where the partially reduplicated form expresses a single intense performance of an action.

Meanings of complete reduplication   The most common meaning
expressed by complete reduplication of verb stems is plurality, either of an
action being performed a number of times (frequentative), of a number of people severally performing an action, or of a number of objects undergoing an
action (distributive plural).

Thus, irrespective of the number of either subject or object, a completely
reduplicated form[58] can be used to designate the repetition of an action, e.g.
pakipaki 'clap, i.e. applaud, or slap frequently' from *paki* 'slap, pat'; *kimokimo*
'blink frequently' from *kimo* 'blink'; *pātaitai* (also *patapatai*) 'ask a number
of questions' from *pātai* 'ask'. The reduplicated form of a verb designating a
'non-countable' action, such as 'go', often means 'to V a lot' rather than 'to V
repeatedly'. Thus, *hāereere* 'wander about' from *haere* 'go'.

Reduplicated forms expressing distributive plural agree with the number of
the object in the case of transitives or of the subject of intransitives. Contrast:

> *I*   *tū*   *ake rātou ki te*   *waiata.*
> TA stand up   3Pl.   P Det. sing
> 'They stood up to sing (together, as a group).'

> *I*   *tūtū*   *mai   ngā   koroua ki te*   *kōrero.*
> TA stand forth Det. elder   P   Det. speak
> 'The elders stood up (individually, one at a time) to speak.'

> *Kua tīmata ia*   *ki te*   *kurukuru rīwai.*
> TA   begin   3Sg. P   Det. throw   potato
> 'He has started to chuck potatoes about.'

Finally, in the case of some adjectives, the complete reduplication signifies a
weakening of the meaning, e.g. *werawera* 'warm' < *wera* 'hot'.

Compounds

Reference has already been made to the property of Māori phrase structure
whereby virtually any base may be used as a modifier to another. Very many
instances of two bases in succession are of this type. However, there are others
in which an analysis as head plus modifier is inappropriate and the sequence is
best regarded as a compound and as a single lexical item.[59]

There are three ways in which these compounds differ from the superficially
similar sequence of two bases.

(1) Phonological. For at least some speakers, short compounds have a different stress pattern from sequences of two bases in at least sentence-final phrases.
It will be recalled from the previous chapter that, in sentence-final phrases, the

main stress coincides with the word stress of the last base in the phrase. This phenomenon allows a distinction between

>*Haere* [*ki te   whárenui*].PHRASE
>Go   P   Det. house-big
>'Go to the meeting house.'[60]

and

>*Haere* [*ki te   whare núi*].PHRASE
>Go   P   Det. house big
>'Go to the big house.'

(2) Semantic. As is the case in many languages, it is often so in Māori that the meaning of a compound is not simply 'the sum of the meaning' of its constituents. Compounds will often have idiosyncratic meanings. The word *wharenui*[61] of the previous example provides a good example: it designates a building with a particular function, and not just any house which is big. That is, not all *whare nui* are *wharenui*, nor are all *wharenui whare nui*!

Māori exemplifies a number of the types of form–meaning relationships to be found in other languages. For example, there are instances of so-called possessive compounds (bahuvrihi), such as *manawa nui* (heart big) 'big-heart**ed**' and *ihupuku* (nose swollen) 'having a swollen nose, in particular, a sea elephant'. Dvandva also occur: *mātua-tīpuna* (parents-ancestors) 'parents **and** ancestors'.

Compounds of a verb plus incorporated object, to designate not the action but an instrument for performing that action, are common, especially in the modern vocabulary, where deliberate coinage plays a considerable role.[62] Thus, for instance, *whakakoi pene* (Caus.-sharp pen), as a compound, means 'pencil sharpener', as well, of course, as occurring as a verb plus incorporated object in the meaning 'to sharpen pencils'.

(3) Syntactic. In general, a base may not be modified by more than one other base at a time. Thus, where for instance English might have two or more items modifying a noun, Māori must use a coordinate structure involving either the repetition of the head or its replacement in the second coordinand by the pro-noun *mea* 'thing':[63]

>*he   whare kōhatu, he   whare/mea nui*
>Det. house stone   Det. house/thing big
>'a big stone house'

Rather, in sequences of three or more bases, each non-initial base modifies the one before it:

te   hunga tito   waiata
Det. people compose song
'those who compose songs'

In this example, *waiata* 'modifies' *tito* as its incorporated object and the phrase *tito waiata* modifies *hunga*. However, where two bases are compounded to form a single lexical item, a third base can be used to modify the whole:

he   roro.hiko   hōu
Det. brain.electricity new
'a new computer', not 'a brain which is newly electrical'!

The preceding discussion, especially concerning lexical categories, has necessarily anticipated aspects of Māori syntax to which we turn in chapter 6.

NOTES

1. Biggs consistently uses the so-called 'double-vowel' spelling for phonemically long vowels – see chapter 4.
2. Though in fact (see below) *rākau* can appear with a tense/aspect marker.
3. Generally speaking, verbs of perception, emotion, and others where the object is not directly affected, such as 'follow'. Both transitive and middle verbs take two arguments. The distinction between them is relatively clear in languages like Tongan, where transitive verbs are accompanied by ergative case marking, and middle verbs by accusative case marking – see chapter 2. However, as will be seen, the distinction is useful in Māori as well.
4. By [Ø Ø *atu*] I mean a phrase with no particles at the beginning (the first Ø) and no lexical head (the second). The next example is to be understood in similar vein.
5. See Harlow (2001:47–50) for a list and some discussion.
6. More detailed reference to generative accounts of aspects of Māori syntax is made in chapter 6. Of relevance to the present issue are works such as Pearce (1997, 1998a, 2003) and Waite (1994).
7. In these paragraphs, I use 'noun', 'verb', etc., to designate classes of words, in anticipation of the discussion below.
8. With the exception of those 'passive' particles and bases, referred to above, which are formed through agreement with a passive head.
9. The double possessive system of Māori and most other Polynesian languages was mentioned in chapter 2 and will be discussed in detail in chapter 6.
10. See Pearce and Waite (1997) for an analysis within the generative framework.
11. Which allomorph is used depends on the number of moræ in the verb. See chapter 4.
12. Waite (1994) regards this *he* as head of an IP, and thus analogous to a tense/aspect marker.
13. That word class assignment often 'leaks', or, to use more familiar terms, can be 'fuzzy', or even 'squishy', is well known generally in linguistics. A particularly good example is Comrie's (1989:107–10) discussion of Russian numerals, which

are increasingly 'nouny' and decreasingly 'adjectivy', the higher the numerical value.

14. In this definition and the next, *ki* stands for a set of prepositions ending in *-i*.
15. The use of *wh-* vs *h-* in this and several other words varies regionally. See chapter 3.
16. The personal article also precedes locative and personal nouns when they are subject of a clause.
17. The days of the week, on the other hand, are common nouns and thus take a determiner. Contrast *i te Mane* 'on Monday', and *i a Hune* 'in June'.
18. A very few PN languages, largely Outliers, have innovative 'plural' forms as well, involving reflexes of PPN *faa 'four', see Hovdhaugen *et al.* (1988).
19. Especially Bauer (1997:275–89) and Harlow (2001:277–87). On the history of numerals within Polynesia, see Clark (1999).
20. The *mā* here represents the only productive reflex in Māori of PPN *maa 'and, with', *me* having this role in the modern language. Biggs (2000a) suggests that *maa also appears in some compound deity names, e.g. *Rongo-mā-Tāne* 'the god Rongo-and-Tane', and that it is related to the particle *mā* 'and others' which can be used after personal names, or to form a plural of *wai* 'who?'; *ko Hōne mā* 'Hōne and others', *wai mā* 'who, plural answer expected'.
21. See also Bauer (1993:553–4).
22. For instance, *kaumātua* 'respected elder', originally derived from *matua* 'parent', is now unanalysable in any useful way.
23. In this and a few other words, there is regional alternation between /i/ and /u/. See chapter 3.
24. On this phenomenon generally, see the remarks in Pawley (1985:99–102).
25. For instance, the closely related Rarotongan: *te 'are* 'the house' ~ *te au 'are* 'the houses'.
26. Historically from a POC transitive suffix *-i* plus either the 3Sg. object suffix or an adjectival derivative suffix *-a*. See Pawley (1973:139), Lynch *et al.* (2002:80).
27. Roger Lass' (1984:222) characterisation of the situation.
28. These are not intended to be taken as reliable reconstructions to POC. In particular, they should not be taken to imply that there was a passive in that language formed in this way. Rather, it is purely a matter of the relationship between suffixed and unsuffixed forms, which eventually became the Māori active and passive forms.
29. See, for instance, Hale (1968, 1973, 1991), Haslev (n.d.), Lass (1984), Sanders (1990, 1991), Schane (1976), and, more recently, Blevins (1994) and de Lacy (1996, 2003a).
30. For many words; for stems of two moræ, the default suffix is *-a*.
31. Similarly, *tatari* goes to *tāringa* when the nominalisation suffix is added – see below.
32. See below on *whaka-* and reduplication.
33. This account is summarised from de Lacy (1996), from which stem the two short passages cited here.
34. *FT bans all feet but the head foot. LAPSE_FT is violated when footable moræ are not parsed into a foot. DEP-C prohibits epenthetic consonants.
35. Pānia was a figure well-known in Māori mythology, a sea creature who married a human but, as a result of a bungled attempt by her husband to prevent her return to the sea, became a rock.
36. Ngā Pōtiki are a tribe from the Bay of Plenty area.

37. In some areas of New Zealand, the body of the deceased lies inside the meeting house during the period of mourning (*tangihanga*). In some places where this is so, the body enters and leaves the house not through the door, but through the window.
38. See further Krupa (1966:53).
39. The variation in the length of the initial vowel in *ārahi* ~ *arahanga*, seen also in the passive *arahina*, is odd.
40. Both *-nga* and *-Canga* are reconstructible to PPN, though the latter form is productive really only in EP languages. See Clark (1981).
41. In fact *-nganga* does not occur, and words with thematic *ng* in the passive have *-nga* by haplology: *kai* ~ *kainga* [*sic*] ~ *kainga* 'eat ~ passive ~ Nom.', *hāpai* ~ *hāpaingia* ~ *hāpainga* 'raise, [etc.]'.
42. *Pakaru* 'be broken', being longer than two moræ, takes *-tanga*.
43. Most adjectives show only zero-nominalisation, as sketched above.
44. Part of a well-known legend in Māori oral tradition.
45. Arguably, these three are the only true colour terms in Māori, all other terms for colours being extensions of words with other meanings, e.g. *kōwhai* 'yellow' from the tree of that name with yellow flowers, *kākāriki* 'green' from a bird of that name. See Bauer (1993:511, 584–5).
46. Pawley (1985:96) connects this prefix with a POC item *kai* 'person'. See also POLLEX under KAI.5 for possible cognates meaning things like 'inhabitant of . . . , person of . . .'.
47. *Kaikite* 'one who sees' is occasionally found, but in the sense of 'witness' (e.g. of a will).
48. See chapter 7 for further discussion of the Commission and its work in vocabulary expansion.
49. Action song is a popular genre of music in modern Māori culture, in which a song is accompanied by hand and body actions.
50. *Ā-tuhi* is the only such adjective in common use derived not from a noun but from a verb.
51. See further on this point in chapter 4. In fact Hawaiian *ho'o-* appears in a number of phonologically conditioned forms. However, *hō-*, the variant which is cognate with Māori *whā-*, has the distribution described. See Elbert and Pukui (1979:76) for Hawaiian and Schütz (1985a:201 note 3) for Fijian. De Lacy (1996), rightly pointing to the irregular distribution of this allomorph in Māori, is sceptical of this explanation.
52. Causation of transitive predicates is biclausal, using the verb *whakamahi*, with a subordinate clause introduced by *kia* as its object.
53. In terms of case marking, as opposed to grammatical relation, the appearance is different. Like most middle verbs, *mōhio* 'know' has an object marked with *ki*; its causative, however, being transitive, marks its direct object with *i*, and its indirect object with *ki*. *Mōhio ki* NP 'to know NP'; *whakamōhio i* NPa *ki* NPb and *whakamōhio i* NPb *ki* NPa 'to cause NPa to know NPb, to inform NPa of NPb'.
54. Mosel and Hovdhaugen (1992:176–7). See also Churchward (1953:253), Simona (1986:59).
55. See, for instance, Maunsell (1842:24, 27, 41, 57f.).
56. See above on *whaka-* and on passive.
57. See also Harlow (2001:114–16) for a summary.

58. This includes 'pattern 4'-type reduplications of longer stems.
59. See Bauer (1993:518–25) and Harlow (2001:131–2).
60. The *wharenui*, or *whare tipuna* (house ancestor), and other terms, is the main building of the marae. See chapter 1.
61. The orthographic conventions set out by the Māori Language Commission (Te Taura Whiri i te Reo Māori) stipulate that compounds with at most four vowel letters in them are to be spelt as a single word, while longer compounds are spelt as separate words.
62. See chapter 7 and Bauer (1993:519–21).
63. Other possibilities also exist, e.g. *he tangata pai, ihumanea hoki* (Det. person good, clever also) 'a good and clever person', but in all cases the second adjective or modifier is in a different phrase from the head.

6   The syntax of Māori

It will be neither possible nor desirable to give a detailed account of Māori syntax in this chapter; for this, the reader is referred to the grammars which are available (especially Bauer 1993, 1997, also Harlow 2001). What this chapter will do instead is provide a sketch of the main characteristics of Māori sentence structure, with excursuses as this approach leads to points which are of interest for typological reasons, which raise problems of analysis, or which have excited discussion in the linguistic literature.

The phrase

Since Bruce Biggs' (1961, see also 1969) detailed treatment of the phrase (in Biggs 1961 called a 'contour word', see Mutu 1989:399–400), it is universally recognised as a fundamental unit in Māori grammar in both phonology and syntax. Phonologically, phrase boundaries are the sites of potential (and in careful or slow speech, actual) pauses, and the phrase has a diagnostic intonation pattern of high tone on the last prominent syllable, followed by a low tone.[1] In syntax, not only are phrases coterminous with predicates, arguments and adjuncts, they are also the units in terms of which variations of order within clauses are to be stated. That is, where variant orders are possible, it is phrases, not words within phrases,[2] whose order varies.

Biggs' Item and Arrangement account of the phrase is very 'flat' and emphasises the similarity of structure found across all phrasal categories. He identifies three 'slots' in phrases:[3] a preposed periphery (PrP), in which certain paradigms of particles occur, in particular, tense/aspect markers, prepositions and determiners; a nucleus (Nuc), the site of lexical material heading the phrase; and a postposed periphery (PoP), which contains yet other particles. The category of the phrase is determined by which paradigms of preposed particles are represented. Biggs distinguishes two types of phrase on this basis: verbal phrases, which contain one of the set of tense/aspect markers in their preposed periphery; and nominal phrases, essentially all others. It will be convenient to make a further distinction between prepositional phrases, those of Biggs' nominal phrases which contain a preposition, and nominal phrases *tout court* – i.e., those which do not.

I shall be making use of Biggs' model of the phrase as a basis for discussing some of the particles and the internal structure of the nucleus. However, before passing to these matters, a few remarks are necessary.

(1) While the correlation between the phonological and syntactic delineation of phrases is valid very generally, phrases whose 'lexical' heads are singular pronouns form exceptions. As noted by Bauer (1993:576–7), when such pronouns follow a preposition ending in /i/, the 'personal article' must intervene, and it is this particle which is stressed. For example: *ki á koe* (P Pers. 2Sg.) 'to you(Sg.)'. Similarly, when governed by possessive prepositions ('of', 'for', etc.), the singular pronouns are represented by suffixal allomorphs which are cliticised to the preposition. For example, *mōku* 'for me' is technically a phrase of the shape: $[[m\bar{o}]_P[-ku]_{PRON}]_{PP}$, and bears stress on the /o:/. Finally, especially in casual, faster speech, singular pronominal subjects are cliticised to the preceding phrase thus creating a Prosodic Phrase[4] containing two grammatical phrases: $\{[E\ pai\ ana]_{PRED}[au]_{SUBJ}\}$ 'I am well' pronounced /e.pái.a.naau/.

(2) As mentioned briefly in chapter 5, there are some phrases which consist only of particles. Some determiners, in particular, are able to stand as phrases without accompanying lexical material:

$[Ko\quad Hera]_{PHRASE}$ $[[t\bar{e}nei]._{PrP}[\emptyset]_{Nuc}[\emptyset]_{PoP}]_{PHRASE}$
Pred. Hera   Det.
'This is Hera.'

(3) More recent analyses within the framework of generative grammar differ radically from Biggs' structuralist view of these units. In work by Pearce (especially 2000, 2003) and Waite (1994, also Pearce and Waite 1997), X-bar phrase structure and Move-α produce representations which not only differ from Biggs', but differ from phrase type to phrase type. The following examples are kept as simple as possible by using phrases without what Biggs calls postposed particles. In generative accounts such particles originate in phrases higher up and to the left of the lexical phrase they turn out to modify and get into their correct position by movement of the lexical head.

(i) The verbal phrase

The phrase *i haere* (TA go) 'went' is, according to Biggs

$[[i]_{PrP}[haere]_{Nuc}[\emptyset]_{PoP}]$,

but in Waite and Pearce's work:

$[_{IP}\ X\ [_{I'}\ [_{I}\ i{+}haere_i]_I\ [_{VP}\ DP_{SUBJ}\ [_{V'}\ [_V\ t_i]_V\ Y]_{V'}]_{VP}]_{I'}]_{IP}$

That is, in underlying structure, the TA is a functional head whose complement is the VP headed by the verb. The surface configuration is the result of adjunction of the verb to the head of IP.

(ii) Nominal phrase

The phrase *te whare* (Det. house) 'the house' =

$$[[te]_{PrP}[whare]_{Nuc}[\emptyset]_{PoP}] \text{ vs}$$
$$[_{DP} \emptyset [_{D'} [_D te]_D [_{NP} \emptyset [_{N'} [_N whare]_N \emptyset]_{N'}]_{NP}]_{D'}]_{DP}$$

The whole phrase is of type Determiner Phrase, whose head is the article, while the noun is the head only of the complement of the article.[5]

(iii) Prepositional phrase

The phrase *ki te whare* (P Det. house) 'to the house' =

$$[[ki \, te]_{PrP}[whare]_{Nuc}[\emptyset]_{PoP}] \text{ vs}$$
$$[_{PP} \emptyset [_{P'} [_P ki]_P [_{DP} te \, whare]_{DP}]_{P'}]_{PP}$$

As indicated above, the particles which occur in Biggs' preposed periphery are tense/aspect markers, prepositions and determiners, all of them heads of functional phrases with lexical phrases as complements within X-bar accounts. Full accounts of all these are to be found in the references given above, and innumerable examples will be encountered throughout this chapter.

Tense/aspect markers

This term designates a paradigm of particles whose presence makes a phrase verbal and whose meanings range over tense, aspect and mood. The most important are as follows.

ka

The particle *ka* serves only to mark that its phrase is verbal, and has no inherent tense, aspect or modal value (Harlow 1989). When no adverbial or previous TA marking determines a tense, the default reading of *ka* is temporally present, aspectually aorist. It is also often encountered in the second and subsequent clauses of a series, in which case it 'copies' its TA meaning from the first clause, e.g.

> *Kia tūpato kei hinga **ka** whara*
> TA   careful TA   fall   TA   be. hurt
> 'Be careful, lest you fall and get hurt',

in which *kei hinga ka whara* are asyndetically coordinated clauses with the same modal force, i.e., 'lest', or 'negative subjunctive'. Successions of clauses beginning with *ka* are often encountered in narrative, where they are used for the sequence of foregrounded events.

i

This is the one TA particle with strict temporal meaning, i.e., 'past':

> *I   tono-a   mai he   tangata e te   Atua.*
> TA send-Pass. Dir. Det. person P Det. god
> 'There was a man sent from God.'

kua

This particle marks perfect, that is, the completion of an action or the achievement of a state as the result of an event: *kua mate* 'has died, is dead', *kua oti* 'is completed'. It is also used for the apodosis of irrealis conditionals:

> *Me i konei koe kua kite koe i   a   ia.*
> If P here 2Sg. TA see 2Sg. Obj. Pers. 3Sg.
> 'If you had been here, you would have seen him.'

kia

The particle *kia* occurs typically in four constructions.
  (i)   Imperative of adjectives, neuter verbs and experience verbs

> *Kia tika.*   *Kia ora.*
> TA correct   TA healthy
> 'Get it right!'   'Be healthy' (standard greeting)
>
> *Kia mōhio (koe)* . . .
> TA know   (2Sg.)
> 'You should know . . .'

  (ii) Temporal clauses for future time

> *Kia oti   te   mahi ka hoki   tātou.*
> TA completed Det. work TA return 1Pl.Incl.
> 'When the work is done, we will go home.'

(iii) Final clauses

> *Kua haere mai rātou kia whakaakona ai   ki te   reo.*
> TA go   Dir. 3Pl. TA teach-Pass. Aph. P Det. language
> 'They have come in order to be taught the language (Māori).'

(iv) Sentential complements of verbs of wishing, ordering, requesting, being right or good

> *E   pīrangi ana a   Mere kia mutu te   patu wēra.*
> TA want   TA Pers. Mere TA stop Det. kill whale
> 'Mere wants the killing of whales to stop.'

e . . . ana

The combination of the preposed particle *e* and the postposed particle *ana* expresses progressive aspect in any tense. See, for instance, the previous example.

me

This particle expresses what is often called in the literature on Maori grammar a 'weak imperative', translated most appropriately as 'should/must/ought'. When it is used in passive sentences, the verb remains in its simple form:

> *Me horoi ngā   rīhi.*
> TA wash Det.Pl. dish
> 'Someone should wash the dishes', lit. 'The dishes should be washed.'

kei te ~ i te

Progressive aspect along with, respectively, present and past tense can also be expressed by the particles *kei te* and *i te*. These are originally preposition + determiner combinations which have been reanalysed as verbal markers:

> *Kei.te mahi rātou i Pōneke.*
> P.Det. work 3Pl. P Wellington
> T/A   work 3Pl. P Wellington
> 'They are working in Wellington.'

e/Ø

Imperative marking varies according to the class of the head of the predicate; adjectives, neuter verbs and experience verbs are marked with *kia*, transitives and intransitives with *e/Ø*. The allomorphy is phonologically conditioned: Ø is chosen if the verb, along with any postposed particles, exceeds two moræ in length, otherwise *e*. Since transitive verbs with an explicit or zero-pronominalised patient are passive in commands in Maori, this rule entails that only bimoraic intransitives with no following particles take *e*:

E noho!	*E noho rā!*[6]	*Haere mai!*
TA sit	TA sit Loc.	Go Dir.
'Sit!'	'Farewell' (said by one leaving)	'Come here!'
Tuhi-a!	*Kōrero!*	
Write-Pass.	Speak	
'Write (it)!'	'Speak!'	

Determiners

The class of determiners contains the familiar subclasses of articles, possessive determiners, demonstratives and interrogatives, and the reader will encounter illustrations of their uses in virtually every example sentence in this and other chapters. The purpose of this section is to draw attention to some generalities of their usage and to point to features of a number of individual determiners which are striking or which have excited theoretical discussion.

As mentioned in chapter 5, it is the determiners which indicate number in most nominal phrases; with a handful of exceptions, determiners show a singular ∼ plural distinction by means of the alternation *t-* ∼ *Ø-*: *tēhea* ∼ *ēhea* 'which (Sg. ∼ Pl.)', and so on. The principal exceptions are: the 'definite' article, which is the pair *te* ∼ *ngā*; the invariant personal article *a*, which occurs before locative and personal nouns when these are subjects of clauses, and before personal nouns and pronouns when these are complements of prepositions ending in /i/; and *he*, the 'non-specific' article, on which see below also.

Some of the determiners, the demonstratives, the possessives, the interrogative *tēhea* ∼ *ēhea*, and the 'indefinite' article *tētahi* ∼ *ētahi*, are unique among 'particles' in being able to occur in phrases without lexical material in the nucleus. When used in this way, the demonstrative, interrogative and indefinite determiners are often followed by a partitive PP: [*tētahi*] [*o mātou*]_PP ([Det.][P 1Pl.Excl.]) 'one of us'.

Except for those headed by personal or locative nouns or pronouns, for which there are particular patterns involving the personal article, nominal phrases are almost always introduced by some determiner or other. NP types which in, for instance, English need no determiner, such as those headed by mass nouns or plural count nouns, routinely contain *te*, *ngā* or *he* in Māori: *he kai* 'food', *ngā tāngata* 'people', and so on.

te ~ ngā

Usually glossed 'definite article', this pair does indeed in large part correspond, as singular and plural, to the definite article of English and similar languages. However, *te* especially has further uses. It is for instance used with nominal phrases whose reference is generic, and can in this case be followed by a plural noun (in those few instances where nouns have a distinct plural form, see chapter 5). Thus, *ngā tamariki* (Det.Pl. child.Pl.) 'the children' designates a particular group of children which the speaker has in mind. *Te tamariki* (Det. child.Pl.) 'children' means all and any children.

Te also appears in contexts where the speaker has in fact no specific entity in mind, and thus is indefinite. Bauer (1997:144f.) provides discussion and good examples. Let one suffice here. Predicate nominals and equative sentences have distinct constructions in Māori. The former have a predicate phrase introduced by *he*; the latter's predicate is a definite nominal phrase marked with *ko*.

> *He   tapuhi a   Hana.*
> Det. nurse   Pers. Hana
> 'Hana is a nurse.'

> *Ko   te   pirimia   tērā.*
> Pred. Det. Prime.Minister Det.
> 'That is the Prime Minister.'

However, the negation of both these sentence types is identical:

> *Ehara a   Hana i te   tapuhi.*
> Neg.   Pers. Hana P Det. nurse
> 'Hana is not a nurse.'

> *Ehara tērā i te   pirimia.*
> Neg.   Det. P Det. PM
> 'That's not the Prime Minister.'

In the negation of the predicate nominal type, there is clearly no specific 'nurse' in mind whose identity with Hana is being denied. Yet, the predicate nominal is marked *te*. The reason for this is, as we shall see, that the semantically appropriate determiner, *he*, which is present in the affirmative, is incompatible with prepositions, yet the complement of *ehara* requires the preposition *i*.

Te also occurs in contexts which are clearly verbal, for instance, as complement to neuter verbs like *oti* 'be completed':

*Kua oti   te   waka **te** peita.*
TA be.completed Det. car   **te** paint
'The car has finished being painted.'

Demonstratives

Like many languages, Māori has three-way deixis, the elements *nei, nā, rā* designating, respectively, location associated with the three persons. These elements occur as postposed locative particles, but also form part of four other paradigms:
- locative nouns: *konei, konā, korā* 'here, there by you, over there';
- adjectives: *pēnei, pēnā, pērā* 'like this, . . .';
- *anei, anā, arā* 'here is, . . .';
- demonstratives: *tēnei, tēnā, tēra* 'this, . . .', with their plurals *ēnei, ēnā, ērā* 'these, . . .'.

The similarity of the first element of these demonstratives and the article *te* is reinforced by the parallellism of the following two constructions:

demonstrative + noun = article + noun + locative particle

tēnei whare = *te   whare nei*
Det. house   Det. house Loc.
'this house'

It is clear that any approach which admits movement in derivations will treat these two constructions as transforms. Pearce (1998b, 2003) has the locative particles occurring in the Spec position of a 'Deictic Phrase' which occurs above a NP complement within a Determiner Phrase. The two orderings are the result of various types of movement within that configuration. For instance, adapting the representation in Pearce (1998b), *tēnei whare* has the structure:

$$[_{DP}[_{D'}[_{D}te]_D[_{FP}nei_i[_{F'}[_Fwhare_j]_F[_{DeicP}t_i[_{Deic'}Deic[_{NP}[_{N'}t_j]_{N'}]_{NP} \ldots]_{DP}$$

Possessive determiners

Theoretically, there are indefinitely many of these in Māori. We shall be returning to possession more generally below. However, for the moment, suffice it to say that possessors are marked by the preposition pair $a \sim o$. Thus, for instance,

te   waka o Rewi
Det. car   P Rewi
'Rewi's car'

Just as the locative particles, as in the previous section, can occur both following a noun and incorporated into a determiner, so too the PP designating the possessor can also occur in a determiner:[7]

[*t-ō*   *Rewi*]_{Det} *waka*
Det.-P Rewi   car
'Rewi's car'

Grammatically, these options are available for all possessum ~ possessor constructions. However, there are very strong preferences one way or the other, depending on variable aspects of the contruction. Thus, if the possessor is a pronoun and the Determiner of the whole construction is *te ~ ngā*, then the use of the appropriate possessive determiner is virtually *de rigueur*:

Ø-ā   *rātou* *tamariki*   *t-ō-na*   *ingoa*
Pl.-P 3Pl.   child-Pl.   Det.-P-3Sg.   name
'their children'   'his/her name'

On the other hand, if the possessor is a phrase of any substance, the dependent PP construction is effectively the only possible one. In constructions where there is no explicit possessum, then the possessive determiner constructed as sketched here forms the entire phrase:

[[*t-ā-ku*]_{Det} Ø]_{Phrase}   *Ø-ō*   *ngā*   *wāhine*
Det.-P-1Sg.   Pl.-P Det.Pl. woman.Pl.
'mine'   'the women's (ones)'

he

Of all the determiners of Māori, it is *he* (usually glossed non-specific and indefinite) which has provoked the most scholarly discussion. It has long been recognised that *he* has a restricted distribution when compared with other determiners, and the succession of contributions has led to ever more accurate description of this distribution. At the same time, the issue of the relationship in meaning between *he* and the determiner *tētahi* (with its plural *ētahi*) has been explored.[8]

He is found introducing predicate phrases of two types – those with adjectives as the lexical head, and predicate nominals:

He *reka* *ngā*   *kai.*
Det. sweet Det.Pl. food
'The food is delicious.'

He *rōia*   *a*   *Rewi.*
Det. lawyer Pers. Rewi
'Rewi is a lawyer.'

Waite (1994:58–9) suggests that *he* in this usage is in fact not a determiner but a tense/aspect marker, and that a phrase such as *he rōia* is of the form:

[_{I'} *He rōia*_i [_{NP} X [_{N'} *t*_i Y]_{N'}]_{NP}]_{I'}

That is, *he* is the head of an IP, to which the noun (head of the complement of I) is adjoined. As mentioned in chapter 5, Waite (1994) takes the view that both D(eterminer) and I(nfl.) heads in Māori may have as their complements projections of N, V or A. De Lacy (2001), on the other hand, regards predicative *he* as a determiner, and the phrase it heads as a DP, which is the complement of a covert copular verb.[9]

Unique among determiners, *he* is incompatible with prepositions (except *me* 'like'). This restriction entails that phrases marked with *he* are not available as adjuncts, or even as objects in most dialects,[10] but only as superficial subject. In fact, however, the restriction to subjects is even narrower. The best account of the facts in this respect is to be found in Chung *et al.* (1995), who distinguish 'existential' and 'relational' uses of indefinites. Existential phrases introduced by *he* can refer to a (or some)[11] actual instance(s) of the entity designated:

> *Kua tae   mai he   ope.*
> TA   arrive Dir. Det. party
> 'A visiting party has arrived.' / 'Some visiting parties have arrived.'

Relational uses of indefinites on the other hand are within the scope of some quantificational expression or construction, such as a conditional, negation or interrogative, and thus do not necessarily refer at all:

> *Ki.te tae   mai he   ope, . . .*
> TA   arrive Dir. Det. party
> 'If a visiting party should arrive . . .'

Expanding on earlier work by Hohepa (1969b), Bauer (1993) and Polinsky (1992), Chung *et al.* (1995) found that, in its existential sense, *he* is not only restricted to subject position (in most dialects), but to subjects of passives, non-agentive intransitive verbs, neuter verbs,[12] and predicates naming transitory states – so-called *state-level* predicates, such as 'be cold' (of a person, for instance), 'be angry'.

It turns out that in its relational usage, *he*, while still restricted to subject position because of its incompatibility with prepositions, is available for subject phrases of all types of predicate:

> *Ki.te whakahoki mai he   wahine i   ngā   pukapuka . . .*
> TA   return   Dir. Det. woman Obj. Det.Pl. book
> 'If a woman returns the books. . . (there will be no fine)'
>
> > (Chung *et al.* 1995:442)

The corresponding 'existential' use, as a main clause, is ungrammatical:

> **I   whakahoki mai he   wahine i   ngā   pukapuka . . .*
> TA return   Dir. Det. woman Obj. Det.Pl. book
> 'A woman returned the books. . .'

In those positions where *he* may not occur, *tētahi* (and its plural *ētahi*) is the only indefinite determiner possible.[13] However, there are environments when both are possible – in particular, as subject of certain types of predicate. Here, the question arises as to any difference in meaning. Two such differences have been identified in the literature. Chung *et al.* (1995:433–5) observe that in narrative *he* is not used to introduce an entity which is 'in the spotlight'. *He* can be used to introduce entities, but these are usually peripheral, or are not further mentioned. Entities which are introduced by an indefinite, but which go on to play a role in the narrative, are usually introduced by *tētahi*.

Chung and Ladusaw (2004) explore a difference between *he* and *tētahi* identified by Polinsky (1992), namely that after, say, negation, *tētahi* may have either wide or narrow scope, while *he* may have only narrow scope. That is to say,

> *Kāore tētahi tangata i   haere mai.*
> Neg.   Det.   person TA go   Dir.

is ambiguous, being susceptible to the two interpretations 'no one came' (narrow scope: 'it is not the case that someone came') and 'someone did not come' (wide scope: 'for someone, it is not the case that s/he came'). However, the very similar *Kāore **he** tangata i haere mai* can bear only the former sense. Chung and Ladusaw exploit this difference to argue that *he* and *tētahi* encode two different ways in which an indefinite expression can be 'composed' with a predicate. The monograph is highly technical, but accounts very neatly for the fact that the two determiners are in many respects identical in meaning and interchangeable, but show the scope difference mentioned here.

Prepositions

The third type of particle which occurs phrase-initially is a paradigm of prepositions.[14]

Prepositional phrases play a variety of roles: adjunct, modifier, argument, even predicate; in fact, the only position routinely occupied by a nominal phrase is superficial subject, as will become plain in the account of sentence structure below.

The paradigm called here prepositions is a closed and rather small class of particles, consisting of just seventeen items. Some of these have extremely circumscribed uses, such as *e* 'agent of a passive verb', or *rā* 'by way of' (archaic), while others have very wide ranges of use. *I*, for instance, marks direct objects, spatial and temporal location, standard of comparison, agent of neuter verbs, and cause. Six of the prepositions are used primarily in possessive constructions, on which see below, though four of these also have other uses. *Nā*, for instance, introduces predicative possessive phrases meaning 'belongs to . . .', but is used also to mark the agent in the so-called Actor Emphatic construction, and to mark focussed causes.

> *Nā Mere tēnā pukapuka.*
> P   Mere Det. book
> 'That book (which you have, near you) belongs to Mere.'

> *Nā Mere tēnā pukapuka i   tuhi.*
> P   Mere Det. book   TA write
> 'It was Mere who wrote that book.'

> *Nā te   makariri rātou i   noho ai   ki te   kāinga.*
> P   Det. cold   3Pl. TA stay Aph. P Det. home
> 'It was because of the cold that they stayed home.'

Māori lacks prepositions expressing the detail of spatial and temporal location, such as 'under', 'inside', 'before'. To supply these meanings, recourse is had to 'relator' nouns.

An important subset of locative nouns is a group of nouns which name relative position, such as *runga* 'on, top, surface above', *roto* 'inside', *mua* 'front, space in front'. These take as complement a prepositional phrase, usually marked by *i*, designating the thing relative to which position is specified. Thus, *runga i te tēpu* (top P Det. table) 'the top surface of the table', which can in turn be the complement of a preposition, e.g. *ki runga i te tēpu* (P top P Det. table) 'to the top surface of the table, onto the table'. Similarly, *kei raro i te tūru* (P below P Det. chair) 'is under the chair', *i mua i te whare* (P front P Det. house) 'in front of the house'. Such constructions are often referred to as 'complex prepositions' in earlier literature.

Finally, three prepositions used to form predicative phrases have tense: *i*, *kei* and *hei* are used to introduce predicate phrases asserting the location of a subject in, respectively, the past, the present and the future.[15]

> *Kei hea   te   poutāpeta?*
> P   where Det. Post.Office
> 'Where is the Post Office?'

> *I Ōtepoti ia   i tērā wiki.*
> P Dunedin 3Sg. P Det. week
> 'S/he was in Dunedin last week.'

Postposed particles

A number of particles may occur following the lexical material in phrases.[16] With very few exceptions, the same particles may occur in phrases of any type.[17] Many of these particles fall into paradigms, of which generally only one member may occur at a time. Again, generally speaking, when more than one of these particles are present, the same ordering is found.[18] In addition to the core meanings of these particles, a number of combinations have idiomatic senses (see especially Harlow 2001:103–6).

The particles which occur nearest the lexical material (follow the nucleus, in Biggs' terms) are a group usually called 'manner' particles. Unique among particles, these undergo 'passive agreement' and optionally also 'nominalisation agreement' (see chapter 5). Examples are *tonu* 'still', *kē* 'other', *rawa* 'intensive', though caution is necessary with these glosses, as the meaning of these particles varies greatly from environment to environment. For instance:

> *Kei.te māuiui tonu* ...
> TA   sick   Manner
> ' . . . is still ill'

> *Tae   tonu   atu   rātou,* ...
> arrive Manner Dir. 3Pl.
> 'As soon as they arrived, . . .'

> *ko   koe   tonu*
> P   2Sg. Manner
> 'you yourself'

The second position is occupied by a set of directional particles: *mai* 'towards the speaker', *atu* 'away', *ake* 'upwards', *iho* 'downwards'. These are used not only to indicate the physical direction of movement or orientation in the case of perception, but also to encode a speaker's viewpoint or perspective. Thus, *haere mai* (go Dir.) 'come', *titiro atu* (look Dir.) 'look (away at something)', but also

> *te   maunga   e   tū   mai   rā*
> Det. mountain TA stand Dir. Loc.
> 'the mountain standing over there',

in which the perspective is created that the mountain is in some sense facing towards the speaker. *Atu* and *ake* are used to form the comparative of adjectives:

> *He   roa   **ake** te   huarahi i   tāna i   kī   ai.*
> Det. long Dir. Det. way   P Det. TA say Aph.
> 'The road was longer than s/he had said.'

The third paradigm consists of the three locative particles listed above in the paragraphs on the demonstratives, plus *ana*, a verbal particle, and *ai*, glossed 'Aph.', which figures in a number of constructions which differ from simple clauses in that some constituent has been moved or deleted. Examples of this particle's use can be found below in discussion of constructions such as focussing and relativisation.

The remaining postposed particles, such as *anō* 'also, again', *anake* 'only', *hoki* 'for (= because), also', *pea* 'perhaps', all of which usually follow the first three positions mentioned, do not form paradigms, but are free to occur with any other postposed particle.

The nucleus

Apart from some phrases introduced by certain determiners (see above), all phrases in Māori have lexical material in the nucleus. In many instances, this material is a single base, giving phrases such as [*ki te* [*whare*]$_{Nuc}$] (P Det. house) 'to the house', [*e* [*haere*]$_{Nuc}$ *mai ana*] (TA go Dir. TA) 'is/was coming'.

When two or more bases occur in the nucleus of a phrase, the general pattern is that the first is the head and every other base modifies the one to its left. See again the example from chapter 5

> te   hunga   tito   waiata
> Det. people compose song
> 'composers, people who compose songs',

in which *waiata* 'modifies' *tito* as an incorporated object, and the resultant expression *tito waiata* modifies *hunga*, itself the head of the phrase. Similarly, in

> kei.te   hanga   whare   hōu
> TA   build   house   new
> 'is/are building a new house'

hōu modifies *whare*, and the expression *whare hōu* is the incorporated object of *hanga*. Chapter 5 draws attention to some qualifications to this general pattern, in particular the existence of some modifiers which precede their head, for instance *kia āta haere* (TA carefully go) 'go carefully!', and the fact that not all bases can act as modifiers. Locative and personal nouns are not used in this way, and there are restrictions on where neuter verbs can modify a base to their left.

The general pattern, base + base = head + modifier, subsumes a number of particular cases, which are susceptible to differing theoretical analyses.

(1) **N+A** Adjectives modifying nouns within a phrase follow the noun. This adjective may in turn of course be modified by a further base or particle(s):

> *he   whare   hōu*   *te   tikanga   tino   tahito*
> Det. house   new   Det. custom   very   ancient
> 'a new house'   'the very ancient custom'

(2) **V+A** Māori has no distinct class of adverb. Adjectives can modify verbs directly, in precisely the same way as they modify nouns.

> *Ka   oma   tere*
> TA   run   fast(Adj.)
> 'ran quickly'

Idiomatically though, one finds much more frequently the adjective as a predicate, with a zero-nominalisation of the verb as subject:

> [*Tino   tere*]PRED [*tana   oma*].SUBJ
> Very   fast   his   run
> 'He ran very quickly', lit. 'His running was very fast.'

In generative accounts (see especially Pearce 1998b and 2002), these attributive adjectives originate, as do any modifying particles, in positions higher and to the left of the verb. This latter is then adjoined to higher heads giving the attested order.

(3) **V+N** Apart from some proverbial sayings in which a juxtaposed noun can modify a verb adverbially,[19] this pattern occurs only as object incorporation. That is, the verb is transitive, and the modifying noun is a patient. As generally in object incorporation, the noun is non-specific, but may have modifiers of its own:

> *Kei.te   kimi   whare   hōu   rātou.*
> TA   seek   house   new   3Pl.
> 'They are looking for a new house', lit. 'They are new-house-seeking.'

As has been mentioned, the non-specific article *he* is incompatible with the object marker *i*, and thus (in most dialects)[20] cannot introduce the object of a transitive verb. There are three ways in which Māori handles this restriction. The first is to use the indefinite determiner *(t)ētahi* instead. This leads to sentences which are ambiguous between specific and non-specific readings:

> *Kei.te   kimi   rātou   i   tētahi   whare   hōu.*
> TA   seek   3Pl.   Obj.   Det.   house   new
> 'They are looking for a new house.'

This sentence can be synonymous with the previous example or refer to some specific new house of which the searchers know, but of whose location they are not sure.

The second way is to use the corresponding passive sentence, in which the non-specific 'object' is the grammatical subject and thus can be marked by *he*:

> *Kei.te kimihia   e   rātou he   whare hōu.*
> TA   seek.Pass. P 3Pl.   Det. house new
> 'They are looking for a new house.'

Object incorporation is the third way, and sentences on the pattern of the example above are very common. Object incorporation is a valence-decreasing device (Whaley 1997:187), and in Māori such V+N headed predicates are intransitive in that they can take no further object phrase. However, they are agentive intransitives and thus cannot have a subject marked with *he*, and the subject of their nominalisation is marked as an *a*-category possessive.

Pearce (1998b) has the noun which is incorporated into the phrasal head raised from a complement position, as opposed to the cases described above, where the modifiers originate in higher Spec positions.

(4) **V+V** Although Māori does not have highly productive verb serialisation as is found, for instance, in many non-Polynesian Oceanic languages, there is some limited scope for combining a verb of motion with another verb naming what one is doing while in motion.[21] For instance, *i tangi haere* (TA weep go) 'went weeping', *e oma pahupahu ana* (TA run bark TA) 'are/were running and barking'. All cases of this type are treated by Pearce (1998b) in the same way as modifying adjectives and particles, that is, as higher heads to which the main (first) verb is raised.

These four types by no means exhaust the possible combinations of lexical classes as complex nuclei, all of which follow the principle given above that each base modifies in some way the base to its left.

Sentence structure

Māori is a highly consistent VSX language. By this is meant not only that in pragmatically unmarked clauses the verb (or better, the head of the predicate) comes first followed by the subject and other constituents, but also that Māori exemplifies all the word order correlations familiar from typological research pioneered by Greenberg's (1963) ground-breaking work.[22] Attributive adjectives (indeed any attributively used base) follow their heads, relative clauses follow their antecedents, adpositions are preposed, possessors follow possessa.[23] This consistent 'head-first' ordering is found both within and between phrases. Vennemann and Harlow (1977), using categorial grammar, propose a single statement for Māori serialisation which covers not only these cases, but also the fact that determiners and tense/aspect markers precede, anticipating the generative view that these categories are heads with lexical complements.[24]

All these aspects of constituent order are illustrated in what follows. However, before proceding to some discussion and examples of the sentence types of Māori, it is necessary to make some qualifications to the claim that the language is VSX in basic ordering.

First, some predicates are not (superficially) verbal; both nominal (DP) and prepositional phrases occur as predicates.

Second, other orders of major sentence constituents occur. In particular, subjects, but also a variety of adjuncts, may occur in initial position when in focus or topicalised. Greenberg's Universal 12 (1963:83) asserts that 'if a language has dominant order VSO in declarative sentences, it always puts interrogative words or phrases first in interrogative word questions'. This is actually untrue of Māori, though wh-questions frequently do begin with the wh-phrase. Rather, wh-phrases in Māori remain *in situ*, and the reason that many occur initially is that this position is focussed; subjects and some adjuncts occur there when focussed, irrespective of whether these are wh-phrases or referential. A wh-question asking about the object of a transitive or middle verb takes the form of a cleft sentence with the wh-phrase as the predicate of a predicate nominal clause with a headless relative clause as subject (see below on focus and topic constructions, and on relative clauses).

Third, even in sentences with initial predicates, it is not always the case that the subject is the second constituent. In fact, the placement of the subject phrase is a matter of some interest in Māori. On the one hand, subjects of passives and neuter verbs especially can follow oblique phrases, giving 'VXS' order, while, on the other, subjects will frequently be found 'raised' to non-predicative fronted material and higher predicates, giving superficial 'XSVY' orders. We return to all these points below.

Predicates

In pragmatically unmarked clauses, the first phrase to occur is the predicate. This may be a verbal phrase, a nominal phrase (with *he*, in clauses with predicate nominals or predicative adjectives) or a prepositional phrase (in clauses asserting equation, location or possession).

> *Verbal predicate phrase*
> E   tangi ana te   tamaiti.
> TA weep TA Det. child
> 'The child is/was crying.'

Nominal predicate phrase
He   kaiwhakaako taku matua.
Det. teacher   my   father
'My father is/was a teacher.' (predicate nominal)

He   uaua   tēnā pātai.
Det. difficult Det. question
'That question is difficult.' (predicative adjective)

Equative predicate phrase
Ko   Pīrongia te   maunga e   tū   mai rā.
Pred. Pīrongia Det. mountain TA stand Dir. Loc.
'The mountain (which is) standing over there is Pīrongia.'

Prepositional predicate phrase
Kei[25] Pōneke   te   Whare Pāremata.
P   Wellington Det. House Parliament
'Parliament is in Wellington.' (location)

Nō Pita tērā waka.
P   Pita Det. canoe/vehicle
'That car belongs to Pita.' (predicative possessive)

All such predicate phrases may have further phrases dependent on them such as objects, possessives, adverbial adjuncts. Usually, the subject phrase, especially if it is light, will intervene:

He   hoa   [ia]SUBJ nō taku tuahine.
Det. friend 3Sg.   P   my sister of male
'S/he's a friend of my sister's.'

I runga [te   pukapuka]SUBJ i te   tūru.
P top   Det. book   P Det. chair
'The book was on the chair', lit. 'The book was at the top surface of the chair.'

I kite [a   Hōne]SUBJ [i   a   Mere].OBJ
TA see Pers. Hōne   Obj. Pers. Mere
'Hōne saw Mere.'

The generative accounts of Māori syntax universally have the subject of transitives originate in the Spec position of VP. A verb and its object thus form a constituent of type V', from which the V is moved to adjoin with the higher Infl thus giving the surface order VSO. Using the example in Waite (1994:58):[26]

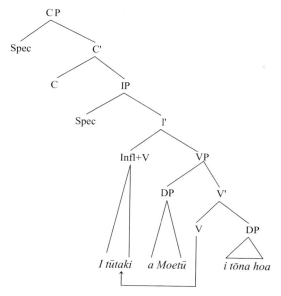

(TA meet Pers. Moetū   Obj. his friend)

'Moetū met his friend.'

Existential sentences

In modern Māori, sentences asserting the existence of something consist minimally of a nominal phrase introduced by *he*. This phrase may be followed by other material – for instance, locative phrases:

> *He   whare   wānanga   kei   Kirikiriroa.*
> Det. house   learning   P   Hamilton
> 'There's a university in Hamilton.'

Otherwise, *he*-phrases occur as the predicate phrase of predicate nominal clauses, or as the subject of a restricted range of clause types (see above on *he*). The question arises as to which, if either, of these can be equated to the use of similar phrases in existential clauses. On the one hand, existentials always occur first in their clauses, as in the example, and in this are similar to predicate nominals. On the other, the negation of the existentials involves the use of the negative verb *kāore* – otherwise used for verbal and some prepositional predicates – not *ehara*, the negative verb used for predicate nominals and equatives (see below, 'Negation').

> *Kāore he   whare wānanga i Taihape.*
> Neg. Det. house learning P Taihape
> 'There's no university in Taihape.'

In older Māori, there was an explicit verb *ai*, which took a nominal phrase in *he* 'a, some' as a single argument. Occasional examples are found in older texts, but some of the earlier descriptions of Māori provide paradigms and examples. For instance, from Smyth (1939:77–8):

> *Kia ai he   moenga mōku i tōku taenga   atu.*
> TA V Det. bed   P.1Sg. P my   arrive.Nom. Dir.
> 'Let there be a bed for me when I reach there.'

Subjects

The major work on the whole matter of grammatical relations in Māori is Chung's (1978) doctoral thesis, already referred to above in chapter 2 (see also Bauer 1993:264ff.).

Subjects are nominal phrases (plus any dependent constructions such as possessors or relative clauses). Nominal phrases headed by common nouns are introduced by a determiner, those with personal or locative nouns as heads are marked with the so-called personal article *a*. In most dialects, pronouns acting as subjects are unmarked.

> *E   tangi ana [te   tamaiti]*.SUBJ
> TA weep TA Det. child
> 'The child is/was weeping.'

> *He   kaiako [a   Rewi]*.SUBJ
> Det. teacher Pers. Rewi
> 'Rewi is a teacher.'

> *Ka haere [tātou]!*SUBJ
> TA go   1Pl.Incl.
> 'Let's go!'

It is by no means just these formal properties which justify referring to the nominal phrases thus identified as subject. Syntactic properties such as raising to higher predicates, and patterns of topicalisation and focussing, to which we turn in later sections of this chapter, unite these phrases in contrast to others which may occur in a given clause.

Further, the subject phrase is unique among arguments in being susceptible to zero-pronominalisation.[27] The pronouns are generally available only for human referents;[28] anaphoric reference to other types of noun phrase involves zero-pronominalisation in the case of subjects and use of an anaphoric determiner *taua* ∼ *aua* or an anaphoric locative noun *reira*.

(A. 'Have you seen *Utu*?')

B. *Āe,   i   kite au   i   taua pikitia i te   tau   1983.*
   Yes TA see 1Sg. Obj. Det. film   P Det. year 1983
   'Yes, I saw it in 1983.'

(A: 'Have you ever been to Australia?')

B: *Kāo, kāore anō au   kia tae   atu ki reira.*
   No   Neg. yet 1Sg. TA arrive Dir. P 'there'
   'No, I've not been there yet.'

(A: 'Where are my glasses?')

B. *Kei runga Ø   i   te   tēpu.*
   P   on, top Subj. P Det. table
   'They are on the table.'

Other sentence constituents

In Biggs' (1961, 1969) model, all phrases in a simple sentence other than the predicate and subject are referred to as comments. What unites them is the fact that such phrases are almost entirely prepositional phrases, and many are marked with the same preposition *i*. However, both meaning and a variety of syntactic tests require the distinction between objects and a range of adjunct types.

Objects   When not passive, transitive and middle verbs take two arguments, a subject, as above, and a further argument marked with the prepositions *i* or *ki*.[29]

Kei.te whāngai a   Tamahae i   ngā kau.
TA   feed   Pers. Tamahae Obj. Det. cow
'Tamahae is feeding the cows.'

Kāore ia   i.te mōhio ki   tēnā waiata.
Neg.   3Sg. TA know Obj. Det. song
'S/he doesn't know that song.'

Both these prepositions have a wide range of functions, especially as adverbial adjuncts, to which we turn below. However, a number of arguments support regarding phrases like those exemplified above as expressing a distinct grammatical relation from the other uses of these prepositions. For instance, it is just these phrases which may turn up as subjects of passive and Actor Emphatic constructions; and relativisation distinguishes these objects from all other phrases marked with these prepositions.

Other oblique phrases   Rather than go through all the possible oblique phrases in turn, this section will simply tabulate, with exemplification, the principle 'meanings' of the main prepositions which mark such phrases. More exhaustive treatment can of course be found in the reference grammars.

Uses of *i* apart from marking direct objects:

Place from which:

> *Kua tae   mai te   ope   i Rotorua.*
> TA arrive Dir. Det. group P Rotorua
> 'The group has arrived from Rotorua.'

Place at which

> *I   tū   te   hui   i Pōneke.*
> TA stand Det. meeting P Wellington
> 'The meeting took place in Wellington.'

Time at which[30]

> *I   tīmata te   kōnohete i   te   rua karaka.*
> TA begin Det. concert P Det. 2   clock
> 'The concert began at 2 o'clock.'

Cause

> *Kua whakamā rātou i   tō.rātou kaha   kūare.*
> TA shame   3Pl. P their   strong ignorant
> 'They became ashamed because of the extent of their ignorance.'

Agent of neuter verb

> *I   mau i   a   Mere he   tuna.*
> TA caught P Pers. Mere Det. eel
> 'Mere caught an eel.'

Standard of comparison

> *He   taumaha ake tēnei toka i   tēnā.*
> Det. heavy   Dir. Det.   rock P   Det.
> 'This rock is heavier than that one.'

Complement of locative relator nouns

> *Kei runga te   pukapuka i   te   tēpu.*
> P   top   Det. book   P   Det. table
> 'The book is on the table.'

Uses of *ki* apart from direct object marking:
Complement of some adjectives and nouns

> *He   tohunga ia   ki te   raranga whāriki.*
> Det. expert   3Sg. P   Det. weave   mat
> 'S/he's an expert at weaving mats.'

Goal of motion

> *E   haere ana mātou   ki Ngāruawāhia.*
> TA go   TA   1Pl.Excl. P   Ngāruawāhia
> 'We are going to Ngāruawāhia.'

'Indirect Object'[31]

> *I   whakamārama te   kaiako   i   te   pātai*
> TA explain   Det. teacher Obj. Det. question
> *ki ngā   ākonga.*
> P   Det.Pl. student
> 'The teacher explained the question to the students.'

Instrument

> *I   tārai-a   te   waka ki te   toki pounamu.*
> TA carve-Pass. Det. canoe P   Det. axe   jade
> 'The canoe was carved with a greenstone axe.'

Other adjuncts can be introduced by, for instance, *mā/mō* 'benefactive', *mā* 'by way of', *e* 'agent of passive'. Dependent possessive phrases are of analogous shape, and in Biggs' model also count as comments. On these, see further below. Waite (1994) regards *i, ki, o/a* (the possessive particles) not as prepositions, but as markers of, respectively, accusative, dative and genitive case. In his approach, these cases are assigned variously by governing lexical heads (accusative and dative) and within DPs (genitive).

Considerations of space preclude more than a brief mention of two other types of 'comment'. Phrases introduced by *hei*[32] name the purpose of some preceding nominal phrase:

>| Kua | tae | mai | a | Hēmi | hei | āwhina | i | a | koe. |
>| --- | --- | --- | --- | --- | --- | --- | --- | --- | --- |
>| TA | arrive | Dir | Pers. | Hēmi | Det. | help | Obj. | Pers. | 2Sg. |
>
>'Hēmi has come to help you.'

Finally, verb stems marked only by *te* (i.e. with no preposition) act as complements to some neuter verbs and the passive *taea* 'be achieved, be possible':[33]

>| Kua | oti | te | whare | te | peita. |
>| --- | --- | --- | --- | --- | --- |
>| TA | completed | Det. | house | te | paint |
>
>'The house has been painted.' / 'The painting of the house has been completed.'

>| Ka | taea | e | koe | tēnei | mahi | te | mahi? |
>| --- | --- | --- | --- | --- | --- | --- | --- |
>| TA | achieve.Pass. | P | 2Sg. | Det. | task | te | do |
>
>'Can you do this task?'

These are the constituents of the pragmatically unmarked simple sentence in Māori. As indicated above, the usual ordering of these constituents is predicate – subject – obliques ('comments'). Within the obliques, there are certain preferred orders – for instance, direct object before recipient, place from which before goal; however, there seems not to be a preferred relative ordering of adverbial expressions of time and place, as there is in some languages.

Various factors can lead to or license orderings which depart from this pattern. For instance, 'heavy' constituents will gravitate to the right. As adumbrated above, the subject is not always to be found in such sentences in second position; under some circumstances, it may follow certain obliques. Non-agentive subjects, in particular, especially if they are less 'salient'[34] than some oblique expression, tend to occur later. This is clearest with passives and neuter verbs, whose agents are oblique, and whose subjects are not only patients, but are often non-human and may be indefinite. Thus, the following is a more natural ordering than strict VSX:

>| Ka | kite-a | e | ia | he | puna | wai | nui. |
>| --- | --- | --- | --- | --- | --- | --- | --- |
>| TA | find-Pass. | P | 3Sg. | Det. | spring | water | big |
>
>'S/he found a big spring of water.'

However, the subject is most frequently the second phrase of a simple sentence. Thus, it intervenes not only between a verb and any complement, but also between a nominal predicate phrase and any complement, modifier or possessor dependent on it:

> *He   ākonga   a   Hēmi   nā   Ihu.*
> Det. disciple Pers. James P   Jesus
> 'James was a disciple of Jesus'.'

The remainder of this chapter will deal with a number of other topics in Māori grammar, taking this simple sentence pattern as basic. These topics are: coordination; negation; possession; transforms, that is, other sentence types plausibly regarded as 'derived' from the basic shape; complex sentences, especially relativisation.

Coordination

Coordination in Māori is handled differently depending on properties of the coordinands. Asyndetic coordination is common between clauses and phrases as well as between expressions modifying a base, often with *hoki* 'also' added:

> *he   tangata māhaki, hūmārie hoki*
> Det. person mild   peaceful also
> 'a mild, peaceful person'

> *Kei.te ua,   kei.te makariri hoki.*
> TA   rain, TA   cold   also
> 'It's raining and cold.'

Clauses are often also conjoined by means of the word *ā*:

> *Ka hiki te   hui,   ā,   ka haere te   katoa ki.te kai.*
> TA raise Det. meeting and TA go   Det. all   TA   eat
> 'The meeting ended, and everyone went to eat.'

Nominal phrases show two different patterns. If both (or all) coordinands have human referents, then a pattern is used exploiting the rich pronominal system of Māori. Pronouns themselves are not conjoined – rather, the single pronoun which captures the requisite number and person is used, thus *māua* (1Du.Excl.) 's/he and I', *koutou* (2Pl.) 'you(Sg.) and they', and so on. Where one of the coordinands would be a pronoun and the other a full nominal phrase, the summative pronoun is again used followed by the second coordinand marked with *ko*.[35] Similarly, this applies to conjunctions of more than two phrases:

> *kōrua ko tō   wahine*   *rātou ko Mere ko Hēni*
> 2Du.   P   your(2Sg.) wife   3Pl.   P   Mere P   Hēni
> 'you(Sg.) and your wife'   's/he and Mere and Hēni'

Finally, if all coordinands are full phrases, the first occurs initially in the construction, followed by the third person dual or plural pronoun which refers to the whole group, followed in turn by the remaining coordinands, each marked with *ko*:

> te   kaumātua rātou ko ana   mokopuna
> Det. elder   3Pl. P his.Pl. grandchild
> 'the elder and his grandchildren'

Otherwise – that is, if any of the coordinands has a non-human referent – the preposition *me* 'with' is used with the second and any subsequent phrases. As a preposition, *me* is incompatible with another preposition, thus in order to conjoin two prepositional phrases, either asyndetic conjunction is used

> mō te   marae, mō te   wharenui   hoki
> P Det. marae P Det. meeting.house also
> 'Concerning the marae and the meeting house',

or, if the prepositions are the same, then the two nominal phrases governed by the preposition can be conjoined with *me*:

> mō te   marae me te   wharenui
> P Det. marae P Det. meeting.house
> 'Concerning the marae and the meeting house'

From this brief account, it should be clear that there is no word in Māori which corresponds to the English conjunction 'and', which can of course conjoin constituents of more or less any category. As a result, one increasingly hears *me* pressed into service, especially by younger, second-language speakers of Māori, to conjoin units of other types:

> *Ka kata   rātou me ka   ūmere.
> TA laugh 3Pl. ?   TA shout
> 'They laughed and shouted.'

Negation

For sentence negation, Māori makes use of a number of different negative words, the selection of which is conditioned by the type of predicate and by the tense/aspect/mood of a verbal predicate. As with other aspects of Māori grammar, it will not be possible to present all the details here, and the reader is referred yet again to the reference grammars. Rather, this section will provide some typical examples and point to those features of negation which have received attention in the scientific literature.

The negative words to be illustrated always stand first in their clause, and are often followed by the subject phrase,[36] which thus precedes the predicate phrase and any obliques.

Clauses with nominal, equative or possessive predicates are negated by means of the form *ehara*.

> He   kaiwhakaako taku matua.
> Det. teacher   my   father
> 'My father is/was a teacher.' (predicate nominal)

is negated as:

> Ehara taku matua i   te   kaiwhakaako.
> Neg.   my   father P Det. teacher
> 'My father is/was not a teacher.'

> Nō Pita tērā waka.
> P   Pita Det. canoe/vehicle
> 'That car belongs to Pita.' (predicative possessive)

is negated as:

> Ehara nō[37] Pita tērā waka.
> Neg.   P   Pita Det. canoe/vehicle
> 'That car does not belong to Pita.'

Prepositional predicates asserting location, existentials and most verbal predicates are negated by means of the form *kāore*.[38]

> Kei Pōneke   te   Whare Pāremata.
> P   Wellington Det. House Parliament
> 'Parliament is in Wellington.' (location)

is negated as:

> Kāore te   Whare Pāremata i   Pōneke.
> Neg.   Det. House Parliament P Wellington
> 'Parliament is not in Wellington.' (location)

> E   tangi ana te   tamaiti.
> TA weep   TA   Det. child
> 'The child is/was crying.'

is negated as:

> Kāore te   tamaiti e   tangi ana.
> Neg. Det. child   TA weep TA
> 'The child is/was not crying.'

The third major negative is *kaua* 'negative imperative', which negates direct and indirect commands, as well as 'optative' clauses:[39]

> Haere!   Kaua e   haere!
> Go   Neg. TA go
> 'Go!'   'Don't go!'

> I   mea[40] atu ia   kia kaua rātou e   haere.
> TA say   Dir. 3Sg. TA Neg. 3Pl.   TA go
> 'S/he told them not to go.'

The primary interest in negation has been in the issue of the class membership and syntax of these negative words. The modern consensus is that they are verbs which take the clause being negated as (at least underlyingly) a single argument. Hohepa (1969b), which argues that these words are not only verbs, but neuter verbs, is the most important single work in this area, but the same approach is used and developed in a number of other publications.[41]

The verbal properties of the words are at their clearest with respect to the form *kore*. This form is used, *inter alia*:

to negate verbal predicates with future tense

> E   kore rawa   au   e   whakaae!
> TA Neg. Manner 1Sg. TA agree
> 'I shall never agree!'

to construct negative nominalisations

> Nā taku kore e   whakaae . . .
> P   my   Neg. TA agree
> 'Because of my refusal to agree, . . .'

to negate final clauses

> kia kore ai   koe e   hinga
> TA Neg. Aph. 2Sg. TA fall
> 'so that you don't fall'

As can be observed from these examples, *kore* is verb-like in being compatible with a variety of tense/aspect markers and postposed particles, most tellingly *ai*. It has both zero- and suffixed nominalisations (example above, and *korenga*). *Kāore* and its cognate forms are in fact 'lexicalised' phrases with *kore* as head, *kāore* itself being from *ka kore*. *Ehara* is etymologically from *e hara* (TA miss, come short of), and seems to be a uniquely Māori negative. *Kore* is an Eastern Polynesian innovation, and *kaua* has cognates throughout the entire Polynesian family. However, in those constructions negated in Māori by means of *ehara*, many of the languages most closely related to Māori have either generalised a *kore*-form, or have independently innovated. Tahitian, for instance, uses the superficially similar *e'ere*, which is in fact not cognate with Māori *ehara*, but formed from a different verb, whose reflex in Māori, *ngere*, means 'having failed in one's object'.

The reflex *tē* of PPN *ta'e 'not' is also found in a few restricted constructions. However, as in the other PN languages in which its cognates occur, this form occurs within the phrase it negates, preposed to the lexical head, not as a separate phrase. Its only really productive use in modern Māori is a negative question form used in northern dialects

> *He   aha   koe   tē   haere   mai   ai?*
> Det.   what   2Sg.   Neg.   go   Dir.   Aph.
> 'Why didn't you come?'

for which other areas use:

> *He   aha   koe   i   kore   ai   e   haere   mai?*
> Det.   what   2Sg.   TA   Neg.   Aph. TA   go   Dir.
> 'Why didn't you come?'

Otherwise, *tē* occurs only in idiomatic expressions such as:

> *Tē   taea   te   aha.*
> Neg.   achieve.Pass.   Det.   what
> 'There is/was nothing to be done.'

Possession

As in many languages, possession in Māori is used for a range of constructions involving two NPs, not just expressions of 'ownership'. Part–whole relationships, partitive ('one/some of . . .'),[42] and the subject of nominalisations, for instance, are all treated the same way as more 'canonical' possession.

All these constructions are dealt with in more detail elsewhere. See especially the reference grammars and Harlow (2000a). In keeping with the tenor of this chapter as a whole, the present section will provide a very brief summary of the constructions themselves and of the aspect of possession in Māori which has provoked the most discussion, the alternation between /a/ and /o/ as the characteristic vowel of the possessive particles.

Attributive ('my book') and predicative ('I own a book' and 'The book is mine') possessive constructions make use of very similar sets of particles. In all cases, it is the possessor which is marked, the possessum showing no sign of the relationship.

Attributive possession

The basic markers in attributive possession are the prepositions *a* and *o*, which mark the possessor:

Te	*waka*	*o*	*Rewi*		*te*	*kai*	*a te*	*rangatira*
Det.	canoe	P	Rewi		Det.	food	P Det.	chief
'Rewi's canoe'					'the chief's food'			

As mentioned above (in the section on determiners), the possibility exists of constructing an indefinite number of possessive determiners by incorporating a dependent possessor of this kind into the pattern: $[t \sim \emptyset + PP]_{Det}$. Thus:

tō   Rewi   waka   =   te   waka   o   Rewi
Det.P   Rewi   canoe   Det.   canoe   P   Rewi
'Rewi's canoe, the canoe of Rewi'

ō   Rewi   waka   =   ngā   waka   o   Rewi
Det.P   Rewi   canoe   Det.   canoe   P   Rewi
'Rewi's canoes, the canoes of Rewi'

Such determiners, as well as being very much the preferred pattern in the case of pronominal possessors, occur with all types of possessor, especially when the head noun of the possessum phrase is not explicit. This may occur because it is readily supplied from the context

He   nui   ake   tōu   whare   i   [[tō   Pita].$_{Det}$ [$\emptyset$]$_N$]$_{NP}$
Det.   big   Dir.   Det.P.2Sg.   house   P   Det.P   Pita
'Your house is bigger than Pita's (i.e., house).'

or in the predicative possessive construction to which we now turn.

Predicative possessives

In order to assert or deny that one has, owns or possesses some possessum, modern Māori usually does not use a verbal predicate.[43] Rather, a predicate nominal construction is used with the indefinite possessum as predicate and the appropriate possessive determiner as subject.

> *He   moni   [ā rātou]?*$_{Poss.Det}$
> Det.   money   their
> 'Have they any money?'

> *He   waka   [tō   Pita]*.$_{Poss.Det}$
> Det.   canoe/vehicle Det.P Pita
> 'Pita has a car.'

The negation of such expressions is not, however, the regular negation for predicate nominals, *ehara*, but *kāore*, which negates, *inter alia*, existentials. Two patterns occur depending on whether the possessor is a pronoun or a full NP. Both deny the existence of an entity possessed by the possessor:

> *Kāore   āku   moni.*
> Neg.   my   money
> 'I have no money.'

> *Kāore   he   moni   a te   kaunihera.*
> Neg.   Det. money P Det. council
> 'The Council has no funds.'

Similarly, Māori disposes of no verb meaning 'belong to', using instead a predicative form of the possessive PP:

> *Nō   wai   tēnei   whare?*
> P   who   Det.   house
> 'Whose is this house?' / 'Who does this house belong to?'

> *Nāu   tērā   pukapuka?*
> P.2Sg.   Det. book
> 'Is that book yours?'

In this instance, the negation is *ehara*, as for equatives and predicate nominals:

> *Ehara nāku   tērā   pukapuka.* = *Ehara i   a   au*
> Neg.   P.1Sg.   Det. book   Neg.   P Pers. 1Sg.

> *tērā   pukapuka.*
> Det. book
> 'That book is not mine.'

The principal area of interest in the possessive system, indeed one of the thorniest matters in the grammar of Māori, is a feature shared with nearly all other PN languages.[44] As will be noticed from the examples given so far in this section, there is an alternation in the characteristic vowel of possessive forms between /a/ and /o/.[45] In general, textbooks and grammars of Māori deal with the issue in part by providing lists of items which typically take possessors marked in one or the other way. Not untypical is the list given in Harlow (1996:20ff.) repeated here.

a-forms are used for:

(1) small portable possessions

> *tāku   pene*
> my   pen
> 'my pen'

(2) kin of lower generation than EGO (except *uri* 'descendant', which takes o-forms), and spouses

> *te   wahine   a Hēmi*   *tāna   mokopuna*
> Det. woman   P Hēmi   his/her grandchild
> 'Hēmi's wife'   'his/her grandchild'

(3) the subject of nominalisations of transitive verbs, including derived nominals

> *te   patunga a ngā tamariki i   te   kurī*
> Det. beating P Det. children Obj. Det. dog
> 'the children's beating the dog'

> *Te   waiata a Horomona*
> Det. song   P Solomon
> 'The Song of Solomon' (traditionally taken to have been composed by Solomon)

(4) all consumables except fresh water and medicine

> *Hōmai he   parāoa māku.*
> Give Det. bread P.1Sg.
> 'Give me some bread', lit. 'Give (me) some bread for me.'

(5) animals not used for conveyance

> *ngā kurī a te   rangatira*
> Det. dog P Det. chief
> 'the chief's dogs'

o-forms on the other hand are used for:

(1) large objects, including means of conveyance, including animals like horses

tōna	*whare*	*ō rātou*	*waka*
his/her	house	their	canoe
'his/her house'		'their canoes/cars'	

(2) the subject of nominalisations of intransitive, neuter and experience verbs

tō rāua	*taenga atu*
their(Du.)	arrival Dir.
'their arrival'	

(3) the subject of nominalisations of passive transitive verbs

te	*patunga o te*	*kurī e*	*ngā tamariki*
Det.	beating P Det.	dog Agt.	Det. children

'the children's beating the dog', lit. 'the dog's being beaten by the children'

(4) all other kin (see above), and friends. Strikingly, though *wahine* 'wife' and *tāne* 'husband' take a-form possessives, their synonyms, *hoa wahine* 'female friend, companion, wife' and *hoa tāne* 'male friend, companion, husband' take o-forms

te	*tuakana*[46] *o*	*Mere*	*ōna*	*mātua*
Det.	older.sister P	Mere	his/her.Pl.	parent.Pl.
'Mere's older sister'			'his/her parents'	

(5) parts of whole, including parts of the body and, by extension, clothing

te	*tuanui o te*	*whare*	*tōna*	*pōtae*
Det.	roof P Det.	house	his/her	hat
'the roof of the house'			'his/her hat'	

Such lists, while perhaps useful for learners of the language as rules of thumb, and arguably used by speakers to select possessive markers, miss what is going on at a more abstract level. W. H. Wilson (1982:14f.) calls the listing approach 'Word-Class Theory' and likens it to grammatical gender; that is, it implies that the nouns of Māori (Wilson's discussion is about PN languages generally, but the same points apply in the specific case) fall into two classes, one requiring a-marking on any possessor, and the other o-marking. Wilson (1982:15) points out, as do many others,[47] that this cannot be the correct approach, not least because there are many examples of the same possessum taking now a-marked possessors and now o-marked ones. For instance, using an example from Biggs (1969:43): *te waiata a te tangata rā* (Det. song P Det. man Loc.) 'that man's song' referring to a song he sang or composed, as opposed to *te waiata o te tangata rā* (Det. song P Det. man Loc.) 'the song of that man', where the song is about the person.

What is encoded in the choice of a-forms or o-forms is rather the relationship between the possessor and the possessum. All textbooks and grammars, as well as other publications, grapple with the characterisation of this relationship, a difficult undertaking given that one must somehow bring together such superficially disparate ideas as those exemplified in the list above. However, there is general agreement that notions of 'dominance' and 'control' play a crucial role. Biggs (1969:43), for example, formulates the generalisation: 'Possession of anything towards which the possessor is dominant, active or superior, is expressed by *a*; possession of things in respect of which the possessor is subordinate, passive or inferior, is expressed by *o*.' Biggs (2000b)[48] proposed a simplified version of this much more recently on the basis of a suggestion of Ross Clark's – namely, that the o-forms are the 'unmarked' item of the alternation, and thus one need only specify when the a-forms should be used: 'In Maori a Possessor that is considered to be active towards or in control over a Possessee is marked *a* "of, dominant possessor". All other Possessors are marked *o* "of, possessor".' This latter modification accounts better for the fact that there are many possessor ~ possessum pairs which are reciprocally marked with o-forms, e.g. siblings, friends, people ~ places:

> *ngā tāngata o tēnei marae*
> Det. people   P Det. marae
> 'the people of this marae'

> *te   marae o tēnei iwi*
> Det. marae   P Det. tribe
> 'the marae of this tribe'

If both a- and o-marking were conditioned by an asymmetrical relationship of superiority ~ inferiority of some kind, then only asymmetrical marking should occur. In fact, there are of course many such asymmetrical pairings, such as parents ~ children, teachers ~ pupils, bosses ~ workers, and so on. However, taking the o-forms as unmarked, i.e. simply the absence of the control relationship, as opposed to its contrary, is not only simpler, but accords better with the occurrence of reciprocal o-marking.

Curiously, there is one pair of terms which uses reciprocal a-marking. These are *tāne* 'husband' and *wahine* 'wife':

> *Ko   Tama te   tāne   a Mere.*
> Pred. Tama Det. husband P Mere
> 'Tama is Mere's husband.'

> *Ko   Mere te   wahine a Tama.*
> Pred. Mere Det. wife   P Tama
> 'Mere is Tama's wife.'

This is inexplicable in an account which posits an asymmetrical relationship as the reason for a-marking. W. H. Wilson's (1982:16–18) 'Initial Control Theory', however, does better justice to this example. He proposes that 'the controller . . . is the noun phrase which *causes or instigates* the relationship' (emphasis added).[49] Under this interpretation, the reciprocal a-marking of the husband and wife pair is due not to some idea that husbands and wives dominate or control each other, but to the idea that both 'cause' their relationship by consenting to it.

Hohepa (1993) proposes that the superordinate criterion is ±location. If the relationship can be seen as +location, then the possessor is o-marked; otherwise, ±control operates as in Biggs' account. However, in order to get this algorithm to predict the correct choice, it is necessary to construe the notion of '+location' extremely widely, allowing it to subsume what are usually regarded as different relationships such as part–whole, even possessor–possession in the narrow sense of ownership.

Along related lines, Thornton (1998), in the conviction that 'any particular language expresses the mind set and spirituality, past and/or present, of the people whose language it is' (1998:381), discusses the issue in the context of two key concepts in Māori thought and values: *mana* and *tapu*. These are very difficult concepts relating to relative status not only between people, but also between people and non-human entities, as well as between the latter.[50] She is able to argue for a good correlation between 'higher' status of possessor over possessum and the use of a-marking, especially, but not exclusively, in the case of relationships between people, but concedes that other instances, such as the treatment of the subject of nominalisations, are best regarded as grammatical.

In this latter connection, the work done on Māori syntax within a generative framework makes an interesting contribution. Waite (1994) tries to account for the different marking, which he regards as Case rather than as prepositional, by positing different underlying positions for possessor phrases. Those which will surface as a-marked phrases originate in the Specifier position of the NP complement of the entire DP, while o-marked possessors start off life in the Complement position of that NP. The determiner then assigns a-case-marking to the Specifier position in its complement, while the noun of the NP assigns o-case-marking to its own complement. Thus (1994:66), [DP [D' te [NP te wahine [N' tamaiti]]]] becomes *te tamaiti a te wahine* (Det. child P Det. woman) 'the woman's child'. *Te wahine* is assigned 'a-Genitive' case-marking by *te*, and *tamaiti* is adjoined to the D. On the other hand, [DP [D' te [NP Ø [N' whaea [DP te wahine]]]]] becomes *te whaea o te wahine* (Det. mother P Det. woman) 'the woman's mother', by both adjunction of *whaea* to the D *te*, and movement of the possessor (assigned 'o-Genitive' case by *whaea*) to the Specifier position of the NP (the Ø in the above structure).

This approach works particularly well for those DPs whose complements are headed by a verb or adjective, i.e. for nominalisations. Exactly those predicates (neuter verbs, non-agentive intransitives, passives) susceptible to an unaccusative analysis take o-marked subjects when nominalised: that is, those verbs whose surface subject is taken to originate in its complement position.[51] On the other hand, transitive and agentive intransitive verbs, whose subjects originate in the Specifier position of the VP, have a-marked subjects when nominalised, as exemplified above.

Pearce (1997, 1998a) further develops this approach in the light of more recent advances in generative theory, in particular Minimalism, and proposes to account for the two types of case-marking by means of two case checking heads between the D and the lexical phrase, be it NP or VP. The case checking which leads to the a- or o-marking is sensitive to the thematic role of the 'possessor'. Pearce's work further incorporates the treatment of possessor phrases into the wider structure of the DP involving other 'modifiers' such as deitics and attributive adjectives.

None of these proposals, grammatical or semantic, accounts fully for the occurrence of a- and o-marking for possessors. Not least, this is because there are cases where speakers vary in usage, and where whatever generalisation one sets up, individual items sometimes select marking contrary to what the generalisation would predict. Thus, for instance, *moemoeā* 'dream' has an o-marked possessor for some speakers, and a-marking for others; *noho* 'stay, sit' regularly takes a-marking on its subject in nominalisations, as if agentive. Further, it is clear that whatever more general principles may underly the choice between a- and o-marking, something like the 'word-class' approach does play a role in speakers' actual usage; possessors are marked according to a speaker's classification of an item in a set of categories analogous to those listed above. This leads to varying results on occasions, particularly for newer words and concepts. Is a watch a tool? Then a-marking is required. Is it, on the other hand, an item of clothing? If so, then o-marking is used. Is a camel a vehicle or a domesticated animal? It is hoped this short section has shown why this aspect of Māori grammar was characterised at the beginning as one of the thorniest, and why, probably more than any other single aspect, it has produced such a diverse range of proposals.

Transforms of basic sentences

Apart from the relative freedom of placement of NPs and PPs following the predicate phrase in Māori basic sentences, there are other patterns available which provide for different encoding of thematic roles to grammatical relations and/or for different ordering of constituents. In particular, Māori has a passive, and a number of constructions in which subjects or some obliques occur first in the clause.

Passive

The formal properties of the passive in Māori are relatively easy to state.[52] What is, however, of particular interest is its usage – the fact that passive clauses are used much more frequently than in comparable languages. In general, passive clauses have a verbal phrase as predicate containing a form marked passive by means of the characteristic suffix. The subject is the patient (or thing perceived, wanted, etc., in the case of middle verbs), and any agent (experiencer) is expressed in an oblique PP marked with *e*. This is clearest if one compares active and passive 'versions' of a canonical transitive clause:

> *I   whakareri   a   Hōne   i   ngā   kai.*
> TA make.ready Pers. Hōne Obj. Det. food
> 'Hōne prepared the food.'

> *I   whakareri-tia   ngā   kai   e   Hōne.*
> TA make.ready-Pass. Det. food Agt. Hōne
> 'The food was prepared by Hōne.'

As noted above, passive clauses are often found in which the oblique agentive phrase precedes the subject phrase.

> *I   whakareri-tia   e   Hōne   ngā   kai.*
> TA make.ready-Pass. Agt. Hōne Det. food
> 'The food was prepared by Hōne.'

Exceptions to this general pattern are clauses with *me* 'should' as their TA and/or *waiho* 'leave' or *hōmai/hoatu* 'give (to me / away)' as their verb, in that the passive suffix does not appear in these cases:[53]

> *Me   waiho   ngā   pukapuka   ki   runga   i   te   tēpu.*
> TA leave Det. book   P on   P Det. table
> 'The books should **be left** on the table.'

As noted, it is not so much the form as the usage of passive in Māori which has provoked discussion – in particular, its relative frequency. Clark (1973:576–80), which is one of the most important contributions to this issue, reports a count of active vs passive versions of agent–object verbs in Orbell (1968), a collection of nineteenth-century prose texts. Of the 432 eligible clauses, 244 (56 per cent) are passive. Clark goes on to identify a range of syntactic environments in which active or passive is the only grammatical possibility. If these are excluded from the count, the preference for passive in these narrative texts is even more pronounced: 172 out of 250. This very high frequency of passives in comparison to actives was among the considerations which led Gibson and Starosta

(1990) to claim that the passive form is in fact the basic transitive construction, the 'active' is thus an antipassive, and Māori is an ergative language (see chapter 2). Clark's own suggestion to explain this state of affairs is that there is an aspectual difference between corresponding active and passive clauses, which are imperfective and perfective respectively. While this does seem to fit a number of examples, Clark himself admits that there are 'difficult cases' as well.

Chung (1978: especially 66–81) suggests that the 'trigger' for passive is rather the degree of affectedness of the object/patient. To some extent, this suggestion overlaps with Clark's in that objects are more fully affected in perfective clauses than in imperfective ones, but goes further in accounting for some of Clark's 'difficult cases'. Bauer (1997:479–84) summarises both positions, pointing out that neither suggestion accounts fully for the occurrences of passive, and that they are at best tendencies. This section of Bauer's grammar does, however, draw attention to some judgements which are of relevance to Clark's idea. In illustrating the formation of the passive, she (1997: 479) uses an active–passive pair similar to the one given above, and reports that in fact the active version is sometimes rejected by informants. Strikingly, examples of active sentences involving, say, continuous tense/aspect marking instead of *i* 'past' are much more readily accepted, which would be quite consistent with the notion that perfectivity is the relevant criterion.

A further possible factor (also at best a tendency) has to do with anaphoric reference. Subjects generally may be readily omitted if recoverable from context. Similarly, in many passive clauses, the agent phrase is not explicit, even though a specific agent is in the speaker's mind. Objects on the other hand do not seem to be so readily omissible in the same way. A transitive verb without overt object would generally be taken to have no specific object.

In a number of examples, it appears that participants in a sentence or scene of the narrative may be introduced by means of an active clause, while further actions involving these participants are encoded with passive verbs with omitted subject and agent phrase:

> *Ka mau a   Tāwhaki ki tētahi o ngā karu o tōna taina,*
> TA grab Pers. Tāwhaki P Det. P Det. eye P his   brother,
>
> *makaia   atu ana ki te   konohi o te   kuia   rā.*
> throw.**Pass**. Dir. TA P Det. eye   P Det. old.woman Loc.
> 'Tāwhaki took one of his younger brother's eyeballs and placed it in the old woman's eye.'
>
> (Ruatapu 1993:30)

Both Tāwhaki and his brother's eye are introduced in the first clause and figure again as agent and patient in the second clause (*makaia*), which is passive so that neither participant need be overt; had the second clause been active (*maka*), *Tāwhaki* could have been omitted, as subject, but the eye would have had to be referred to again. It is not clear that the 'taking' (*mau*) is any less perfective than the 'placing' (*makaia*), or that the eye is any less affected when 'taken' than when 'placed'. Further down the same page of narrative is a similar example:

> *Ka horoi ia   i   tōna tipuna,   ka   rākaitia,   ka   pai*
> TA wash 3Sg. Obj. his   ancestor, TA adorn.**Pass**. TA good
>
> *ki tāna titiro.*
> P his   view
> 'He washed his grandmother and adorned her, and then she looked good to him.'

Apart from its frequency, a further striking feature of the use of passive in Māori is its role in imperative clauses with transitive verbs. Such verbs with specific (though not necessarily overt) patients are passive when used as a direct command (thus the patient is subject, and the addressee agent):

> *Katia   te   kūaha!*   *Tuhia!*
> Shut.Pass. Det. door   Write.Pass.
> 'Shut the door!' 'Write it!'

Above all, this use of the passive, so different from imperatives in English, along with its clearly much higher frequency generally, has led to 'hypercorrect' overuse of passive especially in younger L2 speakers of the language. There are constructions in which passive morphology may not appear – for instance, the so-called Actor Emphatic, on which see below. However, increasingly, one hears gratuitous passive suffixes added in this and similar places where it historically did not occur.

Focus and topic constructions

As noted above, Māori has a number of constructions which place constituents other than the predicate phrase in initial position. All such constructions serve to place the fronted material in focus or topic position. By no means all non-predicate phrases may be fronted in these ways. Objects, for instance, may not, and in order to place an object in focus, recourse is had to a kind of cleft construction in which the 'object' to be focussed is a predicate nominal or equative predicate with a headless relative clause (see below on the possessive strategy for relative clause formation) as subject:

*[He aha]*PRED *[tāu e   kimi nā?]*SUBJ
Det. what   your TA seek Loc.
'What are you looking for?' lit. 'What you are looking for is a what?'

Ko   Hēmi tāku e   mea   nei.
Pred. Hēmi my   TA say/do Loc.
'It's Hēmi I mean.' / 'I mean **Hēmi**.'

Subject fronting Superficially, any subject may be placed in initial
position with no necessary change to the rest of the clause. If the subject is
definite, it is marked with the preposition *ko*, already encountered as the marker
of equative predicates. The fronting of a subject marked with *he* 'indefinite'
results in an existential sentence:

He   rōpū   kei.te haere mai.
Det. group TA   go   Dir.
'There's a group approaching.'

Fronted definite subjects have two quite different meanings, each associated
with a different intonation pattern.[54] Bauer (1991), which is the major source
of information and analysis on this construction outside the reference grammars, gives the example of the following string, which has two distinct stress
placements and correspondingly two pragmatically different meanings:

Ko Rewi e   whāngai ana i   te   kūao   kau.
P   Rewi TA feed   TA Obj. Det. young.of cow
'Rewi is feeding the calf.' (My glosses)

With heavy stress on the first phrase *Ko Rewi*,[55] the sentence has the reading
'It is Rewi who is feeding the calf.' That is, Rewi is in focus, and the sentence
is an appropriate answer to the question, 'Who is feeding the calf?' In this case,
ko must be present in the focussed phrase.

With the major sentence stress on the predicate phrase, its normal position
in pragmatically neutral sentences (and with *ko* able to be omitted), the initial
phrase is topicalised, and the sentence is appropriate, for instance, in a discussion
about what Rewi (and perhaps others) are doing. Bauer (1991) and Pearce (1999)
regard only this second construction as subject fronting, Bauer analysing the
example sentence as:

*[Ko Rewi]*Su/Topic *[[e whāngai ana]*V *[i te kūao kau]*DO]Pred

Pearce, following work by Cinque and Rizzi, posits the existence of FocusP
and TopicP nodes within an expanded CP. In particular,

ForceP (= CP) > TopicP* > FocusP > TopicP* > FiniteP > IP.

This general formula allows for the presence of one or more topicalised phrases, which may either precede or follow a focussed phrase. In the case of Māori, Pearce locates the fronted phrase in the Spec of a Topic position just below Force. As she rightly points out, in sentences containing both topicalised and focussed material, the topic phrase is initial. Examples with topicalised constituents other than subject are also found, but by no means so frequently as fronted subjects, and usually with a resumptive pronoun in the body of the sentence (see Bauer 1997:657–9).

Bauer (1991) and Pearce (1999) likewise agree in their analysis of the focus construction, arguing that, in this case, the *ko*-phrase is in fact a predicate, and thus the whole sentence is an equative, with a headless relative clause as subject:

$$[Ko\ Rewi]_{Pred}\ [[e\ wh\bar{a}ngai\ ana]_V\ [i\ te\ k\bar{u}ao\ kau]_{DO}]_{Su}$$
$$(Bauer\ 1991:5)$$

Within Pearce's framework, *ko* is the head of a combined Force/I, while the rest of the phrase (here *Rewi*) is situated in the Spec position of an XP complement of Force/I.[56]

Essentially, this analysis is a claim that such sentences are clefts: '(The one) who is feeding the calf is Rewi'. This approach to these sentences in fact brings the focussing of subjects into line with that of objects (see above). This view gains support from the fact that such sentences do sometimes have explicit antecedents for the clause claimed to be the subject:

$$Ko\ Rewi\ [te\quad mea]\ [e\ wh\bar{a}ngai\ ana\ i\ te\ k\bar{u}ao\ kau.]_{RelCl}$$
$$Det.\quad thing/person/one$$

A problem is, however, the headless relative clause required in this analysis. Headless relatives do occur in Māori, but they are all examples of the possessive strategy (see below), whereas the clause in the present instance would be an example of the zero strategy, which is never otherwise used without an antecedent. In all other instances of the meaning 'the one who . . .' (with subject as target of the relative clause), an explicit antecedent must be present.

Actor Emphatic   As reported in chapter 2, this construction is an innovation in Eastern Polynesian languages, all of which share the pattern, though in no two are the details identical.[57] Clark (1976) and Harlow (1986) speculate on the historical origins of the pattern, Clark seeing it as a predicative version of the possessive relative strategy to be described below, while Harlow connects its formation with the cross-linguistically not uncommon relationship between possessive constructions and perfectivity. For the main characteristic of this construction is the fronting of an agent phrase and its marking as if it were a predicative possessive:

Nā Rewi te   kūao   kau i   whāngai.
P   Rewi Det. young.of cow TA feed
'It was Rewi that fed the calf.'

Mā Rewi te   kūao   kau e   whāngai.
P   Rewi Det. young.of cow TA feed
'It is for Rewi to feed the calf.' / 'It is Rewi who will feed the calf.'

The three core elements of this construction are: an agent phrase placed first and marked with *nā/mā* (past or future), prepositions otherwise used for marking predicative possessors, as above; a patient phrase as subject (hence no preposition/object marker); a verb phrase marked with *i/e* (past or future). The patient/subject phrase may precede or follow the verb phrase, or indeed, as subject, be topicalised with *ko* and placed before the agent phrase:

Nā Rewi i   whāngai te   kūao   kau.
P   Rewi TA feed   Det. young.of cow
'It was Rewi that fed the calf.'

Ko te   kūao   kau nā Rewi i   whāngai.
P   Det. young.of cow P   Rewi TA feed
'As for the calf, it was Rewi that fed it.'

The fronted agent phrase is focussed, so that these constructions are very common in wh-questions and corresponding answers where the action is presupposed, and the identity of the agent is the new information. At the same time, such sentences also occur in sequences in which the agent is already topical, and the assertion is the attribution of some action to that agent. For instance:

. . . Māui . . . Nāna hoki te   whenua i   hī   ake.
. . . Māui . . . P.3Sg. for Det. land   TA fish Dir.
'. . . Māui . . . For it was he who fished up the land.'[58]

This construction is restricted to transitive verbs with specific (though not necessarily overt) objects, and past and future tenses. For some speakers, its use with some agentive intransitives is possible, especially for the future: *Māna e haere* (P.3Sg. TA go) 'S/he is to go, s/he is the one who is to go.'

Most of the discussion of this construction in the literature focusses on its analysis, the approaches being very usefully summarised in Waite (1990). Before proposing his own analysis within a GB framework, Waite sketches three models which he sees implied or stated in previous work. In two of these models, the agent phrase, being similar in form to a predicative possessor phrase, is seen as the predicate, the patient phrase as a subject, and the *i/e* + V a subordinate clause. Carstairs (1970) and Chung (1978:175), who discuss Actor Emphatic as an example of promotion of direct object to subject, thus establishing direct object as a grammatical relation in Māori, see the construction as:

[$_S$ agent phrase [$_S$ [i/e V] NP]]

Here the agent phrase is the entire predicate of the main clause, while the subject is a lower clause consisting of the verb complex with the patient as its subject. The other admissible order of these constituents – agent phrase NP i/e +V – is due to 'raising' of the NP to the higher clause.[59]

Clark (1976) and Harlow (1986), on the other hand, posit a structure:

[$_S$ [agent phrase [$_S$ i/e V]] NP]

in which the verb phrase is a relative-clause-like subordinate to the agent phrase, and the patient is the subject of the main clause.

Finally, Bauer (1981a), Hohepa (1967) and Reedy (1979) prefer a mono-clausal analysis with the TA + V complex as the predicate. It is this basic position for which Waite himself argues, positing an underlying structure in which the VP has an empty Spec position, the V and patient NP form the V′ phrase, and the agent PP is an oblique sister of V′:

[$_{CP}$ Ø Ø [$_{IP}$ Ø i/e [$_{VP}$ Ø [$_{V'}$ V NP] PP]]]]

Movements motivated by case assignment lead to superficial structures:

[$_{CP}$ PP$_i$ Ø [$_{IP}$ NP$_j$ i/e + V$_k$ [$_{VP}$ t$_j$ [$_{VP}$ [$_{V'}$ t$_k$ t$_j$] t$_i$]]]]

or

[$_{CP}$ PP$_i$ i/e + V$_k$ [$_{IP}$ NP$_j$ t$_k$ [$_{VP}$ t$_j$ [$_{VP}$ [$_{V'}$ t$_k$ t$_j$] t$_i$]]]]

This analysis requires suppression of the accusative case usually assigned by V to its object. However, this is a phenomenon already needed in Māori for passives and for unaccusative accounts of the syntax of some intransitives and neuter verbs.

Pearce (1999) extends Waite's analysis using an expanded CP domain, and locates the agent phrase in the Spec position of a FocusP, which forms part of the CP complex.

Fronting of adjuncts   Adverbial phrases of time, means of transport, reason and place can also occur in initial position. The details of these constructions are not uniform across all these types, but here only temporal expressions will be described to illustrate this phenomenon, and, as always, the reader is referred to the reference grammars for further detail.

In pragmatically neutral sentences, temporal adverbials follow predicate, subject, and other argument phrases, and are usually marked with *i* or (for future time only) *ā*.

> *I   tae   mai rātou* [*i te   whā karaka.*]
> TA arrive Dir. 3Pl.   P Det. 4   clock
> 'They arrived at four o'clock.'

When in initial position, such phrases are more usually marked with the prepositions *nō* for non-future time, and *ā*, *mō* or *hei* for future. The rest of the clause then appears in two patterns.

(1) The rest of the clause remains unchanged, and there is free choice of tense/aspect marker, though *ka* is very common. Shorter subjects especially may follow the time expression directly:

> *Nō te   whā karaka ka   tae   mai rātou.*
> P Det. 4   clock TA arrive Dir. 3Pl.

and

> *Nō te   whā karaka rātou ka   tae   mai.*
> P Det. 4   clock 3Pl. TA arrive Dir.
> 'At four o'clock, they arrived.'

(2) Available only for past and future – the tense/aspect marking is restricted to *i* (past) and Ø (future), and *ai* is inserted in the verb phrase. Again, subjects, especially if short, may follow the time expression directly:

> *Nō te   whā karaka rātou i   tae   mai ai.*
> P Det. 4   clock 3Pl. TA arrive Dir. Aph.
> 'It was at four o'clock that they arrived.'

> *Hei tērā Rāhoroi te   whakaaturanga Ø   huakina   ai.*
> P Det. Saturday Det. exhibition   TA open.Pass. Aph.
> 'The exhibition opens **next Saturday**.'

The two patterns impart different types of emphasis to the time expression. The first pattern serves to topicalise the time expression and occurs, for instance, when a series of events, labelled by the times at which they occur, are presented. The second pattern, on the other hand, as the translations are supposed to suggest, focusses the time expression. Accordingly, questions about the time of some event normally use this pattern, with the interrogatives *nō nahea* and *āhea*, for past and future times respectively, in initial position. As noted above, however, these interrogatives occupy the initial position, not because they are interrogatives, but because that is the focussed position for such adverbials.

Notwithstanding this basic difference in the type of emphasis imparted to the time expression by these two patterns, they are often interchangeable and even appear side by side in narrative with little apparent difference of force:

> Nō te 15 o ngā [rā] i rere mai ai mātou [i]
> P Det. 15 P Det. day TA fly Dir. Aph. 1Pl.Excl. P
>
> Vancouver, nō tēnei rā ka tū ki tēnei tāone.
> V P Det. day TA stop P Det. town
> 'On the 15th we left Vancouver, and today (on this day) we stopped at this town.'[60]

This sentence contains two clauses, each stating a time and an event which occurred at that time. Notice, however, that the first clause follows pattern (2), and the second pattern (1).

The fronting of other adjuncts very much follows these patterns, with some difference of prepositional and tense/aspect marking depending on the type of adjunct.

Complex sentences

Māori disposes of a variety of ways of subordinating one clause to another in the roles typical of subordination in other languages: adverbial clauses, complement clauses and relative clauses.

Adverbial clauses

Some adverbial clauses are introduced by forms which can be compared with subordinating conjunctions in other languages. These forms are all originally phrases which have become lexicalised: *mehemea* (P Det. thing) introduces some conditional clauses, *nō/nā/i te mea* (P Det. thing) clauses of reason, and *ahakoa* (what particle), which can also take a nominal phrase as complement, concessives:

> **Mehemea** e tika ana tana tohutohu, me whai.
> If TA right TA his/her advice TA follow
> 'If his/her advice is correct, it should be followed.'

> Kaua e whāia **nō te mea** e hē ana.
> Neg. TA follow.Pass. because TA wrong TA
> 'Don't follow (it) because it is wrong.'

> **Ahakoa** e tika ana kāore i whāia e rātou.
> Although TA right TA Neg. TA follow.Pass. Agt. 3Pl.
> 'Though it was correct, they did not follow it.'

Ahakoa   he   aha   tana   tohutohu,   *me   whai.*
Although   Det. what   his/her   advice   TA   follow
'Whatever his/her advice, it should be followed.'

Nominalisations following a preposition are a frequently encountered way in which subordinate clauses are encoded. This is particularly so for temporal clauses for the past

Nō   tō.rātou   taenga   mai . . .
P   their   arrival   Dir.
'When they arrived'. / 'on their arrival',

or cause

Mā   tā.rātou   kōrero   i   te   reo   e   ora   ai.
P   their   speak   Obj. Det.   language   TA alive   Aph.
'It is through their speaking the language that it will survive.'

A further pattern is a clause governed by a preposition. Older texts, including Bible translations, provide examples of a clause directly governed by the preposition *nō*, a possessive preposition, which appears also in temporal phrases:

ā,   nō   ka   noho   ia, (Matt. 5:1)
and   P   TA   sit   3Sg.
'and when he was sat down [his disciples came unto him . . .]'

In modern Māori, in all those cases where it makes sense to think of a clause as governed in this way, the subject of the clause is 'raised' to become itself the complement of the preposition, leaving a gap in the clause, which can be marked by the insertion of *ai* if the TA is *i* 'past':

Nōna   ka   rongo, . . .
P.3Sg.   TA   hear
'When s/he heard, . . .'

I   a   Hēmi   i   uru   ai   ki te   kura . . .
P Pers.   Hēmi TA   enter   Aph. P   Det.   school
'When Hēmi went to school, . . .'

A similar phenomenon is found in a class of causal clauses introduced by *mō* 'for'. These are clauses giving the reason why thanks or acknowledgement are conveyed to someone. The subject of the lower clause is 'raised' to the preposition, where it is followed by the remnant of the lower clause:

Ka   nui ngā   mihi   mōu   i   whakaae ki te   tono.
TA   big Det.   greeting   P.2Sg.   TA   agree   P   Det.   request
'Many thanks (to you) for agreeing to the request.'

Clauses of purpose, so-called final clauses, are usually introduced by one or the other of the verbal particles *kia* (with *ai* after the verb) or *ki te*.[61]

> *Me tū   he   hui   **kia** kōrerotia **ai**   te   take.*
> TA stand Det. meeting TA speak.Pass. Aph. Det. issue
> 'There should be a meeting in order that the issue might be discussed.'

> *Ka tū   ia   **ki te** whakatakoto i   tana   whakaaro.*
> TA stand 3Sg. TA   lay.out   Obj. his/her idea
> 'He/she stood up to present his/her idea.'

The two forms are not interchangeable and the factors which determine the choice between them will arise again below with respect to complement clauses after verbs of wishing, in which the same two markers also occur.

Complement clauses

With the exception of the recent use of *mehemea* 'if' to introduce indirect questions, Māori has no conjunctions for complement clauses. Complements of verbs of saying, thinking, etc., simply follow the higher clause, with pronouns adjusted but no 'sequence of tense' alterations:

> *Ka mea mai ia   [kei.te hiakai rātou].*
> TA say Dir. 3Sg. TA   hungry 3Pl.
> 'He told me they were hungry.'

The actual words reported here were

> *Kei.te hiakai mātou.*
> TA   hungry 1Pl.Excl.

where the present tense TA is preserved in the indirect speech, but the pronoun becomes third person.

Indirect wh-questions as complements of interrogative verbs or nouns such as *pātai* 'question' similarly show adjustment of pronouns only, while reported polarity questions tend in modern Māori to be introduced by *mehemea* 'if':

> *I   pātai mai ia   mehemea e   hiakai ana mātou.*
> TA ask   Dir. 3Sg. if   TA hungry TA 1Pl.Excl.
> 'S/he asked if we were hungry.'

Otherwise, indirect polarity questions can be formed by the insertion of *rānei* 'or' after the predicate:

> *Kāore au   e   mōhio ka haere mai rānei rātou.*
> Neg. 1Sg. TA know TA go   Dir. 'or' 3Pl.
> 'I don't know whether they will come.'

Complements of verbs of wishing and, more generally, 'indirect commands' are marked with the same pair of tense/aspect particles encountered above with final clauses, *kia* and *ki te*. Here, as there, the issue arises as to which is used when – what conditions the choice.

Kei te pīrangi ia	*ki te ako*	*i*	*te*	*reo*	*Māori.*
TA want 3Sg.	TA learn	Obj.	Det.	language	Māori

'S/he wants to learn Māori.'

Kei te pīrangi ia	*kia whakatūria*	*hei*	*tiati.*
TA want 3Sg.	TA appoint.Pass.	Det.	judge

'S/he wants to be appointed judge.'

Most accounts point out that the choice is conditioned by the subjects of the higher and lower clauses, and by the predicate of the lower clause. In particular, *ki te* can be used only if the subjects of the two clauses are identical and if the predicate of the lower clause is an active agentive verb; with unlike subjects or passives, neuter verbs, middle verbs, even negatives in the lower clause, *kia* is the only possibility.

Pearce and Waite (1997), who provide a good summary of previous accounts and a wide range of examples, suggest an analysis within the Minimalist framework. In particular, they assign the feature [-tense] to *ki te*, likening *ki te*- complementation to the non-finite constructions of other languages, and posit PRO as the subject of such clauses. This accords with the requirement that the subject of both clauses must be the same for *ki te* to be possible. They further point out that the predicates which cannot take *ki te* are exactly those for which there are good reasons to propose an underlying unaccusative structure.[62] On this approach, the lower clause, whether a complement or a final clause, would have the underlying structure

$$[_{IP} \text{ (Spec) } ki \ te \ [_{VP} \text{ (Spec) } [_{V'} \text{ V PRO}]]]$$

which is excluded, because this PRO finds itself in a governed position. The article is an important contribution containing much more detailed analysis than it is possible to present here, and contrasting the situation in Māori with that of infinitives in other languages, e.g. Italian.

Relativisation

Although relative clause formation in Māori presents some interesting features, it has not produced the same level of comment in the linguistic literature as some of the other aspects of grammar referred to above. Outside the textbooks (in which it is generally poorly handled) and the reference grammars (among which Bauer's 1997:564–88 treatment is the fullest), there is only one systematic discussion: Bauer (1982). The interest lies in the range of strategies, and the extent to which Māori accords with cross-linguistic generalisations in this area.

Māori makes use of four strategies in the formation of relative clauses. Which one is appropriate depends on properties of the clause being used to modify the antecedent and on the target (i.e. the position within the relative clause which is indexed to the antecedent). All four strategies have in common that the clause follows its antecedent, and there is no marker which is peculiar to relative constructions – in particular, there is nothing which could be taken as a relative pronoun.[63]

Zero strategy   Under this strategy, the clause is in the same form as for main clauses with simply a gap at the site of the target:

Koirā   anake te   waiata [e   mōhio ana ia   Ø].
There.is only   Det. song   TA know   TA   3Sg. Obj.
'That's the only song s/he knows.'

Apart from the gap in object position, this relative clause is of the same form as the main clause:

E   mōhio ana ia   ki te   waiata.
TA know   TA   3Sg. P Det. song
'S/he knows the song.'

Such clauses may also include one of the locative particles *nei, nā, rā*, after the verb.[64] If included, such a particle replaces the TA *ana*.

This 'zero-strategy' is available when the target is the subject of any type of verb, the object of a middle verb (as in the example above) or (with reservations) the possessor of the subject of the clause.

Tokomaha ngā   tāngata [i   tae   mai ki te   hui]
Many   Det. people   TA arrive Dir. P Det. meeting
'Many people came to the meeting', lit. 'The people who came to the meeting were many.' (target – subject)

ngā   tamariki [kua neke   ake ngā   tau   i   te   rima]
Det. children   TA   exceed Dir. Det. year P Det. 5
'the children older than five', lit. 'the children whose years have exceeded five' (target – possessor of 'the years')

ai-strategy   A frequent relative clause type involves the postposed particle *ai*, already encountered above in focus constructions. The tense/aspect marking of relative clauses of this type is restricted to *e* (non-past) and *i*

Table 6.1. *Marking of predicates in* ai-*strategy relative clauses*

tense/aspect	TA	postposed particle
past	*i*	*ai, rā*
future	*e*	*ai*
present	*e*	*nei, nā, rā*
habitual	*e*	*ai*

(past), and *ai* to non-present. In the present, *ai* is replaced by one of the locative particles with which it forms a paradigm.[65] This gives the patterns in Table 6.1.

Ko   Tōrere te   marae [*i   tū   ai   te   hui*].
Pred. Tōrere Det. marae TA stand Aph. Det. meeting
'Tōrere is the marae where the meeting took place.' (past)

Ko   Tōrere te   marae [*e   tū   nei   te   hui*].
Pred. Tōrere Det. marae TA stand Loc. Det. meeting
'Tōrere is the marae where the meeting is taking place.' (present)

This strategy is found with the widest range of target types. It is found with subjects of verbs whose agents are oblique (passives and neuter verbs); most adjuncts, such as temporal, locative (as in the above examples), causal, instrumental phrases; agents of neuter verbs. For some speakers, particularly younger ones, it is possible where the object of a transitive clause is target, and isolated examples are also found where the agent of a passive verb is relativised on in this way.[66]

te   poaka i   pupuhi ai   taku matua
Det. pig   TA shoot Aph. Det. father
'the pig which my father shot' (object)

te   poaka [i   pūhia   ai   e   taku matua]
Det. pig   TA shoot.Pass. Aph. P Det. father
'the pig which was shot by my father' (subject of passive)
                                        (Biggs 1969:122)

Pronoun strategy   For a number of targets, a resumptive personal pronoun, or the anaphoric locative pro-form *reira* 'there, the aforementioned place' is used. This strategy is used particularly when the target of relativisation is the NP in a predicative prepositional phrase:

te   marae [*kei reira te   hui*]
Det. marae P   there Det. meeting
'the marae where the meeting is'

te   *iwi*   [*nō-na te   whenua*]
Det. tribe P-3Sg. Det. land
'the tribe to whom the land belongs'

Further, though, this strategy is used for a range of targets in roles which are
typically human, such as indirect object, agent of Actor Emphatic, possessor:

te   *tangata* [*i   tukuna   te   moni   ki a   ia*]
Det. person   TA send.Pass. Det. money P Pers. 3Sg.
'the person to whom the money was sent' (ind. obj.)

ngā   *tamariki* [*kua neke   ake ō rātou tau   i   te   rima*]
Det. children TA   exceed Dir. their   year P Det. 5
'the children older than five' (possessor, cf. above)

ngā   *tohunga* [*nā-na (nei)   te   waka   i   tārai*]
Det. expert   P-3Sg. (Loc.) Det. canoe TA carve
'the experts who carved the canoe' (Actor Emphatic)

In older Māori texts, the pronominal copy in Actor Emphatic clauses was
always singular, as in the last example, whatever the number of the antecedent. In
more modern Māori, number agreement applies, and the pronouns *rāua* '3Du.'
and *rātou* '3Pl.' are used with non-singular antecedents. Thus, nowadays the
following are more frequent than the last example above:

Ko ngā tohunga [*nā rāua te waka i tārai*] (dual)

Ko ngā tohunga [*nā rātou te waka i tārai*] (plural).

Possessive strategy   In common with many other PN languages,[67]
Māori makes use of a strategy for targets other than subjects in which the subject
of the relative clause is 'raised' to a possessor position on the antecedent. The
clause itself thus has two gaps, one at the target and the other for the subject.
Further, the clause is marked according to the *ai* strategy.

tō rātou ara [*i   heke   iho ai*]
their   path TA descend Dir. Aph.
'the path by which they descended'

Here the target is an instrumental adjunct ('path by way/means of which . . .'),
and the subject ('they') of the subordinate clause is realised as a possessive
determiner on the antecedent *ara*. This strategy is found with direct objects and

with a range of oblique adjuncts as targets, but is most common in modern Māori where the object of a transitive or middle verb is the target and the antecedent contains no explicit noun. A good example is provided by the line from the Lord's Prayer

> *Kia meatia   tāu   e   pai   ai*
> TA do.Pass. your TA like Aph.
> 'Thy will be done', lit. 'Let be done that which you like.'

or more colloquially

> *Ko   tāku e   mea   nei . . .*
> Top. my   TA do/say Loc.
> 'What I mean is . . .'

It will be clear from these few examples that both o- and a-marking of the possessors occur in this construction. In general, this is conditioned by the target, a-marking appearing with objects as targets, and o-marking with adjuncts.

Māori relativisation and the Noun Phrase Accessibility Hierarchy

Important and well-known work by Keenan and Comrie (see especially 1977 and 1979[68]) makes some very interesting claims about the typology of relative clauses cross-linguistically. In particular, they propose that there is an ordered arrangement of NP functions to which they refer as the Noun Phrase Accessibility Hierarchy:

$$SUBJ > DO > IO > OBL > GEN > OCOMP$$

The abbreviations stand for 'subject', 'direct object', 'indirect object', 'oblique', 'genitive' (i.e. possessives) and 'object of comparison' (i.e. standard of comparison ('than . . .')), and '>' means 'is more accessible to relativisation'. They claim that languages can form relative clauses with targets making up a continuous section of this list from the left. That is, there are languages which can target only subjects, and, if a language can target some position on this list, then it can target all positions to the left.

This seems to be true in the case of Māori. Examples are given above which show relative clauses constructed on all positions except OCOMP. Bauer (1997:582–3) shows that, while odd, grammatical relative clauses can be formed even for this last position on the hierarchy.[69]

Of greater interest is another proposal in Keenan and Comrie's work. This is the idea that if a language has more than one strategy for relative clause formation, then distribution of these strategies will also follow the hierarchy, each strategy covering a continuous segment of the list.

Table 6.2. *Distribution of relativisation strategies by target*

target/strategy	zero strategy	*ai* strategy	pronoun strategy	possessive strategy
subjects	✓	✓ (possible with non-agentive subjects)		
objects[70]	✓ (middle verbs)	✓/?		✓
adverbial adjuncts		✓		✓
agent of neuter verb		✓	✓	
agent of Actor Emphatic			✓	
possessor	✓		✓	
standard of comparison			✓	

A glance at Table 6.2, which summarises the distribution of the four strategies in Māori, shows that this position would be hard to defend in this instance.

This concludes our review of the major aspects of Māori syntax. Clearly there is more that could be said at every juncture. However, space precludes more detailed discussion, and recourse must be had to the reference grammars, especially Bauer (1993 and 1997).

NOTES

1. See especially Bauer (1993:559ff.), and de Lacy (msa). De Lacy equates Biggs' phrase with his Prosodic Phrase in pragmatically neutral clauses. In clauses with a focussed constituent, on the other hand, there is only one Prosodic Phrase, the focussed constituent, and the rest of the clause is not parsed prosodically.
2. There is some slight freedom for particles which follow the lexical head of a phrase to occur in variant orders.
3. Not all of which are necessarily occupied in any given phrase.
4. De Lacy's term, see note 1. De Lacy uses curly brackets to designate Prosodic Phrases.
5. The idea that it is the TA markers and the determiners which are the heads of their phrases is anticipated in Vennemann and Harlow (1977), who show, using categorial grammar, that this approach allows much of Māori word order to be stated in a version of the 'head-first' parameter setting.
6. Uniquely, *rā* does not count in the calculus determining the choice of allomorph.
7. And generative accounts treat the derivation of possessive constructions in the same way as that of the demonstratives. See especially Pearce (1998a, 1998b and 2003) and Waite (1994).
8. The major contributions to this research are Polinsky (1992), Chung *et al.* (1995), Clark (1997), Chung and Ladusaw (2004), all of which contain further references. Chung and Ladusaw (2004) is by far the fullest treatment, as well as the most recent, and usefully summarises the earlier work.

9. This is analogous to Chung and Ladusaw's (2004) treatment of *he* in existential clauses. See below.

10. In some eastern dialects, *he*-phrases can occur as objects, but then lack the object marker *i*: *Kei.te hanga rātou he whare* (TA build 3Pl. Det. house) 'They are building a house.'

11. Unlike most determiners, *he* has no distinct plural form; *he*-phrases can have both singular and plural referents.

12. I.e., so-called *unaccusative predicates*, those which on some views have no underlying subject; their superficial subjects are underlying objects.

13. Apart from being compatible with prepositions, *tētahi* (*ētahi*) differs from *he* in being one of the types of determiner which can occur without an overt lexical complement.

14. Some work in the generative tradition regards some of these as case markers rather than prepositions, see for instance Waite (1994).

15. *Kei* is often used for the future as well as for the present. Northern dialects have *ko* as the future locative preposition.

16. Though these particles always follow a lexical head, work in the generative tradition treats them as higher functional heads which underlyingly precede the lexical material. See Pearce (2002).

17. The main exception is *ana*, which occurs in the locative 'slot', but is found only in verbal phrases. Even *ai*, which occurs in the same position and is characteristic of verbal phrases, is occasionally found in other phrases.

18. Exceptions are found to both these generalisations. See Mutu (1982).

19. For instance, *Me mate ururoa, kei mate wheke* (TA die shark, TA die octopus) '(One should) die like a (fighting) shark, lest one die like an octopus!'

20. Recall that for some speakers, particularly from the east, *Kei te kimi rātou he whare hōu* is grammatical.

21. *Haere* 'go' can also be used to modify particularly neuter verbs and adjectives, imparting a progressive sense 'to become more and more . . .'.

22. For useful summaries of this research, see Song (2001) and Whaley (1997).

23. But see below, 'Possession', for preposed possessors.

24. Taking an item of category x to be a 'modifier' of another of category y/x with which it 'merges' as a y, and similarly an item of the category z/z to be a 'modifier' of another of category z, then the statement that 'modifiers' follow accounts for (nearly) all aspects of basic word order in Māori.

25. *Kei* (present or future) is one of three tensed prepositions in this function. The others are *i* (past), *hei* (future) and *ko* (in Northern dialects, future).

26. De Lacy's analysis of predicate nominals and equatives (2001) has these phrases originate as complements of a covert verb. This 'verb' moves to Infl and further to C, while the complement DP moves beyond this position to [Spec, CP] (and in the case of equatives, on again to [Spec, TopicP]), producing the correct surface order.

27. See also Hohepa (1981).

28. Third person pronouns, especially the singular forms, are found referring to entities other than human beings, but this usage is restricted and idiomatic. See Bauer (1997:262) and Harlow (2001:37, 72).

29. Middle verbs mostly take *ki*, and transitives *i*. However, in some cases the converse is true, and there are some instances where both are possible with the same verb, often with differences of meaning such as degree of affectedness. See, especially,

Johansen (1948:29–42), Bauer (1983, 1997:195–200), Chung (1978:169ff.) and Mark (1970).

30. Future 'time at which' can also be marked with *mō* or *ā*; however, *i* can be used for any time.

31. There are no grounds for identifying Indirect Object as a grammatical relation distinct from other obliques. See Bauer (1993:271ff.). What is meant here is simply recipient after verbs of saying, giving, etc.

32. There is also a preposition *hei* used for future time: *hei tērā wiki* (P Det. week) 'next week'. The *hei* referred to here stands immediately before the lexical material in a phrase. In some ways its distibution parallels that of predicative *he*, so it will be labelled Det. here. However, its exact category, whether determiner or verbal particle, is debatable. For more detail than is possible here, see Bauer (1997:esp. 156f., 202f., 215f.).

33. The main work on this phenomenon is to be found in Hooper (1984) and Waite (1989). Waite's view is that this *te* is not in fact the determiner, but a verbal particle of restricted distribution.

34. It is difficult at this stage of our knowledge to be very precise about what this means. However, relative 'definiteness', relative topicality, relative position on an animacy hierarchy, all seem to lead to VXS ordering.

35. Bauer (1991) discusses this use of *ko*, along with its employment in focussing and topicalising functions, to which we turn below. She labels this *ko* 'specifying' and speculates that it is related to the *ko* seen in the predicates of equatives.

36. This 'raising' of the subject to follow a negative is an instance of a more general phenomenon which sees subjects able to precede their (underlying) predicate in a variety of constructions in which material other than that predicate is clause-initial. The 'raising' is always optional, and the conditions which favour it are not fully understood, but have to do with phrase-weight and 'salience'.

37. In older Māori and in the speech of many modern speakers, *nō/nā* in this construction is replaced by *i*: *Ehara i a Pita tērā waka*.

38. There is some regional variation in this form: *kāhore, kāre, horekau, karekau* all occur with similar distribution.

39. I am here using 'optative' as a label for modal clauses such as those of obligation and 1st person imperatives. *Ka haere tātou!* (TA go Pl.Incl.) 'Let's go!' > *Kaua tātou e haere!* (Neg. Pl.Incl. TA go) 'Let's not go!', etc. *Kaua* is also used in some dialects to negate phrases: *I haere rātou ki Rotorua, **kaua** ki Taupō!* (TA go 3Pl. P Rotorua Neg. P Taupō) 'They went to Rotorua, not to Taupō.'

40. *Mea* is a very versatile word in Māori. As well as its nominal sense 'thing', it is also used as a verb meaning variously 'say' (as here), 'do', 'put'; as a personal noun meaning 'So and so'; and as a determiner meaning 'such and such'.

41. See especially Waite (1987) Chung (1978:132–45).

42. Though Māori, like German, uses simple juxtaposition where specific quantities are named: *kotahi pounamu miraka* (one bottle milk) 'a bottle of milk'.

43. There do exist verbs, especially *whai, whiwhi* meaning 'to acquire, become possessed of', which are increasingly used in parallel to English 'have'. In older Māori, the existential *ai* referred to above could also be used in predicative possessive expressions.

44. See papers in Fischer (2000).

45. There exists also a set of so-called 'neutral' possessive determiners where the possessor is a singular pronoun. These do not show the alternation, but are of very restricted distribution. See Harlow (2000a).
46. In fact, *tuakana* means 'older sibling of same sex as EGO', so in this instance 'sister'. *Teina* is the term for 'younger sibling of same sex as EGO', while *tungāne* is the brother of a female EGO, and *tuahine* the sister of a male EGO.
47. For instance, Biggs (1969:43), Bauer (1997:390ff.), Harlow (2001:157f.).
48. This publication is in a newsletter in a series edited and circulated by Biggs until shortly before his death in 2000. Unfortunately, no one has assumed the mantle since then.
49. In Hawaiian, the language with which Wilson is primarily concerned in work which led to this theory, there is a striking pair of terms with reciprocal a-marking; teacher and pupil. Wilson's theory accounts for this pair on the basis that, though a teacher may have 'control' of his/her pupil, the relationship between them is instigated by mutual consent.
50. Crudely, the two terms can be glossed as 'authority, status' and 'subject to ceremonial restriction, set apart' respectively. For discussion, see Barlow (1991) and the references in Thornton (1998).
51. This works even for middle verbs, which normally have two surface arguments, a subject and direct object. In quite a different connection, Pearce and Waite (1997) propose an unaccusative analysis for middle verbs. Under this approach, surface subjects of middle verbs are thus underlying in the complement position and receive o-marking in nominalisation.
52. The morphology of the passive forms of verbs is discussed above in chapter 5. See there for examples of 'passives' of other parts of speech besides transitive and middle verbs.
53. Some speakers do use passive suffixes in all these cases, using forms like *waihotia*, *hōmaingia*, and clauses like *me mahia* 'It should be done.'
54. Pearce (1999) presents a Minimalist analysis of these two sentence types within her broader discussion of topic and focus in Māori.
55. Recall from much earlier in this chapter de Lacy's (msa.) analysis of such sentences as having only one Prosodic Phrase, the focussed phrase, while the rest of the sentence is not parsed.
56. De Lacy (msa.), which also deals with initial *ko*-marked phrases, argues that all of them – equatives, focussed subjects and topics – are in the same Spec position under CP.
57. The ways in which the EP languages differ from each other in respect of this construction are to do with the tenses in which it is available, the marking of the patient (whether as subject or object) and the verbs with which it is compatible. Harlow (1986) argues that Māori is relatively conservative, while it is the other languages which have reanalysed or extended the original innovation.
58. Māui was a mythological hero widely known in the Pacific for his (often mischievous) exploits, such as fishing up islands, and causing the sun to go slowly.
59. More recently, this is the analysis favoured by Bauer (1997:503).
60. An excerpt from a letter dated 18 April 1898 published in Orbell (2002:32). The material in brackets is missing from the original.

61. *Ki te* is superficially like the string consisting of *ki* 'to', a preposition, and *te* 'the', a determiner, which figures in PPs of, for instance, goal, *ki te whare* (P Det. house) 'to the house'. This is surely the original of *ki te* in verb phrases of the sort illustrated below; however, modern descriptions of Māori concur in regarding this string as now a tense/aspect marker. Final clauses introduced by *hei* or *e* also occur, but space precludes further illustration of these.

62. See above on *he* and on possession.

63. In this section, the concentration will be on those relative clauses which have verbal phrases as their predicate. Considerations of space preclude dealing with clauses with nominal or prepositional phrases as predicates, though these too may act as relative clauses.

64. Though these particles are deictic, signifying 'near the speaker', 'near the hearer' and 'distant from either', respectively, they do not contribute any locational meaning when used in this way.

65. Note that, in the present, relative clauses formed in this way are not formally distinct from some possibilities under the zero-strategy.

66. In general, passive agents are not targets of relativisation. The agents of transitive verbs are relativised either as subjects of active clauses, or as agent in an Actor Emphatic clause.

67. See papers in Fischer (2000) and Clark (1976:116–19).

68. In this second paper, the authors present some data from Māori. Unfortunately, one of their example sentences, which purports to show that some obliques can be targets of a relativisation strategy using question words, is hopelessly ungrammatical and almost certainly due to very severe interference from English in the Māori of their informant.

69. Since this case entails the pronoun strategy, only human targets are possible.

70. Although it appears that there is some choice in how objects are relativised on, in fact, it is far more frequent for patients to be made subjects by passive or Actor Emphatic and thus relativised by zero or *ai* strategies, than for the object position to be the target of relativisation directly. See, especially, Bauer (1997:569ff.).

Until the final decades of the eighteenth century, Māori was the only language spoken in New Zealand. There is no evidence of any substrate influence on the Eastern Polynesian language(s) brought to New Zealand some 800–1,000 years ago. Neither had the brief visit of Abel Tasman in 1642 any impact whatsoever on the language. However, after James Cook's voyages in 1769–74, contacts with the outside world began which would in time have near-fatal consequences for the Māori population, culture and language. Chapter 2 sketches some of the consequences of the contact with English[1] for the shape of the language; this chapter will concentrate on the development of the symbiosis of Māori and English and its consequences for the demography of knowledge of the language, the status of the language, policy, education, language maintenance, attitudes to the language, and related areas. On all aspects of these topics there is considerable and widespread literature so that the goal of this chapter will be to provide an overview with relevant references,[2] but at the same time to present something of the personal perspective of the writer, who has been involved in a variety of roles in some of these areas over the last twenty years or so.[3] Some of the following material is thus necessarily more anecdotal in character than the result of formal research.

Language shift

Demography

King (2003:90–1) estimates the population of New Zealand in the eighteenth century at 100,000 to 110,000.[4] However, the nineteenth century saw a steady reduction in the Māori population, due in very large part to imported diseases to which Māori had little immunity, but also as a result of dispossession, reaching the low point of 42,113 in the 1896 census (King 1981:280). The decline which led to this figure was widely taken to indicate the imminent extinction of the Māori race; however, a range of initiatives in areas such as public health turned the trend around. The twentieth century saw a dramatic rise in the number of people who identified themselves as of Māori descent in the five-yearly censuses. In the 2001 census as many as 604,110 people claimed Māori descent, while 526,281 identified themselves as of Māori ethnicity.[5] The New Zealand censuses have distinct questions about Māori descent and ethnicity; the former simply asks if one is descended from a Māori, while the latter is more interested in how one identifies oneself, in the culture and social groupings of which one feels oneself to be a member. Clearly, a number of people in New Zealand have some Māori ancestry without themselves feeling that they are part of Māori culture and identity.

The overall impact of contact with Europeans, particularly with settlers of British origin, on Māori life and culture is beyond the scope of this book and the interested reader is referred to general histories such as Oliver (1981) and King (2003), as well as to sources more directly dealing with Māori society and culture, such as Metge (1976) and Walker (2004). With respect to the language, the last 200 years of contact could hardly have had more radical effects. Following the pattern which is so familiar from other similar settings, the Māori population has gone from being essentially monolingual in Māori throughout much of the nineteenth century, through a period of bilingualism to a situation in the later twentieth century when eventual monolingualism in English was a real possibility.

This characterisation is of course a simplification, and communities and areas of the country differed greatly in the timing of this shift.[6] In particular, smaller isolated rural communities were in general more resistant to the pressures which led to the shift, and to which even they would ultimately not remain immune.

Clearly there were bilingual Māori throughout much of the nineteenth century and increasingly towards the end of the century, not least because of the way schooling was offered and funded, a matter to which we return below. However, Māori was definitely the language for communication within the Māori community and between the Māori community and institutions such as the state and the churches. For much of the period from the foundation of the apparatus of government in the 1840s,[7] there was at least a policy, even if the practice was patchy, of publishing in Māori any bills and other documents which were judged to affect the Māori people.[8] When Māori representation in the House was instituted in 1867 in the form of four regionally distributed seats, it was necessary to provide interpreters, and the first of these Māori MPs were unable to participate in debate and deliberations held in English. The right to speak Māori in the House and have interpreters provided continues to exist and is still exercised, though nowadays more for politico-cultural reasons than of necessity.

Indicative of the progress of the language shift which occurred throughout the twentieth century is Table 7.1 taken from Biggs (1968:75).[9] Biggs himself concedes that the figures are not entirely comparable. However, there are few figures of any sort on this matter for this period, and these are certainly indicative of the trend.

Table 7.1. *Knowledge of Māori language among Māori schoolchildren*

	Proportion speaking Māori	Proportion understanding Māori
1913	90%	—
1923	80%	—
1950	55%	79%
1953–8	26%	62%

The figures for 1913 and 1923 are for children attending Native Schools who spoke only Māori at home. The figure in the first column for 1950 represents children attending Māori schools who spoke some Māori at home, and those for 1953–8 are the result of the testing of 277 Māori pupils entering four high schools in the Auckland region.

The first substantial survey of the knowledge and use of Māori was conducted by Richard Benton under the auspices of the New Zealand Council for Educational Research between 1973 and 1978. The survey[10] covered some 33,000 people in nearly 6,500 households in over 350 communities in the North Island. The survey was not extended to the South Island because it has been clear for many years that the shift to English had largely been completed in the South Island communities at a time when many North Island communities were still mostly Māori-speaking (Benton 1997:8). People in the south who belong to the generation which in the north had still acquired Māori as at least a first-equal language can remember their grandparents speaking Māori amongst themselves, but their own parents, let alone they themselves, did not acquire Māori through intergenerational transmission.

The survey identified only seven communities which it classified as 'truly Māori-speaking' in the mid-1970s (Benton 1984:3), all of them small rural communities situated either in central Northland or the eastern Bay of Plenty, areas with very high proportions of Māori vs Pākehā in the population. Even in the two least 'anglicised' of these, the trends were beginning to show, with older children increasingly using English amongst themselves, though still speaking Māori with their parents and grandparents (Benton 1997:21).

Overall, extrapolating from the survey, Benton (1981:15) estimated that there were at that time some 70,000 native speakers of Māori, and a total of some 115,000 people who could understand spoken Māori readily. This means that in fact there were probably more native speakers of Māori at that time than at the turn of the twentieth century. However, a number of aspects of the situation differed so much from the earlier period that the results of the survey were cause for great concern. Native speakers of the language were now a minority in the Māori population as a whole; age-grading in the knowledge of Māori is marked throughout all the communities studied (though, as mentioned, there are differences in the rate from one community to another); many speakers now found themselves in contexts which did not provide opportunities to speak Māori: mixed marriages, workplaces with predominantly monolingual English-speaking staff. These factors allowed the prediction that a few decades would see a radical reduction in the number of speakers and this has indeed proved to be the case.

In 1995, Te Taura Whiri i te Reo Māori (TTW, 'The Māori Language Commission') conducted a survey of 2,441 Māori aged 16 and over to determine their level of fluency in Māori (Te Puni Kōkiri 1998). Extrapolating the results to the corresponding total Māori population of over 270,000, the survey found that only about 10,000 people (c. 4%) have 'high' or 'very high' fluency in Māori,[11] while as many as 78% have no Māori at all or only 'very low' or 'low' fluency. Of the '(very) high' fluency group, 73% were aged over 45, and the vast majority had acquired Māori at an early age in the home and community. An unfortunate aspect of this research is that, by surveying the Māori population aged 16 and over at that time, it very neatly missed investigating the very generation of Māori who might have been benefitting from the revitalisation endeavours, especially as seen in the education system.[12]

This information gap is made up for in some part by the results of a survey, Te Hoe Nuku Roa, begun in 1994 by the Department of Māori Studies at Massey University, Palmerston North. Christensen et al. (1997:25, see also Christensen 2001) report that, of their informants aged 0–15, '35% had command of a few basic sentences, and 64% had either no ability or knew only a few basic words.' They rightly point out that this result is not very encouraging with respect to the effectiveness of the educational initiatives for the maintenance of Māori; 24% of their informants had enjoyed at least some Māori-immersion education.

Since that time, the only large-scale surveys have been the censuses of 1996 and 2001. For the first time, these contained a language question, specifically: 'In which language(s) could you have a conversation about a lot of everyday things?' In 1996, just over 22% of the Māori population of over half a million (15% of the total New Zealand population) gave Māori as (part of) their answer. There were a further 23,000 people, not of Māori ethnicity or descent, who did likewise. Similar figures are found in the 2001 census:[13] 160,000 total speakers of Māori, of whom nearly 140,000 are of Māori ethnicity or descent (c. 26% of the Māori population). In these results, the age-grading seen in the earlier surveys is still clear: in 1996, 56% of Māori over 60 years of age claimed to speak Māori, while the lowest proportion (21%) was found in the 25–29 year band (Statistics New Zealand 1997: 'Māori', 16). Interestingly, lower-aged bands showed slightly better levels of ability to speak Māori, perhaps showing the effect of revitalisation initiatives.[14]

The discrepancy between the 1995 survey results and the two censuses are clear (see Benton and Benton 2001:423) and are probably due to differences in the elicitation of information and the vagaries of self-reporting. In any event, speakers of Māori, especially highly fluent ones, are a minority in their own community.

Domains

It is clear also that the decreases in the proportion of the Māori population who can speak Māori go hand in hand with a reduction in the domains in which Māori is used. The surveys referred to above, apart from the censuses, also investigated the use to which speakers were putting their knowledge of Māori. Both surveys found that in very large part Māori was a preferred language only in the context of the marae, particularly for the formal activities of speechmaking, calling and singing. There is some preference for Māori in religious contexts such as formal church services. In all other domains, such as home, workplace, school, neighbourhood, literacy, English had gained a very strong foothold.

The factors which have led to this shift to English are the familiar ones encountered in comparable cases of endangerment of minority languages, and many of them, such as education, media, attitudes, policy, will be dealt with below. A further important factor in the case of Māori has been the urbanisation of the Māori population since the time of the Second World War. Before this time, the Māori population was essentially rural, living in small tightly knit communities. However, primarily for economic reasons, large numbers of Māori moved to the urban centres. As a result, many Māori, though fully fluent in their mother tongue, found themselves in situations where English was the default language. Not only was English the preferred language for work environments, the policy of 'pepper-potting', that is, of encouraging the distribution of Māori evenly through the urban areas, as part of a policy of integration, meant that for many the language of neighbourhood interaction was also English. Urbanisation also brought together Māori from different tribal areas, and it was not unknown for English to become the preferred language for ordinary conversation between Māori from different areas of the country, because of a fear of ridicule over dialect differences.

Reversing language shift

The trends in the decline of knowledge and use of Māori among the Māori population seemed to point inexorably to the loss of Māori as a living language.[15] Biggs (1968:84) felt able to predict that 'there will be a slow and inevitable further retreat of Māori before the overwhelming pressure of English'.[16]

He also predicted that Māori would retain its 'ritual and ceremonial' uses, and be increasingly the object of scholarly interest. These last two predictions are certainly true, but since the 1970s we have seen developments which have given hope that the first may prove inaccurate.

There was not one single trigger for these developments, neither is there a consistent policy driving them, beyond the desire to prevent the loss of Māori. There had been voices in earlier decades expressing concern about the maintenance and adaptation of Māori. For instance, Sir Āpirana Ngata (1874–1950), the great Ngāti Porou leader and politician, often referred in the 1920s and 1930s to the desirability of maintaining the language, and to the need for the Māori vocabulary to be enriched by 'the interplay between local and foreign cultures'.[17]

However, the coincidence of a number of factors, all with antecedents, and all mutually dependent and reinforcing, in the late 1960s, 1970s and 1980s provided the impetus for the attempts on many fronts to reverse the trend. This is the period in which the first generation of young Māori who were in large part brought up in the cities and whose parents raised them in English reached adulthood and were attending tertiary education in unprecedented numbers. Aware of what they individually had been denied and of the history of disadvantage to which their ancestors, and indeed their own generation, were subject, they formed action groups such as Ngā Tamatoa (the 'young warriors'),[18] which sought redress on a number of fronts, including language. In 1972, for instance, Ngā Tamatoa presented a petition to Parliament, for which they had collected 33,000 signatures, calling for Māori to be made available to all pupils who wanted to learn it (Benton 1981:50).

A second factor was a growing awareness of the results of Benton's survey and generally of the precarious position the Māori language was in with respect to continued natural transmission. This was, for instance, a concern of the annual Hui Whakatauira – meetings of Māori leadership, inaugurated in the late 1970s by the Department of Māori Affairs – and led directly to the foundation of the Kōhanga Reo (Walker 2004:237–8).

A further factor was the general ethos of the times. Since the 1970s, New Zealand has been experiencing a phenomenon often referred to as the 'Māori Renaissance'. This is a reawakening of pride in Māori identity and culture, an assertion of Māori claims to a fair participation in national life as *tangata whenua* ('people of the land'), a seeking for redress of past injustices, a flowering of Māori arts, including literature (though primarily in English).[19] This 'movement' did not spring up out of nothing, but has its seeds in a variety of developments throughout the twentieth century, including the Young Māori Party, of which Ngata himself was a leading member.[20]

Māori as an official language

Reference has already been made to the use of Māori for official purposes in the nineteenth century. The practice of providing translations for (some) legislation and of allowing speeches in Parliament to be held in Māori (with interpretation for non-Māori-speaking members) was based purely on necessity.

It was not until 1974, with the passage of the Māori Affairs Amendment Act, that the language received any statutory recognition at all. Section 51 of that Act recognised 'the Māori Language . . . as the ancestral tongue of that portion of the population of New Zealand of Māori descent' and authorised the Minister of Māori Affairs to 'take such steps as he deems appropriate for the encouragement of the learning and use of the Māori language' (Benton 1981:21). This statute did not, however, have the effect of making Māori an official or national language or of creating any rights with respect to its use. That had to wait until 1987, when the Māori Language Act was passed, in the preamble to which reference is made to the Crown's obligation under the Treaty of Waitangi.

On 6 February 1840, at Waitangi in Northland, a treaty was signed between the representative of the British Crown, Captain W. Hobson, and a number of Māori chiefs from that region. Over ensuing months, other signatures were obtained from different parts of the country and the so-called Treaty of Waitangi became the primary instrument for the assertion of British sovereignty over New Zealand.[21] Among other provisions, it guaranteed (at least in the Māori-language version) to the Māori continued possession of their *taonga* 'treasured possessions, property'. Under the Treaty of Waitangi Act 1975, the Waitangi Tribunal was empowered to hear claims of alleged infringement of the Treaty of Waitangi by the Crown and to recommend settlements to the Crown. In 1985, a claim was made by Huirangi Waikerepuru and the Kaiwhakapūmau i te Reo ('The Māori Language Board') to the Tribunal, making the case that the Māori language is a *taonga*, and that the Crown had been delinquent in not guaranteeing the Māori people its continued possession. The Tribunal accepted this argument and made some recommendations to the government.

The Tribunal recommended (Waitangi Tribunal 1986:76) that:
- legislation be introduced enabling any person who wishes to do so to use the Māori language in all courts of law and in any dealings with government departments, local authorities and other public bodies;
- a supervising body be established by statute to supervise and foster the use of the Māori language;
- an inquiry be instituted into the way Māori children are educated to ensure that all children who wish to learn Māori be able to do so from an early age and with financial support from the state;
- broadcasting policy be formulated in regard to the obligation of the Crown to recognise and protect the Māori language; and
- amendments be made to make provision for bilinguism [*sic*] in Māori and in English as a prerequisite for any positions of employment deemed necessary by the State Services Commission.[22]

In the preamble to the report, the Tribunal also recommends that Māori should be made an official language of the country. The government's main response was the passage of the Māori Language Act 1987, which made Māori 'an official language'[23] of New Zealand, founded TTW,[24] created the right to limited oral use of Māori in courts and tribunals with a range of jurisdictions, and set up a system for the certification of translators and interpreters to be run by TTW.

Apart from the specific right of any party to a wide range of types of hearing to speak Māori,[25] the Act gives no guidance as to what official status should mean. I have tried to argue (Harlow 2000c), on the basis of the example of Rhaeto-romansh in Switzerland, that the term 'official language' implies a much wider range of language rights and governmental obligations. Little has happened in this direction by means of regulation or statute; however, TTW, very early in its existence, began urging government departments to develop policies and practices to make Māori more visible in their operations, beginning with adoption of a Māori name, and progressing through signage and letterheads to the provision of Māori-language 'front-desk' services. This persuasive rather than dictatorial approach has borne fruit.[26]

TTW, as well as having the specific function of administering the certification of translators and interpreters,[27] had the more general function of promoting Māori. Three main prongs of this general goal were high priorities for TTW in its early stages:[28]

- urging those who know Māori to speak it. This goal led TTW members to visit a number of marae to expound the nature of the problem, and its view of the absolute necessity of increasing the use of the language by those who know it or are learning;
- vocabulary development (on which see further below). TTW adopted the view that people, especially younger people, would speak Māori only if it were equipped to express what they wanted to talk about;
- promotion of standards of correct Māori. Because of the precarious state of Māori, and the fact that many speakers in influential positions, such as teachers and broadcasters, were second-language speakers, TTW initiated a series of intensive week-long schools with the goal of making the exemplars of language heard by learners as good as possible.

Other parts in the Tribunal's recommendations, though not addressed directly by the Crown at that point, have attained some level of fulfilment through other developments, particularly in education and broadcasting.

Māori in education[29]

It goes without saying that Māori was the language of tuition in the traditional education system of precontact Māori society. *Whare wānanga*[30] existed in many parts of the country and served for the transmission of historical traditions, cosmology, *whakapapa* ('genealogy'), medical knowledge, *karakia*[31] and so on. The emphasis was on verbatim learning; the actual words themselves, especially in *karakia*, were effective, and mistakes were inauspicious and subject to sanction. To this day, a *whati* 'break' in a traditional song, or *karakia*, used on formal occasions excites comment and misgiving.

For at least the first half of the nineteenth century, *whare wānanga* continued to operate beside the system of schooling initiated by the missionaries.[32] From very early in their ministries, the missionaries established schools with the goal of making Māori literate in their own language. Typical of the materials used is a small booklet prepared by James Watkin, the first missionary in the south of New Zealand, which consists of alphabets, nonsense syllables and short sentences, and progresses to religious sayings, prayers and hymns (Harlow 1994b). Largely for practical reasons, the language of tuition was Māori, but, from as early as 1858, the government imposed the use of English as a condition for grants to mission schools. In 1867, the Native Schools Act established secular schools in Māori communities, which taught through the medium of English. As time progressed, this policy was extended to an 'encouragement' to use only English within schools, and there are many elderly people alive now who suffered sanctions, often physical punishment, for speaking Māori at school.[33] This policy, which remained *de facto* in place until the early 1980s, was based on the overriding ideology of assimilation, and was by no means without its supporters within Māoridom. The acquisition of English was widely seen as essential for Māori in order to better their circumstances. In 1877, a petition from 337 Māori was presented to Parliament asking that teachers appointed to native schools should have no knowledge of Māori. Other petitions supported the construction of native schools everywhere so that Māori children could acquire English (Walker 2001:221). Sir Apirana Ngata himself famously said that if he were designing the curriculum for Māori schools, he would make English four out of five subjects (Walker 2004:193).

While it is true that this policy is one of the factors which led a whole generation, themselves fluent in Māori, to bring up their children speaking only English, and that there is still much resentment about this policy, it is possible to encounter older people who, although they suffered the sanctions themselves, regarded the policy as positive, in that it made them bilingual; Māori was their home language, indeed their only language, until formal schooling made them competent English speakers as well.

Māori as a subject of tuition

Māori as a language of tuition thus disappeared from New Zealand schools from about the middle of the nineteenth century till its reintroduction in Kōhanga Reo and Kura Kaupapa Māori in the 1980s. However, Māori as a subject has been available to varying degrees for quite a lot longer. As a result of the efforts of Ngata, and against some opposition, Māori was admitted as a subject for the BA degree in the University of New Zealand in 1925, although there were no courses till Biggs introduced first-year Māori at Auckland in 1951 (Walker 2004:194). About the same time it became a subject for University Entrance Examinations and, somewhat later, for School Certificate (taken at the end of the third year of secondary education) (Benton 1981:25). In general, until recently, teaching of Māori in secondary schools has paralleled the teaching of foreign languages in approach, and older School Certificate exams looked almost like the contemporary Latin ones, with passages for translation, and 'life and customs' questions. This already difficult format, which did not encourage the learners, mostly Māori pupils, to regard the language as a living means of communication, was made even worse by the iniquitous scaling system used to determine marks in School Certificate. This had the effect of reducing the raw scores in the Māori examinations, making it much harder to reach the passing mark.

As the teaching of modern languages gravitated more to the acquisition of oral fluency, so too did that of Māori. Important resources in this area in recent decades have been Hoani Waititi's books *Te Rangatahi*, which began appearing in 1962 (Waititi 1970, 1974), and Tīmoti Kāretu's *Te Reo Rangatira* (1974), which follows Waititi's patterns of text, vocabulary list, grammatical explanation and exercises in each chapter, but pitches the language at a more advanced level. More recently again, Moorfield's (1988, 1989, 1992, 1996) series *Te Whanake* ('progress', 'development') is an invaluable resource.

Māori as a subject is now very widely available in secondary schools and to all levels, and while acquisition of language skills – especially oral, but also written – remains the main focus, the subject entails much more involvement with Māori culture than was perhaps the case earlier. Traditional Māori arts, including canoeing, weapons skills, oratory, weaving, *haka*, form part of the course as well. In 2004, 24,251 pupils were enrolled in Māori as a subject throughout the five levels of secondary study in 366 schools (Ministry of Education 2004).

As already mentioned, Māori was admitted as a subject in the University of New Zealand as early as 1925. However, the first courses were not taught until 1951, introduced by Bruce Biggs at the University of Auckland. The expansion of the offering to higher stages in the early 1950s met the same sort of opposition that Ngata's efforts had encountered in the 1920s, the objection 'that there was no Māori literature'. On both occasions,[34] this argument was answered by pointing to what publications were in existence, especially Grey's *Ngā Mahi a ngā Tūpuna* ([1854] 1971); however, both occasions also prompted the main participants, Ngata and Biggs, to turn to the production of editions for literary study: Ngata's invaluable series *Ngā Mōteatea* (1959, Ngata and Te Hurinui 1961, 1970[35]), and Biggs' editions of Māori prose manuscripts often circulated in mimeographed form at Auckland.

Māori Studies is now available as a subject at all eight New Zealand universities, and can be taken to Honours, MA and even doctoral level at many. Especially at undergraduate level, the main content of these programmes is the acquisition of language skills, though – depending on the interests of the staff in the respective universities – a wide range of other aspects of Māori life and culture is taught. The use of Māori as the language of tuition in these programmes varies widely; at some universities, e.g. Waikato in Hamilton, the policy is to use Māori in all but very introductory courses, while at others, English plays a rather greater role.

University Māori Studies programmes are sometimes caught in a tension between two distinct purposes: on the one hand they are academic units engaged in the study and teaching of a subject area like any other, on the other they have a unique role in 'teaching Māori to be Māori'. Many ethnically Māori students enrol in these programmes in order to acquire 'their' language and culture, a socialisation process which would under other circumstances have occurred in the home and community, but which is very largely not available there, especially among urban Māori. For these students, the goal of critically researching the language, literature and culture is a poor second behind the goal of the faithful transmission of received knowledge.

Māori Studies departments generally have been slow to respond to the fact that students are now at university who have had their entire primary and secondary education through the medium of Māori, and thus have quite different needs and expectations of the subject from the generations of students who mostly came to university with little or no knowledge of the language. At the same time, Māori tertiary institutions called *wānanga*, set up by Māori initiative to promote Māori participation in tertiary education, and recognised in the Education Act 1989, have increasingly been taking over the second role of the university departments, as have also similar units in polytechs.

Māori as language of tuition

As mentioned, education through the medium of Māori essentially disappeared in the nineteenth century. In recent decades, however, its reintroduction represents perhaps the main hope for the maintenance of the language. A combined initiative of the Department of Māori Affairs and local Māori communities, Te Kōhanga Reo ('nest', 'language') was founded in 1982.[36] 'TKR' is a preschool centre in which children are immersed in both Māori language and Māori practice/custom. Ideally, the teachers are native speakers, preferably older people, and the administration is the responsibility of the *whānau* – this word, which also means 'be born', is usually translated as 'family', but is wider in sense. Māori social structure places much more significance on the 'extended family' in any case, but this word can also be used to designate a group of people 'related' not so much by genealogy as by commitment to a common purpose, in this case the parents and caregivers, and indeed, wider family, of the children enrolled in a TKR. The *whānau* fulfils the role which might in the case of other similar institutions be played by a committee or elected board. The movement as a whole is administered by the Kōhanga Reo National Trust, situated in Wellington, which not only acts as a conduit for the funding which TKR receive, on the same basis as any other preschool centres, but also provides resources and training.

After the founding of the first TKR, the movement gathered considerable momentum. By 1993, there were 809 centres throughout the country, though this has since fallen to 513 in 2004. The number of children enrolled also peaked at that time (1993: Māori children, 14,027 – just under half of all Māori children in preschool centres of any kind – non-Māori, 487; but 2004: Māori children, 10,600 (30 per cent), non-Māori, 9). If TKR is at all successful in its goal of producing bilingual five-year-olds, then a very significant proportion of the Māori population is regaining its language. However, that is a big question. Both the effectiveness of the TKR movement itself and the support from home and subsequent schooling are important factors. Beside highly effective and committed *whānau*, one hears of cases where the TKR is little more than a childminding centre and/or social gathering point for parents, with little in the way of a structured programme or even much opportunity for the children to interact usefully with the adults in Māori. The vast majority of the homes from which TKR pupils come are monolingual in English. Many *whānau* have policies encouraging parents to acquire Māori in parallel with their preschool children, but even in cases where this is done conscientiously, it is doubtful whether it is generally effective in reinforcing TKR's work.[37]

The issue of subsequent schooling raised its head only a few years later when the first TKR children started to reach the age of compulsory primary education. Despite vague promises, the state system was not ready, so a number of TKR centres began retaining their pupils and extending their education into the primary curriculum themselves. The first Kura Kaupapa Māori (*kura* 'school', *kaupapa* 'policy/ideology', 'Māori': KKM) was founded in 1985 at Hoani Waititi Marae in Auckland, and numbers have subsequently grown to sixty-two. KKM are now recognised under the Education Act 1989[38] and receive government funding – however, particularly in the earlier days of the movement and in the early history of individual schools, opposition from the state extended even to threats of prosecution. When it became clear that both the movement itself and the individual schools were not going to yield to such pressure, the state system began considerable funding and administrative support. Curriculum statements for key learning areas were developed for Māori-medium education;[39] extra funding was provided not just to KKM but to any school, depending on the proportion of tuition delivered through Māori; resources in the form of reading material and syllabus support are being developed, though they remain at a level woefully lower than corresponding English-language material.

Like TKR, KKM are also run by *whānau* rather than boards. In 2004 there were 62 such schools with 5,995 enrolments, of whom 5,976 were Māori. In addition, other 'mainstream' schools offer various levels of tuition through the medium of Māori, and a total of 29,579 school pupils were receiving at least some Māori-medium tuition in 2004 – 12,580 of these for 81–100 per cent of the time.

More recently again, a number of KKM, and even one or two schools which, while not officially KKM, follow similar goals – e.g. Rākaumanga at Huntly – have extended tuition to year 13, the final year of secondary education in New Zealand. The first students from these schools began arriving at university in the early 2000s.

Clearly, extending Māori-medium education to this sort of level raises a variety of problems and questions; the provision of resources and of teachers with an appropriate level of sophistication in the language coupled with subject knowledge is very difficult; the development of any idea of the levels of linguistic knowledge which might be appropriate as criteria for the different stages of secondary school must occur in virtually a complete vacuum; whether, particularly in the more science-oriented subjects, one should perhaps use English anyway, since this is the language of further study and international discourse, is a question with no clear answer.

Māori-medium education at tertiary level has been available rather longer, at least to the extent that some Māori Studies courses at the universities are taught in this way. However, initiatives to extend this practice and to make it possible to conduct one's entire tertiary study through the language have also taken place. In the early 1990s, a programme of study, Te Tohu Paetahi, was developed at the University of Waikato, Hamilton, which made it possible to complete an entire BA in this way. If one then proceeded to an Honours degree and MA in Māori, and exercised the right to submit a doctoral thesis in Māori (see below), one could gain a Ph.D. without ever having attended a lecture or written an assignment in English. Such a BA had Māori Studies as its major subject but had also to contain a number of course credits from other disciplines where staff were able to teach their subjects through Māori. The first years of this programme attracted very viable numbers of students, many of whom have gone on to important roles in Māori broadcasting, policy and academic work. However, since the end of the 1990s, there has been a noticeable falling-off of interest; many students who enrol in the first year of the programme change their enrolment to an ordinary BA for subsequent years and follow the full range of subjects available in English.

While the presence of Māori in the whole range of educational levels, both as subject and as language of tuition, is vastly greater than it was in the mid-1980s,

it remains to be seen whether success awaits this attempt to restart intergenerational transmission – which is clearly recognised by all concerned as a *sine
qua non* – by creating a generation of 'native' speakers who will bring up their
own children through their traditional language and at the same time instill in
them the commitment to continue the process.

Māori in the media

To quite an extent, the use of Māori in mass media parallels its use in education, and for the same reasons. Beginning very soon after the establishment of
British rule, and extending well into the twentieth century, newspapers in Māori
fulfilled an important role in Māori community, political and religious life. The
earliest was a government publication which appeared first in 1842, and the
latest a church newspaper which appeared well into the 1930s.[40] There were
three principal publishers of Māori newspapers: the government, for the purpose of informing Māori of legislation, etc.;[41] the churches; and Māori political
movements, such as Te Kotahitanga and the King movement.[42] Few newspapers enjoyed long life, and many were ephemeral, sometimes reincarnate in a
successor within a few months. However, for nearly 100 years there was continuous journalistic publication in Māori. The papers contain news, debate, the
transcription of traditional material, and are a mine of material which is only
very recently being exploited again.

Since that period, periodicals and newspapers in Māori have not enjoyed
much success. The most important Māori journal of the more modern period
was *Te Ao Hou* ('the new world'), published by the Department of Māori Affairs
between 1952 and 1974. It contains material in both languages, continuing
the sort of content found in the earlier publications. More recent publications
intended for Māori audiences have been almost entirely in English.

However, in recent decades the broadcast media have been much more important than print journalism.[43] At the same time as pressure was mounting for support for the language in other ways, so too the presence of Māori in radio and
television became an issue. Since 1983, there has been a daily news broadcast
Te Karere ('the message'), initially only five minutes, but growing to fifteen,
on one of Television New Zealand's mainstream programmes. In 1988, *Waka
Huia*,[44] an hour-long archival programme entirely in Māori, began being broadcast. More significant, however, than such almost token efforts on the part of
mainstream media has been the development of specifically Māori broadcasting.
This has taken two forms, *iwi* radio and Māori television, and while in virtually
no case is Māori the only language used, it is gaining far more exposure than
ever before through these media.

In its ruling on the Māori language, the Waitangi Tribunal found, as has subsequent litigation, that the Crown has an obligation to promote the language

through broadcasting. This has led to the provision, sometimes forced, of considerable resources for radio stations and, more recently (2004), a television station both directly from government, and through a special funding agency, Te Māngai Pāho, established in 1993, which until 2000 distributed a proportion of the Public Broadcasting Fee (TV licence) for the production and transmission of Māori programmes.[45]

This new funding environment has led to some twenty *iwi* (local, 'tribal') radio stations. An option would have been a centralised network, which would have had the advantage of concentrating the resources, both in money and in personnel with relevant experience and knowledge of Māori. Instead, locally controlled stations were preferred.

The other initiative has been a Māori television station Whakaata Māori, which began daily broadcasts of about eight hours in 2004. The material being broadcast shows a very imaginative approach to programming, the extent to which Māori is being used shows a firm commitment to the use of this medium to support the language, and it is fascinating to watch the spontaneous adaptation of the language to quiz shows, cartoons, news and sports broadcasts, debates, and so on. Whakaata Māori is to be sincerely congratulated.[46]

Likewise worthy of congratulation and a real contribution to the exposure and status of Māori was the production of *The Māori Merchant of Venice*. In 1946, Pei Te Hurinui published a translation into Māori of Shakespeare's *Merchant of Venice*.[47] Long an ambition of Māori director and actor Don Selwyn, the project to make a film of the play came to fruition in 2002, and won instant acclaim for the quality of the production. While such achievements will not by themselves revitalise the language, the contribution they make to its exposure and to the nation's attitudes to the language cannot be overestimated.

Attitudes

The attitudinal motivation and support for these developments is widespread, not only among Māori themselves.

The importance of Māori language as an aspect of Māori identity, even the importance of taking measures to ensure its survival, is supported time and time again not only in the rhetoric of Māori proverbs such as *Ko te reo Māori te hā o te Māoritanga* (Pred. Det. language Māori Det. essence P Det. Māori-ness) 'The Māori language is the essence of Māori identity',[48] but also in numerous surveys of attitude which have been carried out in recent times.[49] The demographic surveys mentioned above (except the censuses) also contained questions eliciting opinions on the place of Māori in New Zealand, the measures taken to assist its revitalisation and its importance to the informants individually. In addition there have been further surveys directed exclusively at gaining a picture of New Zealanders' attitudes. For instance, Mary Boyce (1992) conducted such a survey as part of a research project on Māori language in a Wellington suburb, Porirua. At much the same time, a survey commissioned by TTW and the Māori Studies Department of Massey University, Palmerston North, was carried out by postal questionnaire (Brown *et al.* 1990, Nicholson and Garland 1991).

More recently and extensively, Te Puni Kōkiri (2002) reports on a telephone survey of over 600 Māori and over 700 non-Māori conducted in 2000. Both groups showed a range of opinions, though overall the value of Māori to the Māori community was recognised. The analysis of the survey identified three groups of Māori respondents: 'Cultural Developers' (68% of respondents); 'Māori Only' (20%); 'Uninterested' (12%). For this last group, learning Māori or participating in Māori culture had very little importance. What distinguishes the two larger groups is not commitment to the language and culture as important for themselves and Māori as a community, but the relative openness to the idea of a role for Māori in the wider nation, as a 'heritage' for all New Zealanders. Non-Māori were similarly divided into three groups in the analysis: 'Passive Supporters' (49%), who would be supportive of a greater role for Māori, and saw it as relevant for their own lives; 'Uninterested' (39%), who were tolerant of Māori language and culture, but saw no relevance for themselves; 'English Only' (12%), who were dismissive of Māori and held English to be the only language for public life. This last group were negative, even fearful, about the recent increased visibility and vitality of Māori culture and interests.

Leaving aside the Māori 'Uninterested' and the non-Māori 'English Only' groups, it appears that the vast majority of New Zealanders see the continued existence of Māori as desirable. However, there the unanimity ends. People differ not only in their view of the relevance of Māori to themselves personally and of the extent to which the state has a responsibility to expend resources on language maintenance, but also, as the analysis of the survey shows, in their view of the role of Māori within New Zealand. The ambivalence over 'Māori as a language for all New Zealanders' vs 'Māori as an exclusively Māori preserve' emerges again in what little discussion there has been of the general direction of the language maintenance policies. We return to this below.

Despite the rhetoric about the place of the language in Māori identity and the generally positive attitudes, there seems to me to be ambivalence also about what people want the language for. I am unable to rid myself of the suspicion that some positions adopted quite widely, even by people who are overtly committed to the importance of maintaining the language, are symptomatic of an underlying ideology inimical to the establishment of genuine societal bilingualism in New Zealand.[50] One can perhaps characterise this ideology as a 'monolingualist' mind-set, which is particularly worrying when evidence for it is found among people who are themselves bilingual and profess support for Māori; it suggests an absence of a true vision of Māori as a co-equal language in the country. This ideology is that of the majority of non-Māori and indeed corresponds pretty much to the status quo. It is the view that English is the default language, the 'working' language for normal life in New Zealand, and that Māori is a dependent add-on, with purely iconic function. Space precludes rehearsal of all the points I try to make in Harlow (2005), but typical of the position I am referring to here is the push to have the Māori names for places made 'co-official' with the English names. Thus, many people use 'Aotearoa-New Zealand' to refer to the country, 'Aoraki-Mt Cook' for the country's highest mountain. This suggests a view that there is only one real name for a place, and that is what it is called when speaking English; the Māori names have a claim to priority so they must be borrowed into English. This view is a 'monolingualist' view and contrasts with what I would take to be the situation in a country with genuine societal bilingualism, namely that any given place has as many names as there are languages in which one refers to it. In New Zealand, with two official languages, one *de jure* and one *de facto*, all places thus have two names, one used in English and the other in Māori. That places have different (in some cases not even etymologically related) names, depending on the language used to refer to them, is normal in other parts of the world. A particularly good example of this is the name for what is called Germany in English; some other languages, such as Romansh and Italian, have related names, in this case *Germania*, but German has *Deutschland*, French *Allemagne*, and Finnish *Saksa*. There is no sense in which any of this is more truly the name of the country than any other; it is a matter purely of the language being used.

Benton and Benton (2001:438) draw attention to the response to one question in the 1995 attitudes survey: only 13 per cent of respondents agree that 'you have to speak Māori to be a real Māori'. That is, despite the rhetoric about the place of the language in Māori identity and culture, it would seem that there is a very high level of acceptance of being 'Xmen through Y-ish' (Fishman's terms, 1991), with perhaps some tokenistic concern for aspects of the language, such as 'correct' pronunciation of placenames borrowed from Māori and the increased visibility of Māori placenames alongside the English ones, to serve as a sort of logo.

Language planning

Technically, any activity deliberately undertaken in order to influence the shape or status of Māori is an instance of 'language planning'. Thus, all the initiatives in education, such as Kōhanga Reo and Kura Kaupapa Māori, in broadcasting and media, in computing and the internet, and so on, would fall under this heading. This notwithstanding, the present section will concentrate on those

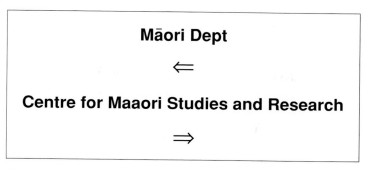

Figure 7.1   Sign at the University of Waikato using different orthographic conventions.

discussions and activities which relate directly to policy (status planning) for Māori, and the deliberate adaptation of the language for the modern world (corpus planning).[51]

A problem which besets all aspects of planning for Māori is the lack of coordination and of authority; there is no one body entrusted with the oversight of planning for Māori. Further, even if there were, it is doubtful whether it would have the authority to prescribe successfully, especially in areas of corpus planning.[52] TTW has by statute the following functions (among others):

7. Functions of Commission – The functions of the Commission shall be as follows:
  (a) To initiate, develop, co-ordinate, review, advise upon, and assist in the implementation of policies, procedures, measures, and practices designed to give effect to the declaration in section 3 of this Act of the Māori language as an official language of New Zealand:
  (b) Generally to promote the Māori language, and, in particular, its use as a living language and as an ordinary means of communication.

(Māori Language Act 1987 section 7)

However, quite independently of what TTW proposes, other government bodies, as well as institutions such as universities and tribal authorities, engage in planning exercises of various kinds. In the case of government bodies, the Ministry of Education, and particularly Te Puni Kōkiri (The Ministry of Māori Development) make very considerable contributions to this area.

The different usages in orthography associated with the University of Auckland on the one hand and most others on the other hand have been referred to in chapter 4. Loyalty to one or the other of these practices, each with a teacher's or institution's authority behind it, has led to sometimes quite ludicrous clashes of orthography. At one time the sign in Figure 7.1 hung in a corridor at the University of Waikato in Hamilton.

More positively, some universities have independently developed policies on Māori. Victoria University of Wellington and the University of Waikato, for instance, have policies allowing the use of Māori in work submitted for assessment. The University of Otago is unique in having promulgated a full Māori Language Policy which not only contains similar provision on the use of Māori in assessment, but also commits the University to a range of measures to promote Māori language within its activities.

Ngāitahu, the major tribe of the South Island, has developed its own language policy in the hope of reviving knowledge and use of Māori among its membership. As remarked above, the South Island underwent shift to English some two generations ahead of the North. Further, the dialect spoken historically in the South was the most divergent of Māori dialects. These two considerations have motivated the tribal authorities to adopt a policy called Kotahi Mano Kāika Kotahi Mano Wawata ('one thousand homes, one thousand desires/aspirations'), which aims to have Māori spoken in 1,000 homes within the tribe by 2025.[53]

Status planning

Many of the activities already described count as 'status planning' in that they are deliberately undertaken in order to make Māori a language for education, a language for the broadcast media, a language for serious modern literature, and so on.

Explicit planning and the discussion and development of goals has also occurred, largely within government circles, but the goals and strategies lack precision. The legislation itself, the Māori Language Act 1987, modelled in large part on the Welsh Language Act 1967, certainly raised Māori to the status of official language and implied, in its definitions of functions for TTW, the goal that Māori should be 'a living language and . . . an ordinary means of communication', but provides little guidance as to what either provision means or how they are to be achieved. Similarly, the government's major statements of Māori Language Policy (Te Puni Kōkiri 1999, 2003) list policy objectives such as 'increasing the numbers of Māori speakers, increasing the opportunities of Māori to be spoken and/or heard', without showing how such goals fit into an overall vision of the linguistic future of New Zealand.

Just as these government documents are vague on the desired outcome, beyond simply strengthening the language in some way, so there is clearly widespread ambivalence about quite what the position of Māori should be in New Zealand. Calls to make Māori compulsory in schools imply the position that Māori is a language for all New Zealanders. If successful, which would be highly unlikely, such a programme would make all New Zealanders bilingual, and lead to the probably undesirable state of affairs that the vast majority of speakers of Māori would be Pākehā.[54] The surveys of attitudes reported above show that there is a range of opinion, especially among Māori themselves, as to whether Māori language and culture are in some sense 'for all New Zealanders' or the exclusive preserve of the ethnically Māori.

Among the very few who have addressed the broader issues are Chrisp (1997) and Christensen (2001, 2003).[55] Chrisp argues that a diglossic model should be adopted as goal, and that efforts should concentrate on the promotion of Māori as preferred language among Māori in clearly Māori domains. To some extent this translates as 'firm up the status quo', but such is the precarious situation of Māori, even in traditional Māori domains,[56] that even this goal will require some considerable effort. Christensen agrees with the concentration on Māori households as the locus for revitalisation, but rejects the explicitly diglossic model as it perpetuates the present power relationships between the two languages.

Until there is more clarity on the matter of an agreed and explicit goal, the specific activities and efforts – effective as many of them are in their own way – will remain to some extent diffuse and rudderless.

Corpus planning

Kaplan and Baldauf (1997:38) list a number of aspects of language planning 'which are primarily linguistic and hence internal to language': 'orthographic innovation, pronunciation, changes in language structure, vocabulary expansion, simplification of registers, style, and the preparation of language material'. In the case of Māori, there has certainly been development in most of these areas in recent times,[57] but one can talk of conscious planning only with respect to orthography, vocabulary expansion and preparation of language materials.

In chapter 4 mention was made of the 'Orthographic Conventions' promulgated by TTW. These were an attempt to standardise practice in a range of aspects of orthography where variation was rife – such as use of hyphens, treatment of compounds – and to promote the use of macrons for the designation of the long vowels. In general, these are well thought out, but contain one or two points where greater consistency could have been achieved. For instance, it was arbitrarily decided that compound nouns should be spelt as one word if there are no more than four vowel symbols in the resulting form, otherwise as separate words. This leads to some pairs, such as *orokati* (*oro* 'phoneme/sound', *kati* 'closed') 'consonant' vs *oro puare* (*puare* 'open') 'vowel', being treated differently.

These conventions have been published on the TTW website, and are followed in all the TTW's own publications, including the monolingual dictionary which is in preparation at the time of writing. Interestingly, though the conventions are ostensibly about Māori and its spelling, the same document contains the Commission's attempt at corpus planning for English, by proscribing the use of English plural suffixes on words borrowed from Māori.

The continued disarray in the detail of Māori spelling to which reference was made in chapter 4 shows, however, that this instance of planning suffers as much as any other from the authority problem outlined above.

Vocabulary expansion

The area of corpus planning in which the most concerted effort has been expended is that of vocabulary expansion.[58] With the advances in Māori-medium education, the specific right to use Māori in courts granted by the Māori Language Act 1987 and, generally, the increased interest in using Māori not only privately but in the media and in government publications such as information brochures, Māori was being pressed into service in domains where it had not been used before or had not been used since the nineteenth century. In the case of these latter domains, a new atmosphere of purism meant that much of the older terminology, which was borrowed, could not be revived and would have to be replaced by modern coinages.

From its very inception, TTW took the view that, for the language to survive, it must be spoken, and for it to be spoken, it must be able to express what people, especially the younger generations, want to talk about. TTW saw the task of creation of new terminologies as part of its statutory function 'to promote the Māori language, and, in particular, its use as a living language and as an ordinary means of communication' (see above). For the first five or six years of its existence, the TTW members themselves spent a great deal of time at the monthly meetings working on sets of terminology. However, more recently this function has devolved to the TTW's staff, particularly those working in its translation and language-quality services. Quite a high proportion of this work has been ad hoc – for instance, in response to requests from Māori-medium broadcasters wanting a term for some news item they were about to present. However, much of the work was systematic, attacking important fields of vocabulary. The very first field to be approached was courtroom terminology, since it was clear people were going to exercise the right to speak Māori in such settings conferred by the Act as soon as possible. Further fields for which TTW developed vocabulary include sports terminology, especially athletics in time for the Commonwealth Games held in Auckland in 1990; public health, requested by the Ministry of Health for information brochures; household terminology, such as kitchenware. TTW's work has been published, primarily in two editions of its full lists, *Te Matatiki* (Te Taura Whiri i te Reo Māori 1992, 1996), and in its quarterly newsletter, *He Muka*.

In its creation of new terminology, TTW adopted a puristic position in the belief, probably correct, that borrowing would be unacceptable to many of the very people for whom the expanded vocabulary was intended. Instead, a range of devices were used which exploited existing vocabulary and the morphological possibilities of Māori.

The following table based on that in Harlow (1993b) illustrates the main types:

(1) circumlocution – the Māori term is an explanation not just a single word, e.g. *te tangata e whakapaetia ana* 'defendant', literally 'the person who is being accused'.

(2) though direct loans are avoided, calquing is frequent, e.g. *waikawa* 'acid', which is based on the same concept as the German *Säure* 'acid' from *sauer* 'bitter'; *tuarā* 'back' in rugby from 'back', part of body; *pōkairua* from Greek 'di-ploma' (*pōkai* 'fold', *rua* 'two');[59] *totomā* 'leukaemia' from Greek *leukos* 'white' and *haima* 'blood' (Māori *toto* 'blood', *mā* 'white').

(3) analogous compounds – from *tapuwae* 'footprint', a compound involving *wae* 'foot', we get *tapumati* 'fingerprint', *mati* from *matimati* 'finger' (Te Taura Whiri i te Reo Māori 1992; in the second edition, 1996, this item has been replaced by *tapukara*, formed in the same way, but based on *koikara* 'finger').

(4) specialisation of existing Māori words. There are many Māori words which used to be current and are found in the classical literature, but which are not part of modern colloquial speech. Many of these are being revived with some specialised meaning – e.g. types of kit, or basket: *kōnae* 'file (paper or computer)'; *pūkoro* 'pocket, condom (*pūkoro ure*)'; *pūtea* 'fund, budget'.[60]

(5) derivation by reduplication, e.g. *pāpāho* 'media' from *pāho* 'broadcast', itself a specialisation of the original meaning 'be noised abroad'; *kōpaepae* 'compact disc', from *kōpae* 'disc, diskette', specialised from 'circular'.

(6) derivation by affixation, e.g. *pūoro* 'music' by affixation of *pū-* to *oro* 'sound', itself specialised as 'phoneme' in linguistic terminology; *whaka-pane* 'to frank (letters)' from *pane* 'head' – 'stamp (head of king/queen)' by affixation of the causative prefix; *hāpono* 'prove' from *pono* 'true' (the causative *whakapono* has already been lexicalised as 'believe').

(7) shortening, e.g. *pū* from *pokapū* 'centre', as in *tuarā pū* 'centre back (sports position)', *Amerika pū* 'Central America'; *maraukoripi* 'cutlery' from *marau* 'fork', *koko* 'spoon' and *maripi* 'knife'; cf. also, above, the use of the simplex *mati* in *tapumati*. Further, *whare kano* 'ovary' from *kākano* 'seed'.

(8) Māorification of borrowings, especially placenames. *Ngāitīria* 'Nigeria', looks as though it includes the tribal name prefix *Ngāi*; *Huiterangi* 'Switzerland'.

Under calques, one must include examples such as *tapuhi*, to which Keegan (2005:137) draws attention. *Tapuhi* is originally a verb, one of whose English equivalents is 'to nurse'. Led by the homophony of English 'to nurse' and 'nurse (n.)', *Te Matatiki* proposes *tapuhi* as the Māori designation for the latter as well, despite the existence of the well-established loan *nēhi*.

An early policy decision of TTW had been that, while its own terminological work would not make use of borrowings, existing widely used loanwords, many of them in the language since the first half of the nineteenth century, would be allowed to stand. As can be seen from the example of *nēhi* 'nurse' just mentioned, this policy was not always adhered to. One of the most controversial lexicological proposals of TTW was the promotion of one set of traditional terms for the months of the year. The pre-contact Māori calendar operated with twelve or thirteen lunar months beginning at about the winter solstice. There were many systems of names in use over the whole country (Best 1973). However, with the introduction of the Gregorian calendar by the missionaries, borrowed names, such as *Hānuere* 'January', *Mei* 'May', and so on, had been in use and widely known since the 1840s. TTW suggested the reintroduction of one particular set of traditional names (from Tūhoe, eastern Bay of Plenty), moving them so that they aligned with the modern calendar, and at the same time urging people to start using their own traditional sets of terms. No one seems to have taken up this last challenge; however, many – especially younger – second-language speakers of Māori and institutions such as the Kura Kaupapa Māori have enthusiastically embraced the new/old terms. Though there are now many other items in the vocabulary of the younger generations which would be unfamiliar to older native speakers, it is this set of terms more than any other which has provoked complaints of unintelligibility.

TTW is by no means the only source of neologisms in modern Māori. Many individuals and, above all, institutions and specific educational projects have contributed. One of the most successful such contributions was the coinage of *rorohiko* (*roro* 'brain', *hiko* 'lightning' and hence 'electricity') for 'computer' by Katarina Mataira in a children's book about space travel (1975). The development of educational materials, especially curriculum statements,[61] usually with the cooperation of TTW, has produced large amounts of specialist vocabulary.

The rather diffuse approach to vocabulary expansion in Māori has meant that this exercise shows signs of the same problems which beset the whole language planning enterprise, and there has been an unfortunate proliferation of often-competing terminologies, and a tendency to reinvent the wheel. The most pronounced example of this of which I am aware is the matter of grammatical terminology; at least five sets have been proposed, many of these related and overlapping, so that a sort of family tree of terminologies is almost possible.[62]

One example chosen at random illustrates a situation which is by no means untypical. Māori has had a word for 'bayonet' since at least the 1870s. *Pēneti*, clearly a loan, appears in newspapers from that time on, though almost certainly, given the fraught history of earlier decades, it was already in use at least thirty to forty years earlier. It remained current throughout the two major wars of the twentieth century, being used, for instance, by Pōtatau (1991) in his reminiscences of war service. However, more recent proposals provide good examples both of the devices used for the creation of neologisms and of the disregard for well-established loans. Cleave *et al.* (1978:45) suggest *okapū*, an innovative compound created from *oka* 'knife' and *pū* 'gun', while TTW in the second edition of its compendium of new words (Te Taura Whiri i te Reo Māori 1996) proposes *matarere*, an already existing word with the meaning of 'detachable spear point'.

The dissemination of new vocabulary proceeds in the first instance through publications of the sort already mentioned – TTW's *Te Matatiki*, its newsletter *He Muka*, and the curriculum documents published by the Ministry of Education. Modern dictionaries such as Ngata's (1993) popular English–Māori dictionary[63] and Ryan's (1995) voluminous bidirectional dictionary incorporated neologisms created up to the time of their publication. In addition, there are electronic resources providing access to the often bewildering range of modern vocabulary. *Kimikupu hou* ('search-words new') is a searchable lexical database founded initially in 1994, and built up and maintained by Richard Benton at the New Zealand Council for Educational Research. It was an attempt to coordinate all the lexical expansion being carried out in schools, the government, universities and so on. At present this database is accessible only through *Wakareo ā-ipurangi*, an online subscription resource[64] which allows searching of a range of dictionaries, such as H. W. Williams (1971), Ngata (1993), *Te Matatiki* (Te Taura Whiri i te Reo Māori 1996), as well as *Kimikupu hou*.

It is of course all very well to have look-up resources and dictionaries listing newly proposed vocabulary items. Just as important are the means whereby these items are brought to the notice of the Māori-speaking population in an intelligible way, so that they have a chance to become part of the living language. Māori-language broadcasting, both radio and television, plays an important role here, and the wide range of types of programme now being broadcast gives a high proportion of the new vocabulary an airing. The only other medium having any effect in this direction is Māori-medium schooling. Not only teachers and pupils, who use new vocabulary in their work with the central curriculum areas, but parents and caregivers, who, as we have seen, are rather more heavily involved in the running of the schools than is normally the case with mainstream establishments, become familiar with at least some of the new vocabulary. Apart from these two channels, however, there would be little effective dissemination of new coinages or usages. Some of the terminological work has been carried out with the purpose of publishing Māori versions of information brochures, especially in the areas of policy and health, but it is very unlikely that such literature would be at all effective in propagating new vocabulary. Indeed, it is unlikely that these publications serve any purpose other than making the language visible in the public domain, in itself a valuable contribution to the status of the language.

There has been no systematic research on the reception of new terminologies – it is, however, possible to say that they have not enjoyed universal adoption. A number of factors contribute to reserve among many, particularly older, speakers, apart from the simple unfamiliarity of the new usages. The existence of competing terms in many instances, and attempts to replace already widely used words with new coinages (see remarks on month names above) do not help the acceptability of the whole exercise. Dialect loyalty, a correlate of the authority issue discussed above, has led to suspicion of any centralised planning at all, and to a rejection of at least some coinages on the grounds that 'these words are not part of my dialect'. Criticism of specific items can also be heard. Keegan (2005:141–2) refers to Reedy's point that *hangarau*, the usual modern term corresponding to English 'technology', is a form already existing in some dialects of Māori and meaning 'to jest with, befool'.

Language materials

Since the earliest contacts, language materials have been produced, particularly in the form of textbooks and dictionaries. These have been briefly reviewed in chapter 1. In the modern period, however, there has been some deliberate preparation of language materials in the pursuit of particular planning goals. Clearly the curriculum statements mentioned above fall under this heading; they are designed to facilitate the use of Māori as the language of tuition for a range of core subject areas in the school curriculum up to year 10 (roughly ages fourteen to fifteen).

In addition, two other items deserve mention. In 1990, TTW published a booklet (revised and expanded in 1997, see Te Taura Whiri i te Reo Māori 1990) designed to help and encourage the use of Māori in business and government by providing vocabulary and phrases for activities such as advertising 'situations vacant', answering the telephone, and writing, or at least heading, business letters. Second, at the time of writing, there are two projects underway to produce monolingual dictionaries of Māori: one in a private publishing house, Huia, in Wellington, and the other government-funded and administered by TTW. The purpose of these projects is not only practical, to provide a resource for Māori-medium schools, but also directed to the status-goal of freeing Māori from dependence upon English for its description. That is, these dictionaries are intended to enhance the perception of autonomy and self-sufficiency of the language.

Language death?

Is Māori dying? Certainly, it is endangered in the sense of Crystal (2000:20), and has a chance of survival only 'in favourable circumstances and with a growth in community support'. Certainly, its continued use will be a matter of conscious and conscientious effort for the foreseeable future. Certainly too, the language has seen a restriction both in the domains for which it is a preferred language, and in the demography of its use within the Māori community. Further than that, the modern language is showing signs in its structure and usage of the types of phenomena often associated with 'language death'.[65]

Very many, especially younger, speakers have acquired Māori as a second language, and, depending on their level of exposure to 'good' Māori, interference from their first language, English, is very often observable.[66] Some instances of this interference are so common that one must concede that they have become part of the language. Space precludes more than a couple of examples here.[67] *Taea* is the passive form of *tae* 'arrive, achieve', and is used to express ability, achievability. In its inherited usage, *taea* as predicate takes an agent marked with *e* (as do passives generally), a patient in the nominative, and a zero nominalisation of the 'main' verb, e.g. (repeated from chapter 6):

> *Ka taea   e koe   tēnei mahi te mahi?*
> TA achieve.Pass. P 2Sg. Det. task   te do
> 'Can you do this task?'

It is now very common to hear this verb constructed with the agent as subject and the 'main' verb as a complement marked with *ki te*[68] with any patient marked as the object of the 'main' verb:

> *Ka taea   koe ki.te   mahi i   tēnei mahi?*
> TA 'be.able' 2Sg. Comp. do   Obj. Det. task
> 'Can you do this task?'

Not only that, it is now frequently in the sense of 'have permission'. Both the usage and the meaning have changed in the direction and under the influence of English 'can'.

As mentioned in chapter 6, complements of transitive and middle verbs are marked with the prepositions *i* and *ki*. However, two common verbs whose translation equivalents in English require 'for', *tatari* 'wait for' and *tono* 'apply for', are now very frequently heard with an object marked with *mō*, the possessive and benefactive preposition 'for'.

Such morphology as there is is being simplified; those few nouns with distinct plural forms are now frequently used invariantly.

As good models become rarer, there is increasing uncertainty about some of the more complex aspects of the grammar. Benton (1991:15) refers to confusion over the possessive *a* and *o* categories (see chapter 6). Similarly, examples of 'wrong' use of negatives are by no means uncommon. Thus, one hears

> *Kāore he   pātai   māma tēnā.*
> Neg. Det. question easy   Det.
> 'That's not an easy question.'

using the negative for verbal and some prepositional predicates instead of the correct *ehara*, which negates nominal predicates.[69]

Teachers report the occurrence in the speech of some of their pupils of a phenomenon which is completely ungrammatical in Māori, but follows an English model. In answering a question, it is normal in English to omit all of a verb phrase except an auxiliary: 'Have you done your teeth?' 'Yes, I have.' Since aspect and to a lesser extent mood are expressed in Māori by means of particles which must be accompanied by lexical material, an analogous deletion is not possible. Nonetheless, exchanges like the following are now encountered:

> *Kua oti   tō   mahi?*
> TA finished your task
> 'Have you finished your work?'

> *Āe, kua.*
> Yes TA
> 'Yes, (I) have.'

Vocabulary is also subject to such interference. In chapter 2 mention was made of the extension of words such as *tapu* to cover the introduced concept 'holy'. Much of the deliberate vocabulary expansion work carried out in recent times has the implicit goal of making the Māori vocabulary more isomorphic with that of English. In addition, however, similar shifts of meaning have occurred in the modern language, leading to words having the same sense as some English model. The most glaring example is that of *puru*, originally 'a bung, plug, to insert, to plug up', which is now widely used exactly like 'put' in English. Similarly, the word *tika* 'correct, right' is now used to mean 'right' as in 'right to free speech', etc.

Crystal (2000:22) identifies an increase in code-switching as an aspect of imminent language death. Despite the prevalent purism, code-switching – Māori speech with the insertion of English morphemes, words and phrases, called *reo māwhitiwhiti* 'grasshopper speech' – is common.[70] However, this is true even of the most fluent elderly speakers, and thus not necessarily a symptom of decreasing knowledge of the language over recent generations. This last point of course raises the question of when a phenomenon of language contact can be seen as threatening and a sign of language moribundity, and when it is a matter of natural, by no means unhealthy contact, and a source of change in the languages concerned. Languages have after all been in contact throughout history, and many examples of stable bilingual/multilingual situations exist. However, language change of the sort sketched above, when it occurs in conjunction with the historical pressures towards language shift, is most plausibly taken to be caused by the reduction of domains and the paucity of good models – that is, by language at least on the slide towards loss.[71]

Conclusion

Māori will certainly survive as an important mark of Māori cultural and ethnic identity; its use for formal speech making, calling, and performing is also assured. However, its survival as a language of conversation and everyday use, even to the extent observable now, not to mention its being extended into yet more domains and a wider cross-section of Māori society, will probably always remain dependent on conscious effort and commitment. Time alone will tell, but both complacency about its security and a defeatist position which gives up the effort now will certainly lead to the loss of yet another instance of human diversity.

NOTES

1. The contact phenomena in the language are due virtually entirely to English. There are one or two loans from other languages (see chapter 2).
2. Important general references on the whole topic of the situation of Māori and its revitalisation are: Benton (1997), Benton and Benton (2001), Fishman (1991:230–51), Reedy (2000), Spolsky (2003, 2005). See also Peter Keegan's website: www.maorilanguage.info/mao_lang_abib.html, for some comment and further references.
3. Over this period, I have participated in a number of aspects of the recent attempts at language maintenance and revitalisation as a teacher, researcher, parent of a child who took part in Māori immersion education, and as a foundation member of Te Taura Whiri i te Reo Māori ('The Māori Language Commission').
4. See also Davidson (1981:11) and Owens (1981:49).
5. 16.16% and 14.08% respectively of the census-night population of 3,737,277 – see Statistics New Zealand (2002). Some of the increases in numbers between one census and the next are quite striking. For instance, there is an increase of over 25% between 1986 and 1991. What is not clear is how far this may be due to increasing pride in Māori ethnicity and descent over the last twenty or so years rather than to actual increases of this order in the people really of Māori origin. We return to the 'Māori renaissance' below.
6. Benton (1997), which is based on the wide-ranging survey to which we return below, contains very considerable detail of the progress of this shift in different localities, along with discussion of the factors leading to the different rates observed.
7. Pursuant to the signing of the Treaty of Waitangi on 6 February 1840, on which see more detail below.

8. See Parkinson (2001c), which contains a great deal of detail on the policy and its implementation, including lists of those documents which actually were translated.

9. See also Benton (1981:16).

10. See especially Benton (1997). Though published quite some time after the survey, this is the fullest account and interpretation in one work. The results for individual communities were published in the 1980s as leaflets, with Benton (1984) providing a summary of the first 100 communities analysed.

11. 'Very high' and 'high' are the top two levels in the seven-point scale of fluency used.

12. Kōhanga Reo and Kura Kaupapa Māori, which began in the 1980s. See further below on these initiatives.

13. Statistics New Zealand (2002). See also Starks *et al.* (2005).

14. Christensen (2003:59–60) is an invaluable summary of the self-assessment language proficiency questions in these surveys and their results.

15. Māori is of course by no means alone in this predicament; very many languages in all parts of the world are endangered, and, in very many such cases, there are efforts being made to ensure the survival of these endangered languages. Most of the issues and approaches have parallels with what is happening in New Zealand. General books on the subject of language revitalisation include Fishman (1991, 2001) and Grenoble and Whaley (2006).

16. Biggs' prediction was by no means the first. As early as 1905, it was claimed that Māori would die out in two generations because of the importance of English (Walker 2001:110–11).

17. Ngata (1986 vol.I:165, 182; vol.II:191; vol.III:199). See also Walker (2004:193). On Ngata's life and work generally, see Walker (2001).

18. King (2003:478, 482–3), Walker (2004:209–12, 221).

19. Each of these areas is of course a wide-ranging topic in its own right with a full and varied literature. With respect to modern Māori writing in both languages, Ihimaera *et al.* (1992–6) give a very good survey of the range of material being produced in recent times.

20. See histories such as King (2003), Walker (2004).

21. On the Treaty of Waitangi and the history of its treatment in New Zealand law, see Orange (1987).

22. This is a summary version of the full recommendations provided by the Tribunal's website, see www.waitangi-tribunal.govt.nz/reports/generic/wai11/, where the full report is also available.

23. The formulation suggests there are other official languages. In fact, at the time of writing (legislation is being prepared to give New Zealand Sign Language similar status), Māori is the only *de iure* official language, though clearly English is so *de facto* and, in very many respects, is clearly the only official language (currency is monolingual; passports, though containing a page of instructions in Māori, have person specifications only in French and English; immigration forms contain the instruction that they must be filled in in English; and so on). On the other hand, much official information – e.g. brochures on health, census forms – now appears in both languages.

24. Designated Te Kōmihana Mō Te Reo Māori in the Act, but changing its name to Te Taura Whiri i te Reo Māori in the Māori Language Amendment Act 1991.

25. The right to submit written material to courts in Māori, or to ask to be addressed in Māori, is not included in the Act.
26. See Chrisp (1998). Some departments have produced bilingual information booklets and brochures, as well as employment advertisements, especially in areas of direct concern to Māori, such as Māori Affairs policy, health, justice.
27. This provision replaced a long-standing system of licensing interpreters, particularly for the Māori Land Court, which was founded in 1865 as the Native Land Court, and which has jurisdiction to determine issues of title to land held under traditional tenure.
28. These remain important aspects of TTW's activities, though emphases have shifted – see www.tetaurawhiri.govt.nz.
29. See, especially, Benton (1981) for detail on developments up to that date, and Walker (2004:238–43) for more recent events.
30. This designation for the traditional house of learning is now used as the equivalent of English 'university'. On the traditional houses, see Best (1974) and Mead (2003:306–12).
31. 'Spells, charms, incantations'. There were *karakia* appropriate for all sorts of activities and occasions, and many are still used, see Te Rangi Hīroa (1949:489–507), Barlow (1991:36–7).
32. The best-known of these, thanks to its members' decision to commit their teaching to writing in the 1860s, was situated in the Wairarapa, the south-eastern area of the North Island. See Smith (1913–15) and Thornton (2004).
33. This was not a linear progression, and the policy 'softened' from time to time depending on the officials involved (Benton 1981:45).
34. Walker (2004:194), Pawley (1981:10–11).
35. Part 4 existed in manuscript without English translation till its publication as Ngata (1990).
36. See especially Fishman (1991), Benton and Benton (2001) and Walker (2004:238–9). The Kōhanga Reo National trust has a website at www.kohanga.ac.nz with information about present structures and goals. For statistics, see the Ministry of Education's site www.minedu.govt.nz, under 'Early childhood'.
37. Parents interviewed in the research for Te Hoe Nuku Roa report this as a concern: Christensen (2001:21).
38. As is the document *Te Aho Matua* ('the main thread') (see www.piripono.school.nz/english_te_aho_matua.htm), which sets out the values and curriculum goals which define and guide KKM. On KKM generally, see the references for TKR above.
39. Ministry of Education (1996a, 1996b, 1996c, 1999a, 1999b, 2000).
40. In recent years, these newspapers have been the subject of considerable academic work, and have been published as web documents (see www.nzdl.org/cgi-bin/library?a=p&p=about&c=niupepa&l=en&nw=utf-8). Curnow *et al.* (2002) is a collection of essays on the Māori newpapers, and Orbell (2002) presents a selection of letters to the editors of these papers with English translation and comment.
41. See Parkinson (2001c).
42. On these movements, as well as the Ratana Church, which combines both religious and political purposes, see Walker (2004).

43. For an account of Māori-language broadcasting and analysis of its goals and effectiveness, see Hollings (2005). See also Walker (2004:331–9).
44. Literally, a container for a much treasured feather of the huia bird, now extinct. Here the meaning is extended to designate a vehicle/medium for the recording of valued recollections and knowledge.
45. This fee is no longer collected, but Te Māngai Pāho continues to be funded at the same level.
46. 'Mainstream' channels continue to broadcast the series *Te Karere* and *Waka Huia*, and occasional single programmes in Māori.
47. See Harlow (2002) for comment on the motivation for this translation, as well as the role of such translations in language maintenance exercises.
48. See Mutu (2001) for a view of the importance of Māori for identity, because the language is the vehicle of the sayings (*pepeha*) by which Māori identify themselves within the geographical, historical and tribal landscape of New Zealand.
49. See Boyce (2005) for a full summary of these surveys.
50. See Harlow (2005). This ideology is not explicitly stated or even consciously held, but directs some actions and opinions, which are in my view at best tangential to the explicitly held goals of revitalisation.
51. Waite (1992), a very thoughtful language policy discussion document which was commissioned by the Department of Education, but which unfortunately has enjoyed no follow-up or implementation, makes proposals about Māori within the wider context of the languages of New Zealand. Waite is of the view that revitalisation of Māori is of the highest priority for any language policy. See also Benton (1996) and Peddie (2005).
52. See Harlow (2003) for fuller discussion.
53. See their site, www.kotahimanokaika.com, which also contains links to resources. See also Hohepa (2000) for examples from other tribal areas.
54. What is sometimes meant by such calls is the idea that a little exposure to the language will improve the general population's attitudes to its importance. However, it is probably the case that this can be achieved in other ways which do not require the entire teaching profession to be language teachers.
55. See also brief remarks on this in Keegan (2005), Spolsky (2005) and Harlow (2003).
56. Chrisp (1997:41) follows Waite's (1992) language policy discussion document in identifying Māori homes and neighbourhoods, schools, religion, marae and workplaces as to target domains.
57. See chapter 2 for remarks on recent changes in phonology, and chapter 6 and this chapter for some examples of changes in language structure probably due to English interference on the language of the younger generations. The deliberate extension of Māori into new domains has led spontaneously, not so much to simplification of registers, as to the creation of new ones – e.g. officialese, legal – as more and more documents appear in both languages.
58. See, especially, Keegan (2005), Harlow (1993a, 1993b).
59. In the second edition of *Te Matatiki* (Te Taura Whiri i te Reo Māori 1996), this is replaced by *tītohu* (*tī-* < '**di**ploma', and *tohu* 'sign', now a general term for 'qualification'). I asked staff at TTW why the change had been made, and was told

that it was because no one could remember the etymology of *pōkairua* when the second edition was being prepared.

60. Among the more interesting examples of this device is the use of *hākinakina* for 'sport' in the sense of games, athletics, etc. The word occurs once in older Māori literature and is indeed glossed in H. W. Williams (1971) as 'sport'. However, the context makes it clear that the word is a verb, and that Williams' gloss is something of a euphemism for sexual intercourse. The word has nonetheless become the usual and widely known term corresponding to English 'sport'.

61. Ministry of Education (1996a, 1996b, 1996c, 1999a, 1999b, 2000). These are curriculum statements for, respectively, Mathematics, Science, Māori Language, Technology, Arts, Social Studies, for use in Māori-medium education. On the development of mathematical terminology, see, especially, Barton *et al.* (1995).

62. See Harlow (2003) for some detail on this. Since publication of that article, a further set of terms has been agreed upon by the monolingual dictionary project. While based on the set devised by Cleve Barlow for his translation of Biggs (1969, = Biggs 1990b), it nonetheless goes its own way at a number of points.

63. Available online at: www.learningmedia.co.nz/ngata/.

64. See www.reotupu.co.nz/wakareo.

65. See, especially, Crystal (2000) and Crowley (1997:279–83).

66. And is a cause for concern among native speakers of the language, see Christensen (2001:26–8).

67. See Harlow (1991a:35–8, 2001:45, 74, 155, 164, 184, 191) for these and others.

68. Literally, 'to the', and used, for instance, for goal adjuncts. However, these particles also introduce the complement of verbs of wanting, *inter alia*; see chapter 6.

69. See chapter 6. It must be conceded that at least Hawaiian and Rarotongan, among closely related languages, have spontaneously generalised the verbal negation in an analogous way. However, in the present case, it is almost certainly due to insufficient exposure to the correct negation.

70. See Benton (1991:14–15) and Eliasson (1989, 1995). On code-switching in the other direction as a feature of Māori writing in English, see Gordon and Williams (1998).

71. On the general phenomenon of language death and loss, see, for instance, Nettle and Romaine (2000).

References

Acson, Veneeta Z., and Richard L. Leed (eds.). 1985. *For Gordon H. Fairbanks*. Oceanic Linguistics Special Publication 20. Honolulu: University of Hawaii Press.

Anttila, Raimo. 1972. *An Introduction to Historical and Comparative Linguistics*. New York: Macmillan.

Aubert, Mother Mary. 1885. *New and Complete Manual of Maori Conversation*. Wellington: Lyon and Blair. Reprinted 1905, 1909, 1914. Appeared subsequently, in 1901, as 1st edition of A. T. Ngata (1926).

Baldi, Philip (ed.). 1990. *Linguistic Change and Reconstruction Methodology*. Trends in Linguistics Studies and Monographs 45. Berlin and New York: Mouton de Gruyter.

Banks, Joseph. 1962. *The Endeavour Journal of Joseph Banks: 1768–1771*. Ed. J. C. Beaglehole, 2 vols. Sydney: The Trustees of the Public Library of New South Wales in association with Angus and Robertson.

Barlow, Cleve. 1991. *Tikanga Whakaaro: Key Concepts in Māori Culture*. Auckland: Oxford University Press.

Barnard, Roger, and Ray Harlow (eds.). 2001. *Proceedings of the Conference 'Bilingualism at the Ends of the Earth', University of Waikato, November 2000*. Hamilton, NZ: Department of General and Applied Linguistics, University of Waikato.

Barton, Bill, Uenuku Fairhall and Tony Trinick. 1995. He Korero Kupu Tatai: Word Stories in Maori Mathematics Vocabulary Development. In Bill Barton and Uenuku Fairhall (eds.), *Mathematics In Maori Education*. Auckland: The University of Auckland, Mathematics Education Unit, pp. 25–32.

Baucke, William. 1922. An Extinct Race. *New Zealand Herald*. Auckland. 8 July – 14 October.

　1928. The Life and Customs of the Moriori. In H. D. Skinner and William Baucke (eds.), *The Morioris*. Memoir 9(5). Honolulu: Bishop Museum, pp. 357–84.

Bauer, Winifred A. 1981a. Aspects of the Grammar of Maori. Ph.D. thesis. University of Edinburgh.

　1981b. *Hae.re* vs. *ha.e.re*: A Note. *Te Reo* 24: 31–6.

　1982. Relativization in Maori. *Studies in Language* 6: 305–42.

　1983. Experience Verbs in Maori. *Te Reo* 26: 3–28.

　1991. Maori *ko* Again. *Te Reo* 34: 3–14.

　1993. *Maori*. London and New York: Routledge.

　1997. *The Reed Reference Grammar of Maori*. Auckland: Reed.

Begg, A. Charles, and Neil C. Begg. 1966. *Dusky Bay*. Christchurch: Whitcombe & Tombs.

　1979. *The World of John Boultbee*. Christchurch: Whitcoulls.

Bell, Allan, Ray Harlow and Donna Starks (eds.). 2005. *Languages of New Zealand.* Wellington: Victoria University Press.

Benton, Richard. 1981. *The Flight of the Amokura. Oceanic Languages and Formal Education in the South Pacific.* Wellington: New Zealand Council for Educational Research.

 1982. *Ko ngā kupu pū noa o te reo Māori. The First Basic Maori Word List.* Wellington: New Zealand Council for Educational Research.

 1984. *The Maori Language in a Hundred Communities.* Wellington: New Zealand Council for Educational Research.

 1991. The History and Development of the Māori Language. In McGregor and Williams (1991:1–18).

 1996. Language Planning in New Zealand: Defining the Ineffable. In Michael L. Herriman and Barbara Burnaby (eds.), *Language Policies in English-Dominated Countries.* Clevedon and Philadelphia: Multilingual Matters, pp. 62–98.

 1997. *The Maori Language: Dying or Reviving?* Wellington: New Zealand Council for Educational Research. (First appeared in the Alumni-in-Residence Working Paper Series of the East-West Centre, Honolulu, in 1991.)

Benton, Richard, and Nena Benton. 2001. RLS in Aotearoa / New Zealand 1989–1999. In Fishman (2001:423–50).

Best, Elsdon. 1906. Maori Numeration: Some Account of the Single, Binary, and Semi-vigesimal Systems of Numeration Formerly Used by the Maori. *Transactions and Proceedings of the New Zealand Institute* 39: 150–80.

 1973. *The Maori Division of Time.* Dominion Museum Monograph 4. Wellington: Government Printer.

 1974. *The Maori School of Learning.* Dominion Museum Monograph 6. Wellington: Government Printer.

Biggs, Bruce. 1961. The Structure of New Zealand Maaori. *Anthropological Linguistics* 3.3: 1–54.

 1966. *English–Maori Dictionary.* Wellington: Reed.

 1968. The Maori Language Past and Present. In E. Schwimmer (ed.), *The Maori People in the Nineteen-sixties.* Auckland: Longman Paul, pp. 65–84.

 1969. *Let's Learn Maori.* Wellington: A. H. and A. W. Reed.

 1971. The Languages of Polynesia. In Thomas A. Sebeok (ed.), *Current Trends in Linguistics,* vol. VIII: *Linguistics in Oceania.* The Hague: Mouton, pp. 466–505.

 1978. The History of Polynesian Phonology. In Wurm and Carrington (1978:691–716).

 1980. Traditional Maori Song Texts and the 'Rule of Eight'. *Pānui* (Anthropology Department, University of Auckland) 3: 48–50.

 1981. *The Complete English–Maori Dictionary.* Auckland: Auckland University Press and Oxford University Press.

 1989. Towards a Study of Maori Dialects. In Harlow and Hooper (1989:61–75).

 1990a. *English–Maori Maori–English Dictionary.* Auckland: Auckland University Press.

 1990b. *Me ako taatou i te reo Māori.* Translation of Biggs (1969) by Cleve Barlow. Auckland: Billy King Holdings Ltd.

 1991. A Linguist Revisits the New Zealand Bush. In Andrew Pawley (ed.), *Man and a Half. Essays in Pacific Anthropology and Ethnobiology in Honour of Ralph Bulmer.* Auckland: Polynesian Society, pp. 67–72.

1994a. Does Maori have a Closest Relative? In Sutton (1994:96–105).

1994b. New Words for a New World. In A. K. Pawley and M. D. Ross (eds.), *Austronesian Terminologies: Continuity and Change*. Pacific Linguistics C-127. Canberra: Australian National University, pp. 21–9.

2000a. POLLEX. (Polynesian Lexicon.) Computer file. *Department of Anthropology, University of Auckland*.

2000b. *Te Paanui A Wai-Wharariki*, February 2000. Māori Department, Auckland: University of Auckland.

Blevins, Juliette. 1994. A Phonological and Morphological Reanalysis of the Maori Passive. *Te Reo* 37: 29–53.

Blust, Robert A. 1977. The Proto-Austronesian Pronouns and Austronesian Subgrouping: A Preliminary Report. *Working Papers in Linguistics, University of Hawaii* 9.2: 1–15.

1978. Eastern Malayo-Polynesian: A Subgrouping Argument. In Wurm and Carrington (1978:181–234).

1984. More on the Position of the Languages of Eastern Indonesia. *Oceanic Linguistics* 23: 1–28.

1987. The Linguistic Study of Indonesia. *Archipel* 34: 27–47.

1990. Patterns of Sound Change in the Austronesian Languages. In Baldi (1990: 231–67).

1993. Central and Central-Eastern Malayo-Polynesian. *Oceanic Linguistics* 32: 241–93.

Boyce, Mary. 1992. Māori Language in Porirua: A Study of Reported Proficiency, Patterns of Use and Attitudes. Unpublished MA thesis. Victoria University of Wellington.

2005. Attitudes to Māori. In Bell *et al.* (2005:86–110).

Brown, Andrea, Marc Cullinane, Andrew Reid and Iain Vernon. 1990. New Zealanders' Attitudes to a Bilingual Society. A research report prepared for the Māori Language Commission and Department of Māori Studies, Massey University, July 1990.

Campbell, Lyle. 1999. *Historical Linguistics: An Introduction*. Cambridge, Mass.: The MIT Press.

Carstairs, Andrew. 1970. Agency and Possession in Maori. Unpublished term paper. MIT.

Chambers, J. K., and Peter Trudgill. 1998. *Dialectology*. 2nd edition. Cambridge: Cambridge University Press.

Chrisp, Steven. 1997. Diglossia: A Theoretical Framework for the Revitalisation of the Māori language. *He Pukenga Kōrero* 2.2: 35–42.

1998. Government Services and the Revitalisation of the Maori Language; Policies and Practices. *Te Reo* 41: 106–15.

Christensen, Ian. 2001. Māori Language Revitalisation and Maintenance: Issues and Insights. *New Zealand Studies in Applied Linguistics* 7: 15–40.

2003. Proficiency, Use and Transmission: Māori Language Revitalisation. *New Zealand Studies in Applied Linguistics* 9.1: 41–61.

Christensen, Ian, T. E. Black, A. E. Durie, M. H. Durie, E. D. Fitzgerald and J. T. Taiapa. 1997. Māori Language in the Manawatū-Whanganui Region: Analysis and Discussion of Preliminary Findings from the Te Hoe Nuku Roa Household Survey. *He Pukenga Kōrero* 2.2: 24–30.

Chung, Sandra. 1977. Maori as an Accusative Language. *Journal of the Polynesian Society* 86: 355–70.

1978. *Case-Marking and Grammatical Relations in Polynesian*. Austin and London: University of Texas Press.

Chung, Sandra, Te Haumihiata Mason and J. W. Milroy. 1995. On Maori *he* and the Use of Indefinites. *Journal of the Polynesian Society* 104: 429–59.

Chung, Sandra and William A. Ladusaw. 2004. *Restriction and Saturation*. Linguistic Inquiry Monograph 42. Cambridge, Mass.: MIT Press.

Churchward, C. M. 1953. *Tongan Grammar*. Oxford: Oxford University Press.

Clark, Ross. 1973. Transitivity and Case in Eastern Oceanic. *Oceanic Linguistics* 12: 559–605.

1976. *Aspects of Proto-Polynesian Syntax*. Te Reo Monograph. Auckland: Linguistic Society of New Zealand.

1981. Inside and Outside Polynesian Nominalizations. In Hollyman and Pawley (1981:65–81).

1994. Moriori and Maori: The Linguistic Evidence. In Sutton (1994:123–35).

1995. From Accusative to Ergative and Back Again. Paper presented at the Second International Conference on Oceanic Linguistics. Suva, Fiji, July 1995.

1997. What is *he* Really Like? Paper presented at the Third International Conference on Oceanic Linguistics. Hamilton, NZ.

1999. Proto-Polynesian Numerals. In E. Zeitoun and P. J.-K. Li (eds.), *Selected Papers from the Eighth International Conference on Austronesian Linguistics*. Taipei: Academia Sinica, pp. 195–204.

2000. The Definite Article and the Authenticity of Moriori. *Rongorongo Studies* 10.1: 13–26.

Cleave, Peter, Katarina Mataira and Rangimarie Pere. 1978. *Oxford Maori Picture Dictionary*. Oxford: Oxford University Press.

Clements, G. N., and Elizabeth Hume. 1995. Internal Organisation of Speech Sounds. In John Goldsmith (ed.), *The Handbook of Phonological Theory*. Oxford: Blackwell, pp. 245–306.

Comrie, Bernard. 1989. *Language Universals and Linguistic Typology*. Chicago: University of Chicago Press.

Crowley, Terry. 1997. *An Introduction to Historical Linguistics*. 3rd edition. Auckland: Oxford University Press.

Crystal, David. 2000. *Language Death*. Cambridge: Cambridge University Press.

Curnow, Jenifer, Ngapare Hopa and Jane McRae (eds.). 2002. *Rere atu, taku manu! Discovering History, Language and Politics in the Maori-Language Newspapers*. Auckland: Auckland University Press.

Davidson, Janet M. 1981. The Polynesian Foundation. In Oliver (1981:3–27).

Davidson, Janet M., Geoffrey Irwin, Foss Leach, Andrew Pawley and Dorothy Brown (eds.). 1996. *Oceanic Culture History: Essays in Honour of Roger Green*. Dunedin: New Zealand Journal of Archæology Special Publication.

Deighton, Samuel. 1889. A Moriori Vocabulary. *Appendices to the Journal of the House of Representatives* (Wellington), 2. G-5: 1–7.

de Lacy, Paul. 1996. Circumscription Revisited: An Analysis of Maori Reduplication. ROA-133–0496. Rutgers Optimality Archive, Rutgers University (URL = http://roa.rutgers.edu).

1997. A Co-occurrence Restriction in Maori. *Te Reo* 40: 10–44.

2001. Predicate Nominals and Equatives in Maori. Rutgers University Minimalist Syntax Archive #179.

2003a. Maximal Words and the Maori Passive. In John McCarthy (ed.), *Optimality Theory in Phonology: A Reader*. Oxford: Blackwell Publishers, pp. 495–512.

2003b. Constraint Universality and Prosodic Phrasing in Maori. In A. Carpenter, A. Coetzee and P. de Lacy (eds.), *Papers in Optimality Theory II*. Amherst: GLSA, pp. 59–79.

msa. *Focus and Prosodic Phrasing in Maori*. University of Massachusetts, Amherst.

msb. *Intonation in Maori*. University of Massachusetts, Amherst.

Duval, Terry. 1992. The French Contribution to the Maori Language. In John Dunmore (ed.), *French and the Maori*. Waikanae: The Heritage Press Ltd., pp. 132–8.

1995. A Preliminary Dictionary of Maori Gainwords Compiled on Historical Principles. Ph.D. thesis. University of Canterbury, Christchurch.

Elbert, Samuel H., and Mary Kawena Pukui. 1979. *Hawaiian Grammar*. Honolulu: The University of Hawaii Press.

Eliasson, Stig. 1989. English–Maori Language Contact: Code-switching and the Free-morpheme Constraint. *RUUL (Reports from Uppsala University Department of Linguistics)* 18: 1–28.

1995. Grammatical and Lexical Switching in Maori–English 'Grasshopper Speech'. *RUUL (Reports from Uppsala University Department of Linguistics)* 28: 63–80.

Fischer, Steven Roger. 1997. *Glyphbreaker*. New York: Copernicus.

(ed.). 2000. *Possessive Markers in Central Pacific Languages. Sprachtypologie und Universalienforschung* 53.3/4.

Fishman, Joshua A. 1991. *Reversing Language Shift*. Clevedon, Philadelphia and Adelaide: Multilingual Matters.

(ed.). 2001. *Can Threatened Languages be Saved? Reversing Language Shift, Revisited: A 21st Century Perspective*. Clevedon, and Buffalo, N.Y.: Multilingual Matters.

Fox, Anthony. 1995. *Linguistic Reconstruction: An Introduction to Theory and Method*. Oxford: Oxford University Press.

Gibson, Jeanne D., and Stanley Starosta. 1990. Ergativity East and West. In Baldi (1990:195–210).

Gordon, Elizabeth, and Mark Williams. 1998. Raids on the Articulate: Code-Switching, Style-Shifting and Post-Colonial Writing. *Journal of Commonwealth Literature* 33.2: 75–96.

Gordon, Elizabeth, Lyle Campbell, Jennifer Hay, Margaret Maclagan, Andrea Sudbury and Peter Trudgill. 2004. *New Zealand English: Its Origins and Evolution*. Cambridge: Cambridge University Press.

Grace, George. 1985. On the Explanation of Sound Changes: Some Polynesian Cases. In Acson and Leed (1985:56–63).

Green, Roger C. 1966. Linguistic Subgrouping within Polynesia: The Implications for Prehistoric Settlement. *Journal of the Polynesian Society* 75: 6–38.

Greenberg, Joseph H. 1963. Some Universals of Grammar with Particular Reference to the Order of Meaningful Elements. In Joseph H. Greenberg (ed.), *Universals of Language*. Cambridge, Mass.: MIT Press, pp. 73–133.

Grenoble, Lenore A., and Lindsay J. Whaley. 2006. *Saving Languages – An Introduction to Language Revitalization.* Cambridge: Cambridge University Press.

Grey, George. [1854] 1971. *Nga Mahi a nga Tupuna.* 4th edition. Wellington: Reed.

Gussenhoven, Carlos, and Haike Jacobs. 1998. *Understanding Phonology.* London: Arnold.

Hale, Kenneth. 1968. Review of Hohepa (1967). *Journal of the Polynesian Society* 77: 83–99.

1970. The Passive and Ergative in Language Change: The Australian Case. In Stephen A. Wurm and Donald C. Laycock (eds.), *Pacific Linguistic Studies in Honour of Arthur Capell.* Pacific Linguistics C-13. Canberra: Australian National University, pp. 757–81.

1973. Deep-Surface Canonical Disparities in Relation to Analysis and Change: An Australian Example. In Thomas Sebeok (ed.), *Current Trends in Linguistics 11.* The Hague: Mouton, pp. 401–58.

1991. Remarks on G. Sanders' 'Levelling in the History of Polynesian Passive Formations'. *Journal of the Polynesian Society* 100: 99–101.

Harlow, Ray. 1979. Regional Variation in Maori. *New Zealand Journal of Archæology* 1: 123–38.

1986. The Actor Emphatic Construction of the Eastern Polynesian Languages. In Paul Geraghty, Lois Carrington and Stephen A. Wurm (eds.), *FOCAL I: Papers from the Fourth International Conference on Austronesian Linguistics.* Pacific Linguistics C-94. Canberra: Australian National University, pp. 297–308.

1987. *A Word-list of South Island Maori.* 2nd revised edition. Auckland: Linguistic Society of New Zealand.

1989. Ka: The Maori Injunctive. In Harlow and Hooper (1989:197–210).

1991a. Contemporary Maori Language. In McGregor and Williams (1991:29–38).

1991b. Consonant Dissimilation in Maori. In Robert Blust (ed.), *Currents in Pacific Linguistics: Papers on Austronesian Languages and Ethnolinguistics in honour of George W. Grace.* Pacific Linguistics C-117. Canberra: Australian National University, pp. 117–28.

1993a. Lexical Expansion in Maori. *Journal of the Polynesian Society* 102.1: 99–107.

1993b. A Science and Maths Terminology for Maori. *SAMEpapers* (Hamilton: Centre for Science and Mathematics Education Research, University of Waikato): 124–37.

1994a. Maori Dialectology and the Settlement of New Zealand. In Sutton (1994:106–22).

1994b. *Otago's First Book.* Dunedin: Otago Heritage Books.

1996. *Māori.* Languages of the World/Materials 20. Munich and Newcastle: Lincom Europa.

1998. Polynesian *f and *s in the Eastern Polynesian Languages. *Rongorongo Studies* 8.2: 47–58.

2000a. Possessive Markers in Māori. In Fischer (2000:357–70).

2000b. Motifs in Māori Prose Narrative. In Steven Roger Fischer and Wolfgang B. Sperlich (eds.), *Leo Pasifika. Proceedings of the Fourth International Conference on Oceanic Linguistics.* Auckland: The Institute of Polynesian Languages and Literatures, pp. 112–26.

2000c. 'He aha te reo 'tūturu'?' *He puna kōrero Journal of Maori & Pacific Development* 1.1: 47–71.

2001. *A Māori Reference Grammar*. Auckland: Pearson Education.

2002. On the Role of Literature and Translation in Language Maintenance. *He puna kōrero Journal of Maori & Pacific Development* 3.1: 73–87.

2003. Issues in Māori Language Planning and Revitalisation. *He puna kōrero Journal of Maori & Pacific Development* 4.1: 32–43.

2004. Borrowing and its Alternatives in Māori. In Jan Tent and Paul Geraghty (eds.), *Borrowing: A Pacific Perspective*. Pacific Linguistics 548. Canberra: Australian National University, pp. 145–69.

2005. Covert Attitudes to Māori. *International Journal of the Sociology of Language* 172: 133–47.

Harlow, Ray, and Robin Hooper (eds.). 1989. *VICAL 1 Oceanic Languages. Papers from the Fifth International Conference on Austronesian Linguistics*. Auckland: Linguistic Society of New Zealand.

Harlow, Ray, Peter Keegan, Jeanette King, Margaret Maclagan, Elizabeth Quinn and Catherine Watson. 2004. NZE Influence on Maori Pronunciation over Time. Paper presented at the Language and Society Conference. Massey University, Palmerston North, New Zealand.

Haslev, Marianne. n.d. Meaningful Statements in Morpho-phonemics: The Case of New Zealand Maori Passive. MS, Bergen.

Hogan, Helen. 1994. *Renata's Journey: Ko te Haerenga o Renata*. Christchurch: Canterbury University Press.

Hohepa, Patrick W. 1967. *A Profile-generative Grammar of Maori*. Indiana University Publications in Anthropology and Linguistics, Memoir 20. Bloomington: University of Indiana.

1969a. The Accusative-to-Ergative Drift in Polynesian Languages. *Journal of the Polynesian Society* 78: 295–329.

1969b. Not in English and Kore and Eehara in Maori. *Te Reo* 12: 1–34.

1981. A Look at Maori Narrative Structure. In Hollyman and Pawley (1981:35–46).

1993. Appendix to H. M. Ngata (1993:541–3).

2000. Towards 2030 (2) – Māori Language Regeneration, Strategies, Government and People. *He Pukenga Kōrero* 5.2: 10–15.

Hollings, Mike. 2005. Māori Language Broadcasting: Panacea or Pipedream. In Bell *et al.* (2005:111–30).

Hollyman, Jim, and Andrew Pawley (eds.). 1981. *Studies in Pacific Languages and Cultures in Honour of Bruce Biggs*. Auckland: Linguistic Society of New Zealand.

Hooper, Robin. 1984. An Unusual Sentence Type: Complements of Verbs of Completion in some Polynesian Languages. *Te Reo* 27: 3–28.

Hopper, P. J., and S. A. Thompson. 1980. Transitivity in Grammar and Discourse. *Language* 56: 251–99.

Hovdhaugen, Even, Ingjerd Hoëm and Arnfinn M. Vonen. 1988. Some Outlier Pronouns in Tokelauan. *Journal of the Polynesian Society* 97: 71–2.

Howard, Irwin. 1981. Proto-Ellicean. In Hollyman and Pawley (1981:101–18).

Huia Publishers. 1995, 1997, 1999. *Ngā pakiwaitara Huia*. Wellington: Huia.

Ihimaera, Witi, Haare Williams, Irihapeti Ramsden and D. S. Long (eds.). 1992–6. *Te ao mārama: Contemporary Māori Writing*. Volumes I–V. Auckland: Reed.

Johansen, J. Prytz. 1948. *Character and Structure of the Action in Maori*. Kgl. Danske Videnskabernes Selskab, Historisk-filologiske Meddelelser, vol. 31, no. 5. Copenhagen: Munksgaard.

Kaplan, Robert B., and Richard B. Baldauf. 1997. *Language Planning: From Practice to Theory*. Clevedon: Multilingual Matters.

Kāretu, Tīmoti S. 1974. *Te Reo Rangatira. A Course in Māori for Sixth and Seventh Forms*. Wellington: Government Printer.

    1993. *Haka: te tohu o te whenua rangatira = The Dance of a Noble People*. Auckland: Reed.

Kearns, Kate. 1990. A Note on the Glottal Fricative in Maori. *Te Reo* 33: 65–81.

Keegan, P. J. 1996. Reduplication in Maori. M.Phil. thesis. University of Waikato.

    2005. The Development of Māori Vocabulary. In Bell *et al.* (2005:131–48).

Keenan, E. L., and B. Comrie. 1977. Noun Phrase Accessibility and Universal Grammar. *Linguistic Inquiry* 8: 63–99.

    1979. Data on the Noun Phrase Accessibility Hierarchy. *Language* 55: 333–51.

Kendall, Thomas. 1815. *A korao no New Zealand*. Sydney: G. Howe.

    1820. *A Grammar and Vocabulary of the Language of New Zealand*. London: Church Missionary Society.

Kern, R. A. 1948. The Vocabularies of Jacob Le Maire. *Acta Orientalia* 20: 216–37.

King, Michael. 1981. Between Two Worlds. In Oliver (1981:279–301).

    1989. *Moriori: A People Rediscovered*. Auckland: Penguin.

    2003. *The Penguin History of New Zealand*. Auckland: Penguin.

Kirch, Patrick Vinton, and Roger C. Green. 2001. *Hawaiki, Ancestral Polynesia: An Essay in Historical Anthropology*. Cambridge: Cambridge University Press.

Kirkham, Francis W. 1917. *Lessons for Beginners in the Maori Language*. Auckland: James N. Lambert.

Krupa, Viktor. 1966. *Morpheme and Word in Maori*. Janua linguarum. Series practica 46. The Hague: Mouton.

    1968. *The Maori Language*. Moscow: Nauka.

    1973. *Polynesian Languages: A Survey of Research*. The Hague: Mouton.

Lass, Roger. 1984. *Phonology*. Cambridge: Cambridge University Press.

Lynch, John. 2002. The Proto-Oceanic Labiovelars: Some New Observations. *Oceanic Linguistics* 41.2: 310–62.

Lynch, John, Malcolm Ross and Terry Crowley. 2002. *The Oceanic Languages*. Richmond, Surrey: Curzon.

Maclagan, Margaret, and Jeanette King. 2001. Māori and English Pronunciation – Where is the Influence going? Paper presented at the Conference on New Ways of Analysing Variation, NWAV 30. Raleigh, North Carolina.

    2002. The Pronunciation of *wh* in Māori – A Case Study from the Late Nineteenth Century. *Te Reo* 45: 45–63.

Maclagan, Margaret, Ray Harlow, Jeanette King, Peter Keegan and Catherine Watson. 2005. Acoustic Analysis of Maori: Historical Data. In Ilana Mushin (ed.), *Proceedings of the 2004 Conference of the Australian Linguistcs Society*. Sydney: University of Sydney, pp. 1–16.

Mahuta, R. T. 1974. Whaikoorero: A Study of Formal Maori Speech. MA thesis. University of Auckland.

Marck, J. 1996. Eastern Polynesian Subgrouping Today. In Davidson (1996:491–511).

    2000. *Topics in Polynesian Languages and Culture History*. Pacific Linguistics 504. Canberra: Australian National University.

Mark, Ann. 1970. The Use of *ki* and *i* in New Zealand Maaori. Unpublished term paper. MIT.

Mataira, Katarina Te Heikōkō. 1975. *Te Ātea*. Wellington: School Publications Branch.
    2002. *Makorea*. Raglan, NZ: Ahuru Press.

Maunsell, Robert. 1842. *A Grammar of the New Zealand Language*. Auckland: J. Moore. Subsequent editions in 1862, 1882, 1894.

May, Stephen, Margaret Franken and Roger Barnard (eds.). 2005. *LED2003: Refereed Conference Proceedings of the 1st International Conference on Language, Education and Diversity*. Hamilton: Wilf Malcolm Institute of Educational Research, University of Waikato.

McGregor, Graham, and Mark Williams (eds.). 1991. *Dirty Silence*. Auckland: Oxford University Press.

McLean, Mervyn. 1981. Text and Music in 'Rule of Eight' Waiata. In Hollyman and Pawley (1981:53–63).
    1996. *Maori Music*. Auckland: Auckland University Press.

McLean, Mervyn, and Margaret Orbell. 1975. *Traditional Songs of the Maori*. Wellington: Reed.

Mead, Hirini Moko. 2003. *Tikanga Māori*. Wellington: Huia.

Metge, Joan. 1976. *The Maoris of New Zealand*. Rev. edition. London: Routledge and Kegan Paul.

Meyerhoff, Miriam, and Bill Reynolds. 1996. On Reduplication and its Effects on the Base in Maori. In Marina Nespor and Norval Smith (eds.), *Dam Phonology: HIL Phonology Papers II*. The Hague: Holland Academic Graphics, pp. 143–64.

Milroy, J. Wharehuia. 1996. Ngā reo-ā-rohe. In Moorfield (1996:51–3).

Ministry of Education. 1996a. *Pāngarau i roto i te Marautanga o Aotearoa*. Wellington: Learning Media.
    1996b. *Pūtaiao i roto i te Marautanga o Aotearoa*. Wellington: Learning Media.
    1996c. *Te Reo Māori i roto i te Marautanga o Aotearoa*. Wellington: Learning Media.
    1999a. *Hangarau i roto i te Marautanga o Aotearoa*. Wellington: Learning Media.
    1999b. *Ngā Toi i roto i te Marautanga o Aotearoa*. Wellington: Learning Media.
    2000. *Tikanga ā Iwi i roto i te Marautanga o Aotearoa*. Wellington: Learning Media.
    2004. Statistical Tables – Subject Enrolments. Downloaded from: www.minedu.govt. nz/index.cfm?layout=document&documentid=6886indexid=6848indexparentid =5611

Mokena, Tanengapuia Te Rangiawhina. 2005. The Structural Framework of the Māori Quest Story. Ph.D. thesis. University of Auckland.

Moorfield, John C. 1988. *Whanake 1 Te Kākano*. Auckland: Longman Paul.
    1989. *Whanake 2 Te Pihinga*. Auckland: Longman Paul.
    1992. *Whanake 3*. Auckland: Longman Paul.
    1996. *Whanake 4 Te Kōhure*. Hamilton: University of Waikato.

Moorfield, John C., and Lachy Paterson. 2002. Loanwords Used in Maori-Language Newspapers. In Curnow *et al.* (2002:60–77).

Mosel, Ulrike, and Even Hovdhaugen. 1992. *Samoan Reference Grammar*. Oslo: Scandinavian University Press.

Mutu, Margaret. 1982. The Manner Particles *rawa, tonu, noa, kee and kau* in Maori. M.Phil. thesis. University of Auckland.

1989. An Overview of Theoretical Orientations to Polynesian Syntax. In Harlow and Hooper (1989:399–412).

2001. Ko Pūwheke te Maunga – Pūwheke is the Mountain: Māori Language and Māori Ethnic Identity – Reaffirming Identity Through Language Revitalisation. *He Pukenga Kōrero* 6.2: 1–8.

Næss, Åshild. 2000. *Pileni*. Languages of the World / Materials 325. Munich: Lincom Europa.

Nettle, Daniel, and Suzanne Romaine. 2000. *Vanishing Voices: The Extinction of the World's Languages*. Oxford: Oxford University Press.

Ngata, A. T. 1926. *Complete Manual of Maori Grammar and Conversation with Vocabulary*. 2nd revised and enlarged edition. Christchurch: Whitcombe and Tombs. (There were four editions from 1901 to 1939.)

1959. *Nga Moteatea. Part 1*. Wellington: Polynesian Society.

1986. *Na to hoa aroha: The Correspondence Between Sir Apirana Ngata and Sir Peter Buck*. 3 vols. Auckland: Auckland University Press in association with the Alexander Turnbull Library.

1990. *Ngā Mōteatea. Part 4*. Auckland: Polynesian Society.

Ngata, A. T., and P. Te Hurinui. 1961. *Nga Moteatea. Part 2*. Wellington: Polynesian Society.

1970. *Nga Moteatea. Part 3*. Wellington: Polynesian Society.

Ngata, H. M. 1993. *English–Māori Dictionary*. Wellington: Learning Media.

Nicholson, Rangi, and Ron Garland. 1991. New Zealanders' Attitudes to the Revitalisation of the Māori Language. *Journal of Multilingual and Multicultural Development* 12.5: 393–410.

Oliver, W. H. (ed. with B. R. Williams). 1981. *The Oxford History of New Zealand*. Wellington: Oxford University Press.

Orange, Claudia. 1987. *The Treaty of Waitangi*. Wellington: Allen & Unwin.

Orbell, Margaret. 1968. *Maori Folktales in Maori and English*. Auckland: Longman Paul.

1985. *Hawaiki: A New Approach to Maori Tradition*. Christchurch: University of Canterbury.

1992. *Traditional Māori Stories*. Auckland: Reed.

2002. *He Reta ki te Maunga / Letters to the Mountain. Māori Letters to the Editor, 1895–1905*. Auckland: Reed.

Owens, J. M. R. 1981. New Zealand Before Annexation. In Oliver (1981:28–53).

Parkinson, Phil. 2001a. The Māori Grammars and Vocabularies of Thomas Kendall and John Gare Butler. [Part 1: The Rotten Branches, 1814–23.] *Rongorongo Studies* 11.1: 4–24.

2001b. The Māori Grammars and Vocabularies of Thomas Kendall and John Gare Butler. [Part 2: 'We have condemned the Grammar . . .', 1824–26.] *Rongorongo Studies* 11.2: 47–62.

2001c. *The Maori Language and its Expression in New Zealand Law*. Victoria University of Wellington Law Review Monograph. Wellington: Victoria University.

2003. The Māori Grammars and Vocabularies of Thomas Kendall and John Gare Butler. [Part 3: Kendall's Revised Grammar, 1827–32.] *Rongorongo Studies* 13.2: 37–55.

2004. The Māori Grammars and Vocabularies of Thomas Kendall and John Gare Butler. [Part 4: Butler's 'New Zealandic Vocabulary', 1839–41.] *Rongorongo Studies* 14.1: 20–37.

Parkinson, Phil, and Penelope Griffith. 2004. *Books in Maori, 1815–1900: An Annotated Bibliography = Ngā tānga reo Māori: ngā kohikohinga me ōna whakamārama.* Auckland: Reed.

Pawley, Andrew. 1966. Polynesian Languages: A Subgrouping Based upon Shared Innovations in Morphology. *Journal of the Polynesian Society* 75: 39–64.

1967. The Relationships of Polynesian Outlier Languages. *Journal of the Polynesian Society* 76: 259–96.

1972. On the Internal Relationships of Eastern Oceanic languages. In R. C. Green and M. Kelly (eds.), *Studies in Oceanic Culture History,* vol. III. Honolulu: Bernice Pauahi Bishop Museum, pp. 1–142.

1973. Some Problems in Proto-Oceanic Grammar. *Oceanic Linguistics* 12: 103–88.

1981. Bruce Biggs: A Foreword. In Hollyman and Pawley (1981:7–23).

1985. Proto-Oceanic Terms for 'person': A Problem of Semantic Reconstruction. In Acson and Leed (1985:92–104).

1996. On the Polynesian Subgroup as a Problem for Irwin's Continuous Settlement Hypothesis. In Davidson *et al.* (1996:387–410).

Pawley, Andrew, and K. Green. 1971. Lexical Evidence for the Proto-Polynesian Homeland. *Te Reo* 14: 1–35.

Pearce, Elizabeth. 1997. Genitive Case in the Maori DP. *Wellington Working Papers in Linguistics* 9: 31–55.

1998a. The Syntax of Genitives in the Maori DP. *Canadian Journal of Linguistics / Revue canadienne de linguistique* 43: 411–34. (Special Issue on Syntax and Semantics of Austronesian Languages.)

1998b. Incorporation in Maori Syntax. Paper presented at the Fifth Meeting of the Austronesian Formal Linguistics Association.

1999. Topic and Focus in a Head-initial Language: Maori. In Carolyn Smallwood and Catherine Kitto (eds.), *Proceedings of AFLA VI: The Sixth Meeting of the Austronesian Formal Linguistics Association, held at the University of Toronto April 16–18, 1999.* University of Toronto Working Papers in Linguistics. Toronto: University of Toronto, pp. 249–63.

2000. Argument Positions and Anaphora in the Maori Clause. In Steven Roger Fischer and Wolfgang Sperlich (eds.), *Leo Pasifika: Proceedings of the Fourth International Conference on Oceanic Linguistics.* The Institute of Polynesian Languages and Literatures, Monograph Series 2. Auckland: The Institute of Polynesian Languages and Literatures, pp. 313–25.

2002. VP versus V raising in Māori. In Andrea Rackowski and Norvin Richards (eds.), *Proceedings of AFLA VIII: The Eighth Meeting of the Austronesian Formal Linguistics Association.* MIT Working Papers in Linguistics 44. Cambridge, Mass.: MIT Press, pp. 225–40.

2003. Iterative Phrasal Movement and the Maori DP. Ms. Victoria University of Wellington.

Pearce, Elizabeth, and Jeffrey Waite. 1997. *Kia* and *ki te* Complementation in Maori: An Unaccusative Analysis. *Te Reo* 40: 45–75.

Peddie, Roger. 2005. Planning for the Future? Languages Policy in New Zealand. In Bell *et al.* (2005:30–56).

Peltzer, Louise. 1996. *Grammaire descriptive du tahitien*. Tahiti: Editions Polycop.

Polinsky, Maria. 1992. Maori *he* Revisited. *Oceanic Linguistics* 31: 229–50.

Pōtatau, Hēmi. 1991. *He Hokinga Mahara*. Auckland: Longman Paul.

Reed, A. W. 1984. *Concise Māori Dictionary*. New rev. edition by T. S. Kāretu. Wellington: Reed.

Reedy, Tāmati Muturangi. 1979. *Complex Sentence Formation in Maori*. Ph.D. thesis. University of Hawai'i.

   2000. Te Reo Māori: The Past 20 Years and Looking Forward. *Oceanic Linguistics* 39.1: 157–69.

Rikihana, T. 1976. *Learning and Teaching Māori*. Auckland: Heinemann.

Ross, Malcolm. 1994. Some Current Issues in Austronesian Linguistics. In Tryon (1994a:45–120).

Ross, Malcolm, Andrew Pawley and Meredith Osmond. 1998. *The Lexicon of Proto Oceanic: The Culture and Environment of Ancestral Oceanic Society*, vol. I: *Material Culture*. Pacific Linguistics C-152. Canberra: Australian National University.

   2003. *The Lexicon of Proto Oceanic: The Culture and Environment of Ancestral Oceanic Society*, vol. II: *The Physical Environment*. Pacific Linguistics C-152. Canberra: Australian National University.

Ruatapu, Mohi. 1993. *Ngā kōrero a Mohi Ruatapu*. Translated, edited and annotated by Anaru Reedy. Christchurch: Canterbury University Press.

Ryan, J. S. 1972. The Form and Range of Borrowings from English into Māori. *Orbis* 21.1: 136–66.

Ryan, P. M. 1974. *The Revised Dictionary of Modern Māori*. Auckland: Heinemann.

   1995. *The Reed Dictionary of Modern Māori*. Auckland: Reed.

Salmond, Anne. 1975. *Hui: A Study of Maori Ceremonial Gatherings*. Wellington: A. H. and A. W. Reed.

   1991. *Two Worlds: First Meetings Between Maori and Europeans, 1642–1772*. Auckland: Viking.

   1997. *Between Worlds: Early Exchanges Between Māori and Europeans, 1773–1815*. Auckland: Viking.

Sanders, G. 1990. On the Analysis and Implications of Maori Verb Alternations. *Lingua* 80: 149–96.

   1991. Levelling and Reanalysis in the History of Polynesian Passive Formations. *Journal of the Polynesian Society* 100: 71–90.

Schane, Sanford A. 1976. The Best Argument is in the Mind of the Beholder. In J. R. Wirth (ed.), *Assessing Linguistic Arguments*. Washington, D.C.: Hemisphere Publishing Corp, pp. 167–85.

Schütz, Albert J. 1985a. *The Fijian Language*. Honolulu: University of Hawaii Press.

   1985b. Accent and Accent Units in Māori: The Evidence from English Borrowings. *Journal of the Polynesian Society* 94: 5–26.

   1990. The Past and Present of Maori Language Policy. In István Fodor and Claude Hagège (eds.), *Language Reform: History of Future*, vol. V. Hamburg: Helmut Buske Verlag, pp. 351–75.

   1994. *The Voices of Eden: A History of Hawaiian Language Studies*. Honolulu: University of Hawai'i Press.

Shand, Alexander. 1911. *The Moriori People of the Chatham Islands: Their History and Traditions*. Memoir 2. Wellington: Polynesian Society.

Simona, Ropati. 1986. *Tokelau Dictionary*. Apia: Office of Tokelau Affairs.

Simmons, D. R. 1966. The Sources of Sir George Grey's *Nga Mahi a nga Tupuna*. *Journal of the Polynesian Society* 75: 177–88.

1976. *The Great New Zealand Myth*. Wellington: A. H. and A. W. Reed.

Sinclair, M. B. W. 1976. Is Maori an Ergative Language? *Journal of the Polynesian Society* 85: 9–26.

Smith, S. Percy. 1913–15. *The Lore of the Whare-wananga, or, Teachings of the Maori College on Religion, Cosmogony and History written down by H. T. Whatahoro from the Teachings of Te Matorohanga and Nepia Pohuhu, Priests of the Whare-wananga of the East Coast, New Zealand*. Translated by S. Percy Smith. 2 vols. New Plymouth: Polynesian Society.

Smyth, Patrick. 1939. *Te Reo Maori. A Guide to the Study of the Maori Language*. Christchurch: Whitcombe and Tombs.

Song, Jae Jung. 2001. *Linguistic Typology: Morphology and Syntax*. Harlow, UK: Longman.

Spolsky, Bernard. 2003. Reassessing Māori Regeneration. *Language in Society* 32.4: 553–78.

2005. Māori Lost and Regained. In Bell (2005:67–85).

Starke, June (ed.). 1986. *Journal of a Rambler: The Journal of John Boultbee*. Auckland: Oxford University Press.

Starks, Donna, Ray Harlow and Allan Bell. 2005. Who Speaks What Language in New Zealand. In Bell (2005:13–29).

Statistics New Zealand. 1997. *1996 Census of Population and Dwellings*. Wellington: Statistics New Zealand.

2002. *2001 New Zealand Census of Population and Dwellings*. Wellington: Statistics New Zealand.

Sutton, Douglas G. (ed.). 1994. *The Origin of the First New Zealanders*. Auckland: Auckland University Press.

Taumoefolau, Melenaite. 1996. From **Sau 'Ariki* to *Hawaiki*. *Journal of the Polynesian Society* 105: 385–410.

Te Hurinui, Pei. 1946. *Te Tangata Whai-rawa o Weneti*. (Translation of Shakespeare's *Merchant of Venice*.) Palmerston North: H. L. Young.

Te Puni Kōkiri. 1998. *The National Māori Language Survey*. Wellington: Te Puni Kōkiri.

1999. *Mātātupu*. Wellington: Te Puni Kōkiri.

2002. *Survey of Attitudes Towards, and Beliefs and Values about the Māori Language: Final Summary Report*. Wellington: Te Puni Kōkiri.

2003. *Te Rautaki Reo Māori. The Māori Language Strategy*. Wellington: Te Puni Kōkiri.

Te Rangi Hīroa (Sir Peter Buck). 1949. *The Coming of the Maori*. Wellington: Maori Purposes Fund Board, and Whitcombe and Tombs.

Te Taura Whiri i te Reo Māori. 1990. *Māori for the Office*. Wellington: Te Taura Whiri i te Reo Māori. (2nd edition, 1997. Auckland: Oxford University Press.)

1992. *Te Matatiki: Ngā Kupu Hou a Te Taura Whiri i te Reo Māori*. Wellington: Te Taura Whiri i te Reo Māori.

1996. *Te Matatiki: Contemporary Māori Words*. 2nd edition. Auckland: Oxford University Press.

Thornton, Agathe. 1985. Two Features of Oral Style in Maori Narrative. *Journal of the Polynesian Society* 94: 149–76.

    1989. *Maori Oral Literature: As Seen by a Classicist*. Dunedin: University of Otago Press.

    1998. Do A and O Categories of 'possession' in Maori Express Degrees of *tapu*? *Journal of the Polynesian Society* 107: 381–93.

    2004. *The Birth of the Universe = Te Whānautanga o te ao tukupū: Māori Oral Cosmogony from the Wairarapa*. Auckland: Reed.

Tiramōrehu, Matiaha. 1987. *Te Waiatatanga mai o te Atua: South Island Traditions*. Recorded by Matiaha Tiramōrehu and edited with translation by Manu van Ballekom and Ray Harlow. Canterbury Maori Studies 4. Christchurch: Department of Maori, University of Canterbury.

Tregear, Edward. 1891. *The Maori–Polynesian Comparative Dictionary*. Christchurch: Whitcombe and Tombs.

Trudgill, Peter. 2004. Linguistic and Social Typology: The Austronesian Migrations and Phoneme Inventories. *Linguistic Typology* 8: 305–20.

Tryon, Darrell T. (ed.). 1994a. *Comparative Austronesian Dictionary: An Introduction to Austronesian Studies*. Berlin and New York: Mouton de Gruyter.

    1994b. The Austronesian Languages. In Tryon (1994a:5–44).

Vennemann, Theo, and Ray Harlow. 1977. Categorial Grammar and Consistent VX Serialisation. *Theoretical Linguistics* 4: 227–54.

Waitangi Tribunal. 1986. *Report of the Waitangi Tribunal on the te reo Maori Claim (wai 11)*. Wellington: Waitangi Tribunal.

Waite, J. 1987. Negatives in Maori: A Lexical–functional Approach. *Te Reo* 30: 79–100.

    1989. Tough- and Pretty-movement in Maori. *Te Reo* 32: 61–94.

    1990. Another Look at the Actor Emphatic. *Journal of the Polynesian Society* 99: 395–413.

    1992. *Aoteareo: Speaking for Ourselves*. Wellington: Learning Media.

    1994. Determiner Phrases in Maori. *Te Reo* 37: 55–70.

Waititi, Hoani R. 1970. *Te Rangatahi I*. Rev. edition. Wellington: Government Printer.

    1974. *Te Rangatahi II*. Wellington: Government Printer.

Walker, Ranginui. 2001. *He Tipua*. Auckland: Penguin.

    2004. *Ka whawhai tonu mātou / Struggle Without End*. Rev. edition. Auckland: Penguin.

Whaley, Lindsay J. 1997. *Introduction to Typology: The Unity and Diversity of Language*. Thousand Oaks, Calif.: Sage.

White, John. 1887–91. *The Ancient History of the Maori, His Mythology and Traditions*. 6 vols. Wellington: Government Printer.

Williams, H. W. 1924. *A Bibliography of Printed Maori to 1900*. Wellington: Government Printer.

    1971. *A Dictionary of the Maori Language*. 7th edition. Wellington: Government Printer. (5th edition, 1917; 6th, 1957.)

Williams, W. L. 1844. *A Dictionary of the New Zealand Language*. Paihia: Press of the Church Missionary Society. (Subsequent editions – 1852 and 1871, both at London: Williams and Norgate; 1892, Auckland: Upton and Co. For the 5th and subsequent editions, see H. W. Williams (1971) above.)

    1862. *First Lessons in Maori with a Short Vocabulary*. London: Trübner. (5th edition, 1904, Auckland: Upton.)

Wilson, Deanne. 1991. *A Study of Spoken Maori in Awarua (Northland)*. MA thesis. University of Auckland.

Wilson, William H. 1982. *Proto-Polynesian Possessive Marking*. Pacific Linguistics B-85. Canberra: Australian National University.

1985. Evidence for an Outlier Source for the Proto-Eastern Polynesian Pronominal System. *Oceanic Linguistics* 24: 85–133.

Wurm, Stephen A., and Lois Carrington (eds.). 1978. *Second International Conference on Austronesian Linguistics: Proceedings*. Pacific Linguistics C-61. Canberra: Australian National University.

Yasuda, Ayako. 1968. The Structure of the Penrhyn Phrase. MA thesis. University of Hawai'i.

Index

Actor Emphatic 27, 31, 32, 105, 146, 175–7
adjective 98, 108, 115
attitudes, language 88, 206–8
Austronesian 1, 10–15

bases 99–102
Bauer, Winifred 6, 26
Biggs, Bruce 5, 43, 96, 135–6
broadcasting 205–6

causative 125–6
clauses
    adverbial 179–87
    complement 181–2
    relative 32, 106, 182
complementation 107
compound words 114, 129–31
consonants 16–17, 26, 62
    aspiration 22–3
    deletion 21–2
    phonetics of 75–81
    regional variation 44–5, 46–7
    wh 22
Cook, James 5, 35, 192
coordination 159–60

derivation 102–3, 120, 121–9
determiners 100, 115, 140–5
    articles 141–2, 143–5
    demonstratives 142
    possessive 142–3
dialects 18, 20, 21, 41–59, 62, 82, 189 n. 38, 196
    eastern 32, 45, 188 n. 20
    loyalty 44, 52
    northern 32
    South Island 20, 39 n. 50, 47–8, 55–6, 86, 89
    western 32, 45
domains of use 196

East Futunan 5
education in Māori 2, 197, 199–205
    Kōhanga Reo 2, 8, 197, 200, 202–3
    Kura Kaupapa Māori 8, 200, 203–4
    tertiary 201–2, 204
English, influence of 31, 160, 173, 217–8
ergativity 24–8, 172

features, phonological 63–6
Fijian 70, 111
focus 85, 173–9

generative accounts 98–9, 136–7, 142, 143–4, 150, 152–3, 157–8, 169–70, 174–5, 176–7, 182
grammar
    changes 23–32
    regional variation 48–9

haka 8
Hawaiian 21, 38 n. 15, 38 n. 27, 40 n. 72, 53, 56, 117
Hawaiki 15

idiom
    regional variation 52
inflection 114–20
intergenerational transmission 2
intonation 84–5

Kendall, Thomas 5

language planning 208
language shift 192–6
    reversing 196–7
Lapita Culture 12
Lee, Samuel 5
lexical diffusion 18
lexicon
    regional variation 49

literature, Māori
  oral 6–8, 14–15, 71
    committed to writing 7
    written 8

Malayo-Polynesian 12, 15
Mangarevan 53, 56
Māori
  grammars, development of 5–6
  lexicography, development of 6
  official status 197–9
  speakers, number of 192–6
Māori and New Zealand English
    Project 39 n. 53, 75, 83, 85
Maori Language Act 1987 199, 210
marae 6–7, 196
Marquesan 53, 55–6
migrations, prehistoric 13–14
  dialects and 52–6
modification 101, 103–4, 130, 148–50
Moorfield, John 5
mora 65, 67, 71–5, 93 n. 23
Mōriori 20, 44, 57–9

negation 153–4, 160–3, 165
New Zealand
  dialects and 52–6
  settlement of 14–15
newspapers 205
Niuatoputapu 5
nominalisation 27, 102, 107, 121–3
  agreement 122
  suffix 121
noun 97, 110–11, 114
  common 110
  locative 97, 110, 146
  personal 98, 110
number 111, 114–15
numerals 112–13, 123

objects 155–6
  incoporation 150
Oceanic 12
oratory 6–7

particles 24, 97, 99–102, 114
  postposed 147–8
  preposed, see determiners, prepositions,
    tense/aspect markers
parts of speech 96–113
passive 16, 25, 26, 28, 74, 104, 105, 115, 171
  agreement 100–1, 104, 116
  pseudo-passive 26
phonemes of Māori 62
  distribution of 68–9

phonotactics of Māori 64, 69, 70–1
phrase 97, 99–102, 120, 135–50
  nucleus 148–50
  peripheries, see particles
POLLEX (Polynesian Lexicon Project) 33–4,
    70
Polynesian 1
  Central Eastern 17, 18, 29, 54, 62
  Eastern 18, 29, 30, 71, 111, 163
  Nuclear 17, 19, 29
  possession 30–1, 48, 163–70, 186
    see also determiners
predicates 151–3
prefixation 73, 83, 123–6
prepositions 30, 31–2, 100, 145–6, 157–8
  i 156–7
  ki 157
pronouns 111–12, 159–60
Proto-Austronesian 10, 15, 16, 26, 32
Proto-Oceanic 10, 12, 15–16, 26
Proto-Polynesian 10, 15–20, 23, 26, 29, 32,
    46, 54, 70, 111
  homeland 14
purism 37

Rapanui (Easter Island) 10, 21, 56
  writing system 6
Rarotongan 40 n. 72, 40 n. 73, 46, 53, 56, 117
reduplication 67, 71, 73, 74, 75, 83, 113,
    127–9

Samoan 25, 38 n. 15
sentences
  complex 179–87
  existential 153–4
sound changes 15–23
  assimilation 19, 20
  consonant deletion 21–2
  metathesis 20–1
  recent 22–3
  sporadic change 19–21
stress 73, 81
subgrouping
  Austronesian 12
  Oceanic 12
  Polynesian 12–13, 14, 34
subjects 154–5
syllable structure 17, 69, 71–5

Tahitian 25, 38 n. 15, 40 n. 70, 40 n. 72, 41,
    46, 53, 56, 117, 163
Tahitic 14, 19, 56, 70
Taura Whiri i te Reo Māori, Te ('The Māori
    Language Commission') 86, 88, 124,
    134 n. 61, 195, 199, 209, 212–4

tense/aspect markers 31, 99, 137–40
  e/Ø 67, 140
  e . . . ana 29, 32, 139
  i 138
  i te 139
  ka 137–8
  kei te 139
  kia 138–9
  kua 138
  me 26, 30, 139
Tokelauan 70
Tongan 25, 29, 30, 70, 120, 121–9
Tongareva (Penrhyn Island) 18
topic 85, 173–9
Treaty of Waitangi 90, 198
Tuamotuan 56

verbs 98, 104–10
  experience (middle) 39 n. 60, 98,
    105–6
  intransitive 106

neuter (stative) 27, 97, 98, 106–8
  transitive 104–5
vocabulary
  adaptation 35, 37
  borrowing 35–7, 64, 69, 84
  change 32–7
  expansion 124, 130, 212–16
vowels 63
  diphthongs 67, 69
  long 12, 17, 66–7, 86–7
  phonetics of 75–81
  regional variation 46
  Waititi, Hoani 5

Williams, William 6
word order 101, 150–1, 158–9
word shape 113–14, 118
writing system
  Māori 85–92, 211–12
    development of 88–92
  Rapanui (Easter Island) 6